The Sexy Science of
The Big Bang Theory

ALSO EDITED BY NADINE FARGHALY

Unraveling Resident Evil: *Essays on the Complex Universe of the Games and Films* (McFarland, 2014)

The Sexy Science of *The Big Bang Theory*

Essays on Gender in the Series

Edited by NADINE FARGHALY
and EDEN LEONE

McFarland & Company, Inc., Publishers
Jefferson, North Carolina

LIBRARY OF CONGRESS CATALOGUING-IN-PUBLICATION DATA

The sexy science of The big bang theory : essays on gender in the series / edited by Nadine Farghaly and Eden Leone.
    p.   cm.
Includes bibliographical references and index.

ISBN 978-0-7864-7641-1 (softcover : acid free paper) ∞
ISBN 978-1-4766-1948-4 (ebook)

1. Big bang theory (Television program) 2. Sex on television. I. Farghaly, Nadine, 1981– editor. II. Leone, Eden, editor.
PN1992.77.B485S49 2015
791.45'72—dc23   2015011466

BRITISH LIBRARY CATALOGUING DATA ARE AVAILABLE

© 2015 Nadine Farghaly and Eden Leone. All rights reserved

No part of this book may be reproduced or transmitted in any form or by any means, electronic or mechanical, including photocopying or recording, or by any information storage and retrieval system, without permission in writing from the publisher.

Cover images © 2015 Hemera/Wavebreak Media/Thinkstock

Printed in the United States of America

*McFarland & Company, Inc., Publishers
    Box 611, Jefferson, North Carolina 28640
        www.mcfarlandpub.com*

Table of Contents

Acknowledgments	vi
Introduction	
Nadine Farghaly *and* Eden Leone	1
Penny and the Politics of Plausibility	
Raewyn Campbell	5
Science in Stilettos: Shaping Perceptions of Women in Science	
Lauren R. Archer	26
The Big Theory on the (Not So) *Bang*in' Jewish Mother	
Julia Spiegel	51
The Adolescent Quest	
Janice Shaw	72
Disciplining Heterosexuality: Interrogating the Heterosexual Ideal	
Andrea McClanahan	88
The Mutual Exclusivity Proposition: Female Intellectualism and Sexuality	
Alissa Burger	112
Failed Genders and Fragile Intimacies: Living in and After the Big Bang	
Benjamin Bateman	132
Sexualizing Two Cultures: C. P. Snow, F. R. Leavis and *The Big Bang Theory*	
Brian McAllister	146
The American Female Dichotomy: Smart *or* Sexy	
Abigail G. Scheg	159

The Androgyny of Rajesh Koothrappali
 Ann-Gee Lee   174

About the Contributors   189
Index   191

Acknowledgments

This book would have never seen the light of day if it weren't for dozens of wonderful people, especially our wonderful contributors. We know that the constant revisions and extra hours you put into this must have been hard; however, our combined work and our countless hours of effort finally paid off in the publication of this collection. Additionally, our thanks to Joe Erickson for proofreading everything so thoroughly. We would also not have been able to complete this project without our loved ones. Thank you all!

Introduction

NADINE FARGHALY *and*
EDEN LEONE

Knock knock knock, Penny! Knock knock knock, Penny! Knock knock knock, Penny! This utterance has been printed on mugs, t-shirts, posters, and many other *Big Bang Theory*–related items, and it has become a repeated as well as a trusted source of entertainment on the CBS hit show featuring Penny, Sheldon, and Leonard, who have become one of TV's most popular threesomes. The smart and funny combination of geeky male protagonists with a pretty, perky female protagonist has been very successful so far. Although the series needed a second pilot to be picked up by the network, it has been going strong since 2007 (Lorre) and it has been steadily making its way up from an original 13-episode starter in season one to one of CBS's biggest hits. According to *Forbes* magazine, the advertising revenue per half hour is $2.57 million. Since its creation *The Big Bang Theory* has captured a steady viewership of nearly 17 million. After the first four seasons the network added an additional three without hesitation and recently renewed the show until 2017. It is more popular than ever before and we want to know why. Does the show's popularity stem from its quirky but loveable characters? Can it be attributed to the clever mixture of science and popular culture? Is it really true that smart is the new sexy? Some of these questions will be answered in this collection, and other questions will probably arise. This collection set out to offer a comprehensive reading of *The Big Bang Theory* in connection to gender and popular culture. We strove to create a well-rounded work that not only helps the audience understand the themes addressed in this show, but also to engage them in an intellectual and meaningful conversation in something they might not have taken as seriously before.

After all, despite its fun, *The Big Bang Theory* is not merely a show about two scientists living across the hall from a waitress/aspiring actress. This show can be used as a lens through which to look at and understand society. As could be said of almost anything discussed in popular culture, one should never make the mistake of saying that a sitcom is not intellectual enough to tell us anything important about our society or ourselves. On the contrary, if one sees popular culture as a lens through which to view highly sophisticated topics such as genetic modifications addressed by a layman, one understands why it should never be disregarded. Popular culture, like nothing else, is able to make complex themes and ideas accessible to everyone. Shakespeare did not belong to highbrow culture when he wrote his poems and plays; he wrote for the masses. Granted, he was sponsored by the Lord Chamberlain's Men, patronized by James I, but his primary audience consisted of all sorts of people, including the lower classes. We are not trying to say that *The Big Bang Theory* will one day be as admired as Shakespeare's works; however, it should not be disregarded just because it is not now. It tackles highly interesting topics such as sexuality (asexuality, homosexuality, queerness, etc.), family, friendship, education, marginalization, and fandom, to name but a few.

As a result, while there are many aspects that make the show a success, there are certain aspects that need to be addressed since the presentation of the characters often is problematic. Throughout its run the show has demonstrated a remarkable capability to reduce women to pretty bedfellows who do not necessarily need a brain or self-esteem; Howard and Raj especially make a point of using (or trying to use) women for sexual gratification and nothing else. Penny, who is also the only character who apparently does not deserve a last name, and her naivete in the first few seasons was hard for many viewers to stomach, and it wasn't until the introduction of Amy Farrah Fowler and Bernadette Rostenkowski that the cast was equipped with long-term female characters whose functions were not as eye candy or sex objects. And, even these characters are problematic. Though she has a Ph.D. and a fabulous job, Bernadette is often portrayed as a stereotypical dumb blonde, who, together with her co-workers, creates super viruses which they then lose track of ("The Desperation Emanation," 4x05) and consumes Jell-O shots from petri dishes that were contaminated with yellow fever ("The Justice League Recombination," 4x11). It often seems women cannot be pretty and intelligent without being punished for it with some unbelievable character flaw. In the same vein, Amy's continued sexual harassment (yes, we are calling it that) of Penny stopped being entertaining several seasons ago, and it finally ended during the last season, coincidentally around the same time Sheldon became a viable possible sexual partner. It is still important to remember all the times Penny was confronted with Amy's not-so-subtle sexual comments; consider when the portrait she had commissioned was originally a nude portrayal of the two women ("The Rothman Disintegration," 5x17), or when she says that Bernadette's bridal shower ought to include naked bridesmaids washing each other, or when she gets the idea that the bachelorette party should embrace the idea of a Native American sweat lodge where women dance around and paint fertility symbols on the bride's naked body ("The Isolation Permutation," 5x08). Amy's continued inappropriate remarks about Penny's body are a constant throughout seasons five and six, but are toned down in season seven.

Another aspect of the show that was entertaining at first is Penny's drinking, which seemed to have gotten out of hand as several episodes in season five demonstrate. The producers reined in this behavior during the last season, and they recently addressed the matter directly. In the "The Locomotive Manipulation" the group discusses what the couples are planning for Valentine's Day. When Bernadette proposes that Leonard and Penny join the other two couples on their trip to Napa, Leonard quickly states, "I'm not sure it's such a great idea to take Penny to where wine comes from." When Penny, holding a big glass of red wine, looks less than amused, Leonard just quips: "What? It's a joke. ... Come on, we bust on each other! I wear dorky glasses, you might have a problem—it's all for laughs." Penny retorts: "That'd really piss me off if I didn't have a buzz going on" ("The Locomotive Manipulation," 7x15). While the situation is meant to be funny, one cannot help but wonder if Penny really is fine or if she does have a problem with alcohol. While the show demonstrated an uncanny sensibility to its viewers' needs, and the ability to capture its attention episode after episode, one has to wonder about the negative portrayal of women in the show's long-term cast members. To be fair, it should be acknowledged that the male characters make equally dumb mistakes, whether it be Leonard and Howard doing almost anything to please women, like bringing home top secret weaponry ("The Staircase Implementation," 3x22) or letting a date drive the Mars rover ("The Lizard-Spock Expansion," 2x08). This collection will not answer all the questions one might have about *The Big Bang Theory*, and, in fact, we hope it brings up more. Offering their opinions on *The Big Bang Theory* in this work are some great scholars.

Like Leonard, Sheldon, Raj, and Howard gearing up for a quest via their computers, the essays herein take readers on a trek through various concepts of femininity, masculinity, sexuality, and relationships.

"Penny and the Politics of Plausibility" by Raewyn Campbell explores the concepts of nerds, masculinity, and marginality, while Lauren R. Archer's "Science in Stilettos: Shaping Perceptions of Women in Science" examines the portrayal of female scientists and their impact on televised media. Julia Spiegel considers female identity and characterization in "The Big Theory on the (Not So) *Bang*in' Jewish Mother," specifically the emergence of the comic representation of a Jewish mother figure, traditionally shaped by females with emphasis on religious or cultural cues of otherness is discussed. Janice Shaw, in "The Adolescent Quest," looks at the traditional notion of the quest in a millennial context.

"Disciplining Heterosexuality: Interrogating the Heterosexual Ideal" by Andrea McClanahan also investigates gender and sexuality, specifically the challenges to hegemonic ideals of masculinity, femininity, and heterosexuality. Female sexuality is further explored in Alissa Burger's "The Mutual Exclusivity Proposition: Female Intellectualism and Sexuality," which examines the dichotomy of women in popular culture and how they are perceived as either intelligent or sexual and how this struggle of perception and characterization is negotiated.

Benjamin Bateman, in "Failed Genders and Fragile Intimacies: Living in and After the Big Bang," focuses on the notions of loving relationships and the perceived failures used for comic relief but that bring about a deeper level of connectedness. Brian McAllister looks at the worlds of scientist and artist in "Sexualizing Two Cultures: C. P. Snow, F. R. Leavis and *The Big Bang Theory.*" The characterization of females on television, specifically what constitutes smart and sexy, and the cultural impact is further explored in "The American Female Dichotomy: Smart *or* Sexy" by Abigail G. Scheg. Metrosexuality, homosexuality, and cultural expectations are explored in "The Androgyny of Rajesh Koothrappali" by Ann-Gee Lee.

Works Cited

"The Desperation Emanation." *The Big Bang Theory*. Perf. Jim Parsons, Kaley Cuoco, and Johnny Galecki. DVD. Warner Home Video, 2013.

Forbes. Forbes Magazine, n.d. Web. 4 Feb. 2014.

"The Isolation Permutation." *The Big Bang Theory*. Perf. Jim Parsons, Kaley Cuoco, and Johnny Galecki. DVD. Warner Home Video, 2013.

"The Justice League Recombination." *The Big Bang Theory*. Perf. Jim Parsons, Kaley Cuoco, and Johnny Galecki. DVD. Warner Home Video, 2013.

"The Lizard-Spock Expansion." *The Big Bang Theory*. Perf. Jim Parsons, Kaley Cuoco, and Johnny Galecki. DVD. Warner Home Video, 2013.

"The Locomotive Manipulation." *The Big Bang Theory*. Perf. Jim Parsons, Kaley Cuoco, and Johnny Galecki. DVD. Warner Home Video, 2014.

Lorre, Chuck. "CLP—Vanity Card #187." Chuck Lorre Productions. October 15, 2007. Retrieved February 7, 2014.

"The Rothman Disintegration." *The Big Bang Theory*. Perf. Jim Parsons, Kaley Cuoco, and Johnny Galecki. DVD. Warner Home Video, 2013.

"The Staircase Implementation." *The Big Bang Theory*. Perf. Jim Parsons, Kaley Cuoco, and Johnny Galecki. DVD. Warner Home Video, 2013.

Penny and the Politics of Plausibility

RAEWYN CAMPBELL

> "They've turned me into one of them. I *am* one of them. That's why you need me: I am your conduit, I am your bridge!"
> —Ich. Bin. Ein. NERD! ("Tramps Like Us")

The above quote from the British sitcom *The IT Crowd* articulates the central concept explored in this essay: the integral role female nerds and non-nerds play in shifting discourses surrounding the signifier nerd. Penny, from *The Big Bang Theory,* is such a character, performing a vital role in the reinforcement of nerd as a male signifier, and participating in the greater incorporation of male nerds into hegemonic masculinity. Drawing from Alan Sinfield's work on the politics of plausibility, this essay explores the ways in which Penny helps bridge cultural faultlines that have opened up or been exposed by shifts in discursive regimes surrounding the signifier "nerd." Penny's friendships with four male nerds—Leonard, Sheldon, Howard and Raj—and her own gradual nerdification facilitate a meeting between nerd identity and plausible conditions of social acceptability and hegemonic masculinity. The increased incorporation of the male nerds into hegemonic masculinity can be used, somewhat paradoxically, as a stepping stone to legitimize and make visible marginalized embodiments of nerd, in this instance female nerds in the form of Amy and Bernadette. Consequently, *The Big Bang Theory* can be seen to challenge the dominance of hegemonic masculinity as, through Penny and the inclusion of Amy and Bernadette, male privilege and female subordination are cunningly renegotiated.

The signifier "nerd" has undergone a dramatic shift in the last twenty years. Once laden with negativity and attracting societal derision, the nerd label is now frequently worn as a badge of pride, even bestowing upon the wearer increased cultural status. The heightened social status and the cultural power that accompanies this shift makes the current state of nerdom a worthy subject of investigation. As maleness continues to be inextricably caught up in the nerd signifier, the influence gender has on both narratives and performances of *nerdity is also a* relevant area of inquiry.

The association of nerd identity with maleness is not because of any intrinsic, essential or biological demand; nerd identity and culture are social constructs, and very recent ones.[1] Origins of this signifier are so murky and contested that attempts to claim the original—and therefore somehow more "authentic"—meaning of "nerd" provide little legitimation for gendering the boundaries of nerdom. Nerd identity and culture is discursively constructed and disseminated. In many ways this simplifies the task of investigating the current state of nerdom, as an understanding of the constructed nature of the identity destabilizes attempts to naturalize the identity or to excuse hierarchies and subjugation within its ranks.

The popularity and commercial success of *The Big Bang Theory* has led to the show being held up—particularly by mainstream journalists—as proof that the figure of the nerd has finally triumphed.[2] Media response provides a pertinent example of how *The Big Bang Theory* participates in the production of what Sinfield calls "bridging stories." Bridging stories are accounts that seek to resolve cultural faultlines ("cultural faultlines" being discursive gaps and incongruities exposed by competing cultural narratives). An example of a cultural faultline is the disharmony between the image of nerd as a "loser," and the social and economic reality of nerds' increasing power within western cultures. Sinfield's image of a "contest of stories" through which action advances is applicable to the shift that nerd identity is undergoing. Such discursive shifts are a process. A story must fight to win some form of consensus. The effects of challenges to discursive regimes are not always immediate or visible; it takes lots of little voices and communal participation to effect a noticeable change in a discursive regime. This is because conditions of plausibility are determined by the collective. Sinfield's theoretical framework helps shed light on the significant role that a successful television show, like *The Big Bang Theory,* is able to play in the discursive shift of the nerd signifier. *The Big Bang Theory* is not unique in portraying nerds as adept in science and computer technology. But its power does not rest primarily in its reiteration of nerds as intelligent and introspective, or even in its challenging longstanding negative attitudes towards the signifier nerd. Rather, much of the power of *The Big Bang Theory* resides in the way in which it renders nerds plausibly masculine, and this is mediated, largely, through the character of Penny.

In "Cultural Materialism, *Othello*, and the Politics of Plausibility," Sinfield states that "conditions of plausibility are crucial. They govern our understandings of the world and how to live in it, thereby seeming to define the scope of feasible political change" (32). *The Big Bang Theory* involves itself in the politics of plausibility in a number of different ways. In-text narrative draws from extra-textual occurrences, thereby anchoring itself in, or tethering itself to, lived experience. *The Big Bang Theory* owes much of its success and popularity to its ability to "authentically" portray nerdom[3]; the stories, the characters, the background details seem *plausible*. As series creator Bill Prady explains in an interview with *Newsarama*, a sense of authenticity and plausibility was important to the program's creators:

> We're writing about ourselves. My highly nerdish background is that I was a computer programmer. I'm also a science fiction fan and an obsessed *Star Trek* fan. Whatever you want to call that group of people, nerds, or geeks, there's a great history of portraying them homogenously; that they are all the same with tape across the bridges of their eyeglasses and have pocket protectors. The thing that I know from living in that world is that it's remarkably heterogeneous. There are great differences and individual passions. What also exists is a greater respect for differences and a greater understanding of difference. The real-life person that I knew that couldn't speak to women [a trait exhibited by Koothrappali], it was just an acknowledged part of his behavior and it was just dealt with. You say that's not the guy to ask to talk to those women over there. All of these things are just matter of fact for us [Bennett, "Big Bang Theory Becoming Favorite of Audience It Lampoons"].

Prady's strategy of writing about what he knows—anchoring the fiction to his own personal lived experience—assists in *The Big Bang Theory* successfully meeting conditions of plausibility for many audience members who participate in nerd culture. Later in the article quoted above, audience member Remy Minnick, "a thirtysomething IT professional in Los Angeles," discusses how much of *The Big Bang Theory's* appeal resides in its effectively linking to his lived experience:

> "There's an episode where Penny sleeps over on the couch. Sheldon comes in to do his Saturday morning ritual of watching 'Doctor Who' only to find Penny sleeping on the couch and it completely throws off his day. That was definitely a 'me' moment," he laughs.
>
> He continues, "The show is smart enough where they don't always go for the 'obvious' joke. The guys are successful, they are sweet, they are the stars of the show and while the show is a comedy they aren't just used for comic relief. If it ever becomes all wedgies and pocket-protector jokes, then it's over for me" [Bennett, "*Big Bang Theory* Becoming Favorite of Audience It Lampoons"].

This quote suggests that meeting conditions of plausibility in the representation of nerd identity is important for self-identifying nerd audiences.[4] Given the immense popularity of the program, however, it is unlikely that every member of the audience has a similarly strong stake in authentic portrayals of nerdom. The plausibility surrounding the four nerd characters' performances of nerdity is less vital for the enjoyment of those who do not identify as or with nerds. Even so, the politics of plausibility still perform a key role in determining not only which stories will be believed but, I suggest, also in which stories will gain traction within a culture.

Penny plays a crucial role in the socialization of Leonard, Sheldon, Howard and Raj. Through her, the four nerds are invited into alternate social spheres that are deemed normative and mainstream. She is the conduit through which the four nerds can move within and make sense of new social spheres. Penny, for example, invites the four nerds to her Halloween party ("The Middle-Earth Paradigm"), organizes a surprise birthday party for Leonard ("The Peanut Reaction"), introduces Howard to Bernadette ("The Creepy Candy Coating Corollary"), invites Leonard to watch football at her house with some of her friends ("The Cornhusker Vortex"), and takes Sheldon to Disneyland with her friends ("The Spaghetti Catalyst"). Penny also performs the roles of interpreter and tutor in regard to social cues and interpersonal skills; for example, she tells Sheldon that the tie on Leonard's bedroom door means Leonard is currently having sex ("The Hamburger Postulate"), and makes it clear to Sheldon that, in friendships, "love trumps hate" ("The Codpiece Topology"),she stands up to Sheldon when his behavior tips from inept to rude, such as when she appropriates his 3-strike system for herself ("The Panty Piñata Polarization"), and is pivotal in the discovery that Raj can overcome his inability to talk to women by consuming alcohol ("The Grasshopper Experiment"). The piece de resistance of Penny's tutelage is arguably her inducement of empathy from the self-centered Sheldon ("The Thespian Catalyst").

More than this, however, Penny is the conduit through which a mainstream audience[5] can make sense of and become comfortable with what has previously been alien: nerdom. Time and time again, Penny makes the choice to maintain her friendship with the boys despite their often deviant and inept behavior, such as when Sheldon breaks into her apartment to clean it while she is asleep ("The Big Bran Hypothesis") and when Leonard makes awkward romantic advances towards her ("The Fuzzy Boots Corollary"). Moments like these can work to position Penny in a place of dominance. Her generosity in the face of social deviancy (and often plain rudeness on the part of Sheldon) can reinforce pre-existing hierarchies of value where already dominant and accepted mainstream beliefs and behaviors maintain the upper hand, by meeting conditions of plausibility. Simultaneously, however, Penny's generous approval of the nerds, despite their very different worldviews, can also reflect positively on the nerd characters—and, by extension, IRL[6] nerds. Penny's acceptance of and fondness for the nerds adds to wider discursive structures surrounding nerdom, thus providing an option in which nerd identity and social acceptability no longer have to be mutually exclusive. Having a character such as Penny, who clearly meets conditions of plausible social acceptability, cheerfully befriending social misfits rather than rejecting, dismissing or ridiculing them, provides an example for the audience. Viewers can potentially see Penny's reaction as a viable performative option in their own lives.

Penny also provides a springboard from which cultural hypocrisies towards nerdom can be exposed and interrogated. An issue that scholars of fan studies have been exploring for decades is the inconsistent cultural distain for fans[7] of popular media texts compared to fans of texts deemed culturally prestigious. Within the show's text, *The Big Bang Theory* has been able to introduce this issue of hypocrisy to its broad audience. In 1992, cultural theorist Henry Jenkins, in his seminal text *Textual Poachers,* suggests that

> fan culture stands as an open challenge to the "naturalness" and desirability of dominant cultural hierarchies.... What may make all of this particularly damning. is that fans cannot as a group be dismissed as intellectually inferior; they often are highly educated, articulate people who come from the middle classes, people who "should know better" than to spend their time constructing elaborate interpretations of television programs.... What cannot easily be dismissed as ignorance must be read as aesthetic perversion. It is telling, of course, that sports fans (who are mostly male and who attach great significance to "real" events rather than fictions) enjoy very different status than media fans [18–19].

The Big Bang Theory frequently challenges these naturalized cultural assumptions that Jenkins highlights in the above quote and is arguably more effectively able to infiltrate and modify dominant discourses than an academic text. One obvious example of *The Big Bang Theory* challenging taken-for-granted cultural hierarchies can be found in "The Nerdvana Annihilation." In this episode Penny chastises Leonard, Sheldon, Howard and Raj for their obsessive enthusiasm towards a replica time machine from the 1960 film *The Time Machine*. Through a series of unfortunate events following the arrival of the time machine, Penny misses out on a shift at the Cheesecake Factory where she works. This leads to the first time in the series that Penny shows overt hostility towards nerdom via an angry outburst directed at Leonard, Sheldon, Howard and Raj:

> PENNY: My God! You are grown men! How can you waste your lives with these stupid toys, and costumes, and comic books, and now that! That...?
> SHELDON: Again, time machine.
> PENNY: Oh please, it's not a time machine. If anything it looks like something Elton John would drive through the Everglades.... Pathetic! All of you. Completely pathetic! ["The Nerdvana Annihilation"].

Here Penny articulates longstanding attitudes towards nerds that, uncannily mirror Jenkins' aforementioned comments: that nerds are immature and waste their time with trivial activities culminating in an unnatural denial of adulthood. By the end of the episode, however, Sheldon confronts Penny and exposes her hypocrisy:

> SHELDON: You hypocrite!
> PENNY: What?!
> SHELDON: Little Miss Grown-Ups-Don't-Play-With-Toys! If I went into that apartment right now, would I not find Beanie Babies? Are you not an accumulator of Care Bears and My Little Ponies? And who is that Japanese feline I see frolicking on your shorts? Hello, Hello Kitty! ["The Nerdvana Annihilation"].

By pointing out the double standards of Penny's accusation, Sheldon, firstly, exposes entrenched and uninterrogated cultural assumptions regarding nerds and, secondly, reveals contradictions inherent in such assumptions. The blatant nature of Sheldon's rebuke—"You hypocrite!"—leaves little room for a multiplicity of interpretations on the part of the audience; the message is clear: if you, like Penny, think of nerds as maladjusted and deviant because they love objects thought to be trivial or immature, then your reasoning is inconsistent and ill-founded. This message is not merely implied, it is explicit. The directness of such a challenge moves beyond the confines of the text, requiring a more active response from audience members who may have held resistant readings. It necessitates that resistant readings must, like Sheldon's argument, be rigorous and supported rather than being simply taken for granted. Penny's character is therefore crucial in displacing uninterrogated attitudes towards nerds, as she becomes the vehicle through which such discrepancies can be highlighted and reformulated to the advantage of nerds.

Simply articulating and directly challenging entrenched prejudices within the text reveals that extra-textual cultural attitudes towards nerds are changing; indeed, that they have already changed significantly. Take for example, again, Jenkin's *Textual Poachers*. A little over two decades ago he observed:

> The fan, whose cultural preferences and interpretive practices seem so antithetical to dominant aesthetic logic, must be represented as "other," must be held at a distance so that fannish taste does not pollute sanctioned culture. Public attacks on media fans keep other viewers in line, making it uncomfortable for readers to adapt such "inappropriate" strategies of making sense of popular texts or to embrace so passionately materials of such dubious aesthetic merit [19].

This is vastly different to portrayals of fans in current media texts such as *The Big Bang Theory*. *The Big Bang Theory* does not hold fans at a distance as Jenkins argues was happening in the 1980s and early 1990s. Rather, *The Big Bang Theory* blatantly exposes hypocrisies inherent in cultural assumptions about pop-culture fans and nerds. It is able to perform a subversive role, challenging and reshaping longstanding attitudes to nerds and fans through a careful balancing act which is dependent on Penny. Through Penny, the show keeps one foot in the realm of the plausible (i.e., the cultural value attributed to being a cute blonde female) while transgressing cultural norms with the other (i.e., the cute blonde female's acceptance of marginalized masculinity).

Furthermore, this process demonstrates that media reception is more dynamic than a "top-down" sanctioned model. *The Big Bang Theory* provides an example of the complex, multidirectional relationship between the media and audiences. As noted earlier, the writers of *The Big Bang Theory* are self-identifying nerds who are themselves passionate consumers of popular media. In order to best increase their chances of cultural (and economic) success they must, write in a way that authenticates themselves among audience members who would likewise identify as nerds. This indicates that the public institutions that, Jenkins argues, promote, control and sanction notions of appropriate media consumption are in fact fluid, changeable and themselves contingent on audience sanctioning. Media production and consumption is not a top-down power model; it is relational. Having audience members producing televisual content for and on behalf of those with whom they feel a kinship is a powerful strategy for instigating cultural change. As is evident in Sheldon's rebuke of Penny's double standards, discourse has shifted so dramatically that "public attacks" are no longer reserved for nerdy fans, rather, they can be aimed at those who denigrate nerdy fannishness.

Prior to the *Big Bang Theory*, very few mainstream popular texts featured nerds as the heroes; many included nerds as sidekicks or comic relief, but very few featured nerdy protagonists. Nerds were stigmatized, marginalized, ridiculed and derided until, so the tale goes, the computer revolution of the 80s and 90s made it possible for a large sub-section of those (either self-identifying or externally labelled) "nerds" to amass wealth on an unprecedented scale. As cultural theorist Lori Kendall so succinctly observes in *Hanging Out in the Virtual Pub*:

> The growing pervasiveness of computers in work and leisure activities has changed many people's relationship to this technology and thus has also changed the meaning of the term "nerd." Since the 1980s, the previously liminal masculine identity of the nerd has been rehabilitated and partly incorporated into hegemonic masculinity [81].

Here Kendall argues that values attached to nerd identity changed, not only because computer technology made many nerds economically and culturally successful, but because this success also entailed a regendering of nerd identity. The behaviours that were encompassed within the nerd signifier did not change, but the connotations of such behaviours did; for example, computer literacy (a significant component of the nerd signifier) enabled nerds to fulfill plausible conditions of hegemonic masculinity, such as accruing wealth and power. As I discuss in "'I Can't Believe I Fell For Muppet Man!' Female Nerds and the Order of Discourse," this reincorporation into hegemonic masculinity protects longstanding male dominated power positions. Though accepting of some modifications to what can be constituted as masculine, it still impedes major shifts within hierarchical gender paradigms. Significantly, this leaves females, and particularly female nerds, in an untenable position, as will be discussed later in this essay in relation to Amy and Bernadette. Given male nerds are largely validated through conforming to notions of hegemonic masculinity, female nerds are unable to sit comfortably within this paradigm (Campbell 180).

Hegemonic masculinity, according to R.W. Connell,

> can be defined as the configuration of gender practice which embodies the currently accepted answer to the problem of the legitimacy of patriarchy, which guarantees (or is taken to guarantee) the dominant position of men and the subordination of women.
>
> This is not to say that the most visible bearers of hegemonic masculinity are always the most powerful people. They may be exemplars, such as film actors, or even fantasy figures, such as film characters.
>
> Nevertheless, hegemony is likely to be established only if there is some correspondence between cultural ideal and institutional power, collective if not individual [77].

Tacit in both Kendall and Connell's observations is that the first step towards hegemonic incorporation requires meeting conditions of plausibility. As Connell asserts, hegemonic masculinity is not only constructed through the existence of powerful IRL individuals who bear certain traits, fictional figures are often exemplars of hegemonic masculinity. This is because hegemonic masculinity is discursive—it is the outcome of a complex dialogue between individuals and institutions, past and present, and belief and performance. Successful shows like *The Big Bang Theory*, therefore, can become instrumental in discursive regime changes that entail a shift in hegemonic gender relations. This is in part because they lay bare the contradictions between cultural narratives and material realities. In the case of *The Big Bang Theory,* it not only fictionally depicts nerd identity as a valid alternative masculinity, extratextually it reveals that nerds are significant behind-the-scenes players in our current media landscape and therefore assumedly meet certain requirements of hegemonic masculinity. The program's success and popularity, therefore, attests that *The Big Bang Theory* provides an accessible and largely accepted bridging story across the cultural faultlines exposed by the rearranging of a culture which believed nerdom to be marginal despite increasing evidence to the contrary. Sinfield asserts the importance of bridging stories in moments of discursive rupture:

> When a part of worldview threatens disruption by manifestly failing to cohere with the rest, then we reorganize and retell its story, trying to get it into shape—back into the old shape if we are conservative-minded, or into a new shape if we are more adventurous [46].

As nerds have gone from social marginalization to being culturally visible and powerful within a remarkably short period of time, this constitutes a threat to deeply engrained worldviews, to the legitimacy of power, to what constitutes masculinity, and even to the increasing cultural presence of technology and those who deal with it. The material conditions that rely upon nerds (such as an increasing reliance on digital technology) are not able to be done away with. These conditions make it impossible for the story of nerds to be reorganized into its old shape. A new story is required. Consequently, texts such as *The Big Bang Theory* become particularly useful. Sinfield states:

> This is why it is not unpromising to seek in literature our preoccupations with class, race, gender, and sexual orientation: it is likely that texts will address just such controversial aspects of our ideological formation. Those faultline stories are the ones that require most assiduous and continuous reworking; they address the awkward, unresolved issues, the ones in which the conditions of plausibility are in dispute [47].

The Big Bang Theory is markedly effective in the process of creating bridging stories regarding nerd identity, because its story revolves around the nerdy male protagonists meeting conditions of plausibility regarding masculinity. In different ways, and through associations with various female characters within the program (particularly Penny, Amy, and Bernadette), each of the four male nerds have their moments of plausibly conforming to traits of hegemonic masculinity. This has extra-textual as well as in-text implications for discourses surrounding nerd identity. By representing sympathetic nerds that meet cultural requirements of plausible masculinity, a cultural space becomes available in which nerd identity can be rendered socially acceptable rather than marginal, and where the performance of power by those associated with the nerd label can be deemed legitimate.

Connell suggests that "in relation to production, masculinity has come to be associated with being a breadwinner" (90) while "hegemonic masculinity is culturally linked to both authority and rationality, key themes in the legitimation of patriarchy" (90). Over the last thirty years, the signifier nerd has slowly come to incorporate particular aspects of hegemonic masculinity associated with authority and rationality, subsequently making cultural inroads regarding the general social acceptability of nerd identity. As the signifier nerd generally connotes rationality (scientific and philosophical), it is not difficult to see how, according to these conditions of plausible masculinity, nerds could successfully be reincorporated into hegemonic masculinity in a 'post-computer revolution' world. Moreover, as seen in real world exemplars such as Bill Gates and Steve Jobs, nerds now have access to an increasing amount of economic, cultural, and political authority. Indeed, Leonard, Sheldon, Howard and Raj each meet the requirements of masculinity noted by Connell, being secure and successful in their jobs at Caltech. While confirming rationality through their occupation as researching scientists, their academic positions also hold a certain cultural authority and prestige.

It has, however, taken longer for nerds to meet conditions of another long-standing aspect of hegemonic masculinity— that is, heterosexual experience and desirability. In a discussion of the performance of sexuality by self-identified nerds in a particular online forum, BlueSky, Kendall observes that participating in heterosexual discourse— whether through talk or physical expression—is a key aspect in displaying allegiance with hegemonic masculinity:

> While not all BlueSky participants are heterosexual, heterosexuality is an important component of the particular style of masculinity enacted on BlueSky.... In keeping with acceptable performance of hegemonic masculinity, both men and women on BlueSky distance themselves from femininity and, to some extent, from women in general. Conversations that refer to women outside the mud,[8] particularly women in whom a male participant might have romantic interest, bluntly depict such women as sexual objects.... In each of these conversations, mere mention of a woman provokes the formulaic question "Didja spike her?" Such joking formulas constitute techniques of group identity construction. Through jokes regarding women's status as sexual objects, the men on BlueSky demonstrate support for hegemonic masculinity [84–85].

While "Didja spike her?" is something you might expect Howard to say in *The Big Bang Theory*, each of the male nerd characters (with the exclusion of Sheldon, at least in the first three seasons) displays this heterosexual hegemonic allegiance in different ways. Moreover, this is facilitated through their friendships with Penny. Not only does Leonard meet requirements of heterosexual masculinity through his romantic relationship with Penny, Howard is also able to better perform heterosexual masculinity through his platonic association with her. It is Penny who introduces him to a number of sexual partners throughout the course of the series, including Christy, an old friend of Penny's from Nebraska ("The Dumpling Paradox"), and Bernadette, who eventually becomes his wife. On several occasions, Penny herself becomes complicit in the sexual objectification of women, thus reinforcing hegemonic masculinity, by pandering to Howard's sexual urges. This can be seen in episodes such as

"The Peanut Reaction," in which Penny bribes Howard to eat a peanut (to which he has an allergy) in order to distract Leonard while she organizes a surprise party for him:

> PENNY: *[on phone]* How about this: you keep him there a little longer, and when you get to the party, I'll point out which of my friends are easy.
> HOWARD: *[long pause]* Don't toy with me, woman.
> PENNY: I've got a hot former fat girl with no self-esteem, I got a girl who punishes her father by sleeping around, and an alcoholic who's two tequila shots away from letting you wear her like a hat.
> HOWARD: Thy will be done. *[Hangs up, takes out granola bar with peanuts, and looks to his crotch]* I'm doing this for you, little buddy.

In this instance, Penny's inclusion of the nerd boys into her normative social sphere is literally contingent on facilitating Howard's masculine heterosexuality. This happens at the expense of female subjectivity and agency as the females alluded to are implicated into Howard's masculinization without their knowledge or consent.

However, the reincorporation of nerds into hegemonic masculinity is far from uncomplicated. For example, while Penny acts as agent for the nerd boys' masculine hetrosexuality and consequently their social normativity, the audience is able to see Penny undergo a concomitant process of nerdification herself. Often these moments are used for comedic affect, however, they reveal that Penny has accepted the four nerdy misfits to the point where she herself has internalized various aspects of nerd culture and identity without it compromising status that comes with being part of the mainstream or her femininity. An example of this is in the episode "The Dead Hooker Juxtaposition":

> PENNY: It's just, you know, that Leonard, Howard and Raj; they aren't like other guys. They're special.
> ALICIA: Okay, they're special. And?
> PENNY: Oh, let's see, how can I explain this ... um... They don't know how to use their shields.
> ALICIA: Shields?
> PENNY: Yeah, like when you're in Star Trek and you're in battle and you raise the shields. *[Beat. Penny looks shocked]* Where the hell did that come from!? Anyways, you know how guys like this are, so please don't take advantage of them.
> ALICIA: Who says I'm taking advantage of them!?
> PENNY: Come on, they're doing everything for you because you're leading them on.
> ALICIA: So I let them do stuff for me? They're happy, I get stuff, who cares? And how's it any different from what you do?
> PENNY: 'Scuse me?!
> ALICIA: I've seen you around them. Are you pretending that you don't do the exact same thing?
> PENNY: Ok lady, you are waaay outta line.

In this exchange, Penny not only reveals she has been nerdified—despite her female biology—through her association with the four nerds, but that she values them as individuals. She is willing to defend and protect them from a society that might only accept them for selfish, utility-based reasons. Through this conversation we can see that Penny is not merely "using" the nerds for her own personal gain, the relationship is two-way. While she socializes the nerds into social acceptability, they socialize her into nerdom. The nerds are not Penny's butt-monkeys, they are her friends. Penny's outrage at the suggestion she too is "using" the nerds is proven genuine by her continued friendship with the them, and particularly by her relationship with Leonard. Moreover, throughout her relationship with Leonard, Penny continues to show signs of nerdification. This can be seen in the exchange between herself and Leonard after they have had sex in the episode "The Wheaton Recurrence":

> PENNY: Having a little trouble catching your breath there, honey?
> LEONARD: If my PE teachers have told me this is what I was training for, I would have tried harder.
> PENNY: "Do or do not. There is no try."
> LEONARD: Did you just quote *Star Wars*?
> PENNY: I believe I quoted *Empire Strikes Back*.
> LEONARD: Oh, my God. I'm lying in bed with a beautiful woman who can quote Yoda. I love you, Penny.

The dual process of acceptance of nerd by the mainstream (as represented by Penny) and Penny's own nerdification might be seen to further coolify nerd identity. If the cool, beautiful Penny accepts the nerdy boys for "who they really are"—nerds—to the point where she herself somewhat proudly performs nerdity, this is a double compliment for nerdom. It also subtly introduces the idea that nerd identity is not exclusively a male domain. However, this remains ambivalent as the sense of surprise that accompanies Penny's moments of nerdity covertly reinforces default understandings of nerd as a male identity. The humor of these moments stems from the subversion of expectations—it is not expected that an attractive socially adept woman would internalize and perform aspects of the male nerdom.

Though a restructuring of previous hegemony takes place through a process in which nerd becomes an acceptable masculinity, even this restructuring is only partial, as Leonard, Sheldon, Howard, and Raj are only deemed acceptable through their plausible conformity to previously accepted traits of masculinity. Yet, the politics of plausibility not only help mend exposed faultlines in culture,[9] they can also be an effective strategy for facilitating dissidence and change within a culture. Sinfield argues:

> In fact, a dissident text may derive its leverage, its purchase, precisely from its partial implication with the dominant. It may embarrass the dominant by appropriating its concepts and imagery.... Deviancy returns from abjection by deploying just those terms that relegated it there in the first place. A dominant discourse cannot prevent "abuse" of its resources [48].

In other words, those people, stories or things that have been exempt or deemed deviant within a culture can ride the coat tails of that which is already accepted, thus gaining legitimacy in the process. Sinfield talks about the way Othello in Shakespeare's *Othello*, uses this strategy (in two different ways) in order to justify his position of power and to gain social acceptance in Venice where he is seen not only as a foreigner, but as an inferior outsider:

> With the conditions of plausibility so stacked against him, two main strategies are available to Othello, and he uses both. One is to appear very calm and responsible—as the Venetians imagine themselves to be. But also, and shrewdly, he uses the racist idea of himself as exotic: he says he has experienced "hair-breadth scapes," redemption from slavery, hills "whose heads touch heaven," cannibals, anthropophagi, "and men whose heads / Do grow beneath their shoulders." These adventures are of course implausible—but not when attributed to an exotic. Othello has little credit by normal upper-class Venetian criteria, but when he plays on his strangeness, The Venetians tolerate him, for he is granting, in more benign form, part of Brabantio's [a voice asserting Othello's otherness] case [30].

The Big Bang Theory uses pre-existing cultural ambivalence in a similar way. While the four male nerds are increasingly able to meet requirements of hegemonic masculinity as the series develops, the text still utilises many of the stereotypical aspects of nerd identity that previously contributed to nerd marginalization, instead employing them to the nerds' advantage. The pervasive narrative that nerds are "not like other men" is drawn upon, particularly in respect to Penny and Leonard's relationship, strengthening the idea that Leonard is worthy of Penny's affections above other men who are more obviously hegemonically masculine. In the first series episode "The Middle-Earth Paradigm," for example, Penny seeks comfort from Leonard after she has a fight with her (very hegemonically masculine) boyfriend, Kurt. When Penny kisses Leonard, he (somewhat reluctantly) refuses to take it any further, and questions Penny's motives:

> LEONARD: How much have you had to drink tonight?
> PENNY: Just ... a lot...
> LEONARD: Are you sure that your being drunk and your being angry with Kurt doesn't have something to do with what's going on here?
> PENNY: It ... might... Boy, you're really smart
> LEONARD: Yeah, I'm a frickin' genius!
> PENNY: Leonard, you are so great. Why can't all guys be like you?
> LEONARD: Because if all guys were like me the human race couldn't survive.

Leonard's response to Penny's question, though tinged with ironic self-reflexivity, highlights the notion that men such as Leonard are unusual, and are even perhaps unnatural. It is tacitly suggested that it is biologically (and therefore naturally) not beneficial for Leonard (and by extension, nerds) to perform and embody maleness in a fashion that is both rational and considerate of the position of women. However, it is the "deviant" masculinity, that which is stereotypically associated with nerd identity, that attracts Penny to Leonard and leads to their eventual romantic relationship. Even after one of their early break ups, it is evident that Penny's expectations for a relationship have changed since dating Leonard. Her short-lived relationship in the third season with the physically dominating yet affable doofus Zach exemplifies the dramatic shift in Penny's attitudes towards men. In the episode "The Lunar Excitation," Penny introduces Zach to Leonard, Sheldon, Howard and Raj while they are in the midst of carrying out a lunar experiment. After an initial explanation of the experiment which involves bouncing light from lasers off reflectors positioned on the moon's surface, the following exchange takes place:

> PENNY: Oh! That's very cool.
> ZACH: One question: how can you be sure it won't blow up?
> LEONARD: The laser?
> ZACH: The moon.
> SHELDON: Now this is a man for Penny.

Here Sheldon reinforces the assumption that Penny is unintelligent, that she is not "one of them" (carrying with it the insinuation that the nerds are unique and exceptional), and that Penny should be with someone from her own metaphorical station. However, after succeeding in their experiment, Sheldon is ready to review his statement:

> ZACH: That's your big experiment? End up with a line on the [computer] screen?
> LEONARD: Yeah! Think about what this represents. The fact that we can do this is the only way of definitively proving that there are man-made objects on the moon, put there by a species that only 60 years before had only just invented the aeroplane.
> ZACH: What species it that!?
> SHELDON: I was wrong, Penny can do better.

Sheldon's admission of error regarding Penny is less a recognition of her intelligence as it is a vindictive statement of derision against Zach and hegemonic "jock" masculinity. More telling than Sheldon's comments, however, are Penny's unspoken responses to both Zach and Leonard throughout the entire scene. Her flinches of embarrassment every time Zach says something ignorant or when one of the nerds makes an underhanded dig at him, alongside her smiles of interest and curiosity as Leonard explains the experiment reveal that Penny's way of thinking about gender performativity has changed since dating Leonard. This is confirmed later in the episode when an apparently inebriated Penny tells Leonard, as she leads him into his bedroom, that he "has destroyed her ability to tolerate idiots!" ("The Lunar Excitation").

Once masculine legitimacy is established in relation to nerd identity, *The Big Bang Theory* can use the politics of plausibility in another way; it can become a wedge of possibility for others inside the label, such as those who are less central or not as visible, like female nerds, to also claim power and legitimacy as nerds and therefore the cultural privileges that come with it. Female nerds, as represented in *The Big Bang Theory* by Amy and Bernadette, are arguably able to use the new acceptance afforded to male nerds to their own advantage. Indeed, the very textual existence of Amy and Bernadette may have been facilitated by the discursive influence of earlier seasons of the show. Just as Penny's response to the male nerd characters is able to inform audience response, so too does her friendship with the female nerd characters. Penny, again, is shown to be the character on which the plausibility of the show pivots. Though ostensibly adopted by Amy, it is Penny who allows their friendship to be maintained, even though Amy oversteps personal, social, and physical boundaries (for example, in "The 21-Second Excitation" Amy misunderstands the conventions of truth or dare, and after conducting research on Wikipedia discovers that experimentation with lesbianism is common at sleepovers. It is implied at the end of the episode that Amy attempts to make-out with Penny off-screen). Though their acquaintance has been relatively short, Amy makes assertive claims that Penny is her "bestie" ("The Love Car Displacement"). Instead of recoiling from Amy, however, Penny endures such awkwardness and forms a strong friendship with her.

Bernadette, alternatively, has a more normative friendship with Penny, formed through working with her at the Cheesecake Factory as a means of supporting herself through her postgraduate degree in microbiology at university. Unlike the four male nerds, Bernadette is less detached from the mainstream as her job allows her to interact with and work alongside people outside specific "nerdy" spheres like universities or comic book stores. Rather than Penny bringing Bernadette into the mainstream, Penny brings Bernadette further into the nerd fold by (albeit reluctantly at first) introducing her to Howard. This can be seen as further sanctioning of nerdom. Bernadette seems to successfully straddle nerdom and non-nerdom, being able to keep up with the male nerds in academic speak (see, for example, "The Gorilla Experiment," where she shows and interest in Leonard's work in physics which results in jealousy from Howard), but also having much in common with Penny, such as interests in fashion and casual conversation (as seen in "The 21-Second

Excitation," when they organize a girls night for themselves, in "The Isolation Permutation" when Penny goes bridesmaid-dress shopping with Bernadette, and in "The Recombination Hypothesis" when Bernadette expresses excitement at the possibility of her and Howard going on double dates with Leonard and Penny).

Amy, conversely, initially has more in common with the male nerds, particularly Sheldon, when it comes to intellect, worldview, and socialization.[10] When Amy first meets Sheldon in a coffee shop after Howard and Raj have secretly subscribed him to a dating website, she closely resembles him in her scientific, rationalist approach to life. Sheldon and Amy both find one another intellectually stimulating and embark upon a firm, yet unconventional friendship. But, once again, it is largely through friendship with Penny that Amy's character develops with more complexity. While Sheldon meets Amy's intellectual needs, it is her relationship with Penny that sees Amy become more aware and expressive of her emotional needs. While Amy's attempts at social interaction are often learned by rote—friendship-by-numbers—she does, however, have a desire for emotional and physical intimacy which is validated by Penny's example, and becomes more practiced in articulating her needs. Amy, through association with Penny, moves closer to straddling the line between nerdom and mainstream expectation. For example, in "The Isolation Permutation" (05:08), Amy seeks and negotiates comfort from Sheldon:

> AMY: At this moment I find myself craving human intimacy and physical contact.
> SHELDON: Oh boy... You know ours is a relationship of the mind.
> AMY: Proposal: one night of torrid love-making that sooths my soul and inflames my loins.
> SHELDON: *[beat]* Counter proposal: I will gently stroke your head and repeat "Aww, who's a good Amy."
> AMY: *[beat]* How about this: French-kissing. 7 minutes in heaven culminating in second base.
> SHELDON: Neck massage, then you get me that beverage.
> AMY: *[Amy thinks it through]* We cuddle. Final offer.
> SHELDON: *[beat]* Very well.

Amy's ability to keep up with Sheldon intellectually, authenticates her status as a legitimate, nerd, while her desires for a more typical sexual relationship simultaneously normalizes her femininity. This works as a challenge to discourses that seek to delegitimize women within the nerd label. It is Amy's ability to sometimes best Sheldon intellectually which makes her a formidable force, giving her a trump card others do not have when it comes to seeking (elusive to most others) compromise with Sheldon.

The episode "The Flaming Spittoon Acquisition" provides another example of Amy's formidableness when comic book store owner Stuart asks her on a date. Spurred by jealousy, Sheldon, on Penny's suggestion goes to ask Amy (mid-date with Stuart) to be his girlfriend:

SHELDON: I believe I would like to alter the paradigm of our relationship.
AMY: I'm listening.
SHELDON: With the understanding that nothing changes what-so-ever—physically or otherwise—I would not object to us no longer characterising you as not my girlfriend.
AMY: *[beat]* Interesting. Now try it without the quadruple negative.
SHELDON: You're being impossible.
AMY: *[leans across to Stuart on her left]* Hi Stuart.
SHELDON: Fine. Amy. Will you be my girlfriend?
AMY: *[long pause]*. Yes.
SHELDON: Well that's enough of that [the conversation].

Sheldon follows up this confirmation with a 31-page Relationship Agreement which Amy deems "so romantic" if not a bit "restrictive." Interestingly, the dynamic of power in Amy and Sheldon's relationship goes beyond valorizing females in nerdom. Amy's refusal to back down in the face of Sheldon's stubborn denials to confirm their relationship can be seen to undermine hegemonic masculinity even as she desires Sheldon to conform to it.

If we look again at Connell's definition of hegemonic masculinity as "the configuration of gender practice which embodies the currently accepted answer to the problem of the legitimacy of patriarchy, which guarantees ... the dominant position of men and the subordination of women" (77), then Amy and Bernadette's characterization as formidable counterparts for Sheldon and Howard challenges this paradigm. Amy and Bernadette are not represented simply as the men's subordinates. What's more, nor is Penny. Penny's friendship with Amy and Bernadette lifts them all from mere objects of male desire (or intellectual interest on the part of Sheldon) and allows each of them characterization beyond that of "girlfriend." Instead of the inclusion of female romantic admiration purely facilitating the male nerds acceptance into hegemonic masculinity, the addition of Amy and Bernadette provides examples of men and women working together to negotiate and compromise within relationships, such as Bernadette and Howard reaching a friendly impasse on the subject of having children in "The Shiny Trinket Manoeuvre," and also in "The Vacation Solution," when Sheldon works with Amy in her neuroscience lab. These examples reinforce that Amy and Bernadette are intellectual and social equivalents to the men. It is also gratifying to see that, in regard to social equivalency, Penny embraces the female nerds just as she embraced the male nerds. This moves her role within the story beyond being based on sexual curiosity.

Significantly, through the inclusion of the female characters, the privilege of Leonard, Sheldon, Howard and Raj is questioned and challenged, not only in terms of their claim to nerdom, but as men. Howard, whose characterization had largely relied on sexual innuendo and sleazy desperation, evades pressures of hegemonic masculinity by forming a stable relationship with Bernadette which is built on respect and intellectual compatibility rather than just sex. Sheldon, somewhat ironically, avoids conforming to the gender paradigms of hegemonic masculinity by succumbing to certain relational norms that Amy, as discussed above, demands of him. Leonard dodges conforming fully to the demands of hegemonic masculinity by recognizing equal value and worth in Penny's personal attributes (such as her social intelligence) compared to his own.

Instead of painting female nerds as inferior to their male counterparts, Amy and Bernadette are worthy partners in the nerd label. They not only match the males in intellect, but they have been increasingly fleshed out in character, largely due to their association with Penny who anchors the show in plausibility. Though, possibly not yet as unequivocally acceptable as the male nerds within the show, the addition of female nerds at least provides an example that is tolerant of gender diversity within the nerd label. It is important, however, to recognize that the treatment of Amy and Bernadette is rife with ambivalence. On the one hand they stand as foils for Sheldon and Howard, working as spring boards from which these male characters develop further in terms of masculinity, emotional intelligence and comedic value. While on the other hand, Amy and Bernadette are public acknowledgements and representations of a marginalized—and often absent from pop-culture—facet of nerd identity: female nerds.

The Big Bang Theory both reflects and participates in a discursive shift in Western culture. The effectiveness of Penny as point of plausibility has assisted *The Big Bang Theory* in taking steps away from nerd as a male-only signifier. Like Othello using the racist narrative of himself to strengthen his legitimacy, *The Big Bang Theory*, by meeting sexist cultural expectations, is paradoxically able to legitimize the visible cultural presence of female nerds. A meeting of these crucial conditions of plausibility is facilitated by the character Penny, who is a conduit between that which is already culturally accepted, and that which has been culturally marginalized.

Notes

1. Only traceable as far as the 1950s where limited written sources suggest the term was already in frequent usage within the United States (Anderegg, 35).

2. See, for example; Michael Idato's " Word's Out, Geeks Rule," and Mary Vanderlinden's "Could it Be? It's Becoming Chic to be Geek."

3. This of course is contested—many self-identifying nerds chastise the programme on the basis of ill-informed representations of nerdery. See, for example, "11 Reasons Geeks Hate *The Big Bang Theory*."

4. For more examples of this see Greg Katzman's "Reasons Geeks Love *The Big Bang Theory*," and Stephen Toulouse's "The Big Bang Controversy."

5. By "mainstream" I am referring to the popular and broad appeal *The Big Bang Theory* has beyond a specifically self-identifying nerd audience; as of May 23, 2013, *The Big Bang Theory* ranked second among the 18– 49 age demographic in the 2012–2013 United States television season's ratings (Patten, "Full 2012-2013 TV Season Series Rankings").

6. IRL is nerdy gamer speak for "In real life."

7. While "fan" is not synonymous with "nerd" they share many attributes in common and, for similar reasons, have analogous histories of being culturally distained. It is useful to think of "fan" and "nerd" as overlapping circles on a Venn diagram: fans are often self-identifying (and externally labelled) "nerds," and nerds are often fans (particularly of popular, "low-brow" media texts).

8. From the acronym MUD, "multiuser dungeon," or alternatively "multiuser domain" or "multiuser dimension."

9. Sinfield makes the observation that "the tendency of ideology is, precisely, to produce good subjects who feel uncomfortable when they transgress" (45).

10. Indeed, it her exasperation towards being taken for granted as one of the guys that prompts Amy to intrude into Penny and Bernadette's girls' night in "The 21-Second Excitation."

Works Cited

Anderegg, David. *Nerds: How Dorks, Dweebs, Techies, and Trekkies Can Save America*. New York: Penguin, 2011. Print.

Bennett, Tara. "*Big Bang Theory*: Becoming Favorite of Audience It Lampoons." *Newsarama*. Tech Media Network. 21 Sept. 2009. Web. 5 Sept. 2012.

"The Big Bran Hypothesis." *The Big Bang Theory: The Complete First Season*. Writ. Chuck Lorre and Bill Prady. Dir. Mark Cendrowski. Warner Bros., 2009. DVD.

Campbell, Raewyn. "'I Can't Believe I Fell for Muppet Man!' Female Nerds and the Order of Discourse." *Smart Chicks on Screen*. Ed. Laura Mattoon D'Amore. New York: Rowman & Littlefield, 2014. Print.

"The Codpiece Topology." *The Big Bang Theory: The Complete Second Season*. Writ. Chuck Lorre. Dir. Mark Cendrowski. Warner Bros., 2009. DVD.

Connell, R.W. *Masculinities*. Crows Nest, New South Wales: Allen and Unwin, 2005. Print.

"The Cornhusker Vortex." *The Big Bang Theory: The Complete Third Season*. Writ. Bill Prady and Maria Ferrari. Dir. Mark Cendrowski. Warner Bros., 2010. DVD.

"The Creepy Candy Coating Corollary." *The Big Bang Theory: The Complete Third Season*. Writ. Chuck Lorre and Bill Prady. Dir. Mark Cendrowski. Warner Bros., 2010. DVD.

"The Dead Hooker Juxtaposition." *The Big Bang Theory: The Complete Second Season*. Writ. Steven Molaro. Dir. Mark Cendrowski. Warner Bros., 2009. DVD.

"The Dumpling Paradox." *The Big Bang Theory: The Complete First Season*. Writ. Brooke D'Orsay. Dir. Mark Cendrowski. Warner Bros., 2009. DVD.

"The Flaming Spittoon Acquisition." *The Big Bang Theory The Complete Fifth Season*. Writ. Chuck Lorre, Steven Molaro and Dave Goetsch. Dir. Mark Cendrowski. Warner Bros., 2012. DVD.

"The Fuzzy Boots Corollary." *The Big Bang Theory: The Complete First Season*. Writ. Chuck Lorre. Dir. Mark Cendrowski. Warner Bros., 2009. DVD.

"The Gorilla Experiment." *The Big Bang Theory: The Complete Third Season*. Writ. Chuck

Lorre, Richard Rosenstock and Steve Holland. Dir. Mark Cendrowski. Warner Bros., 2010. DVD.

"The Grasshopper Experiment." *The Big Bang Theory: The Complete First Season*. Writ. David Goetsch and Steven Molaro. Dir. Ted Wass. Warner Bros., 2009. DVD.

"The Hamburger Postulate." *The Big Bang Theory: The Complete First Season*. Writ. Jennifer Glickman. Dir. Andrew D. Weyman. Warner Bros., 2009. DVD.

Idato, Michael. " Word's Out, Geeks Rule." *The Sydney Morning Herald*. Fairfax Media. 16 June 2011. Web. 5 Sept. 2012.

"The Isolation Permutation." *The Big Bang Theory: The Complete Fifth Season*. Writ. Chuck Lorre, Eric Kaplan and Tara Hernandez. Dir. Mark Cendrowski. Warner Bros., 2012. DVD.

Jenkins, Henry. *Textual Poachers: Television Fans and Participatory Culture*. New York: Routledge, 1992. Print.

Jensen, K. Thor. "11 Reasons Geeks Hate The Big Bang Theory." *UGO Entertainment*. IGN Entertainment. 12 Jan. 2012. Web. 4 Sept. 2012.

"The Justice League Recombination." *The Big Bang Theory: The Complete Forth Season*. Writ. Lee Aronsohn and Maria Ferrari. Dir. Mark Cendrowski. Warner Bros., 2011. DVD.

Katzman, Gregg. "Reasons Geeks Love The Big Bang Theory." *UGO Entertainment*. IGN Entertainment. 19 Jan. 2012. Web. 4 Sept. 2012.

Kendall, Lori. *Hanging Out in the Virtual Pub: Masculinities and Relationships Online*. Berkeley: University of California Press, 2002. Print.

"The Killer Robot Instability." *The Big Bang Theory: The Complete Second Season*. Writ. Richard Rosenstock and Bill Prady. Dir. Mark Cendrowski. Warner Bros., 2009. DVD.

"The Love Car Displacement." *The Big Bang Theory: The Complete Forth Season*. Writ. Chuck Lorre, Bill Prady and Dave Goetsch. Dir. Anthony Rich. Warner Bros., 2011. DVD.

"The Lunar Excitation." *The Big Bang Theory: The Complete Third Season*. Writ. Chuck Lorre, Bill Prady and Maria Ferrari. Dir. Peter Chakos. Warner Bros., 2010. DVD.

"The Middle-Earth Paradigm." *The Big Bang Theory: The Complete First Season*. Writ. Dave Goetsch. Dir. Mark Cendrowski. Warner Bros., 2009. DVD.

"The Nerdvana Annihilation." *The Big Bang Theory: The Complete First Season*. Writ. Bill Prady. Dir. Mark Cendrowski. Warner Bros., 2009. DVD.

"The Panty Piñata Polarization." *The Big Bang Theory: The Complete Second Season*. Writ. Bill Prady and Tim Doyle. Dir. Mark Cendrowski. Warner Bros., 2009. DVD.

Patten, Dominic. "Full 2012–2013 TV Season Series Rankings." *Deadline*. PMC. 23 May 2013. Web. 12 June 2013.

"The Peanut Reaction."*The Big Bang Theory: The Complete First Season*. Writ. Lee Aronsohn and Bill Prady. Dir. Mark Cendrowski. Warner Bros., 2009. DVD.

"The Recombination Hypothesis." *The Big Bang Theory: The Complete Fifth Season*. Writ. Chuck Lorre. Dir. Mark Cendrowski. Warner Bros., 2012. DVD.

"The Shiny Trinket Maneuver." *The Big Bang Theory: The Complete Fifth Season*. Writ. Chuck Lorre, Steve Holland and Tara Hernandez. Dir. Mark Cendrowski. Warner Bros., 2012. DVD.

Sinfield, Alan. *Fautlines: Cultural Materialism and the Politics of Dissident Reading*. Oxford: Oxford University Press. 1992. Print.

"The Spaghetti Catalyst." *The Big Bang Theory: The Complete Third Season*. Writ. Chuck Lorre, Bill Prady, Lee Aronsohn and Steven Molaro. Dir. Anthony Rich. Warner Bros., 2010. DVD.

"The Thespian Catalyst." *The Big Bang Theory: The Complete Forth Season*. Writ. Chuck Lorre, Lee Aronsohn and Jim Reynolds. Dir. Mark Cendrowski. Warner Bros., 2011. DVD.

Toulouse, Stephen. "The Big Bang Controversy." *Stepto.com*. n.p. 24 Sept. 2012. Web. 24 Sept. 2012.

"Tramps Like Us." *The IT Crowd: The Complete Third Season*. Writ. Graham Linehan. Dir. Graham Linehan. 2 Entertain, 2009. DVD.

"The 21-Second Excitation." *The Big Bang Theory: The Complete Forth Season.* Writ. Chuck Lorre, Bill Prady and Jim Reynolds. Dir. Mark Cendrowski. Warner Bros., 2011. DVD.

"The Vacation Solution." *The Big Bang Theory: The Complete Fifth Season.* Writ. Chuck Lorre, Anthony Del Broccolo and Tara Hernandez. Dir. Mark Cendrowski. Warner Bros., 2012. DVD.

Vanderlinden, Mary. "Could It Be? It's Becoming Chic to be Geek." *Flow.* Department of Radio-Television-Film. 25 Sept. 2012. Web. 29 Sept. 2012.

"The Wheaton Recurrence." *The Big Bang Theory: The Complete Third Season.* Writ. Chuck Lorre, Steven Molaro, Nichole Lorre and Jessica Ambrosetti. Dir. Mark Cendrowski. Warner Bros., 2010. DVD.

Science in Stilettos
Shaping Perceptions of Women in Science

Lauren R. Archer

Popular images of science reflect contemporary views on science while also shaping public understanding of scientific endeavors (LaFollette, *Making Science Our Own* 79; Dudo et al., 762). At a time when, for most Americans, exposure to scientific issues primarily comes from media, the images of science conveyed in primetime television can have an even greater influence in shaping how Americans see both science and scientists (Dudo et al.; Steinke). As David Kirby argues in "Scientists on the Set," "The representation of natural phenomena, scientists, and research spaces, whether they represent 'good science' or not, are all rendered 'realistic' within the filmic framework, making it difficult for the public to separate fact from fiction" (273). Thus, the images of scientists contained within primetime television can shape the perception viewers have of scientists as real people even when those images represent fictional personas.

Overwhelmingly males have dominated the images of scientists in mass media (LaFollette, *Making Science Our Own* 79; Dudo et al., 762). This domination is significant because research shows that television and film characters can significantly impact younger viewers as they develop an understanding of gender roles and begin imagining their future professional identities (Steinke 28; Long, Boiarsky, and Thayer 257). Such studies posit the idea that cultural depictions of science as male-dominated and unwelcoming to women may be partially responsible for the low numbers of girls who want to enter into science, engineering, and technology professions. Despite a historically male-dominated vision of science, recently a number of primetime television shows have included female scientists as key characters, from *Bones* to the *CSI* franchise to *The Big Bang Theory* (hereafter *BBT*). Given this increase, the portrayal of female scientists in primetime television deserves more attention in order to understand how these characters might be influencing American perspectives about science more broadly and the role of women in science more specifically. *BBT*'s popularity as well as its inclusion of multiple female scientist characters (including two main characters and a number of minor characters) makes it an excellent text for exploring the image of female scientists conveyed on primetime television.

Through a rhetorical analysis of the CBS sitcom *BBT*, I explore how the show aids in the creation of character types for female scientists. Examining the show across its six seasons, I trace how two dominant character types emerge: the "hyper-feminized" female scientist and the "ultra-rational" female scientist. On the surface the female scientists introduced on *BBT* may seem to provide intellectual challenges to the foundational male characters on the show and offer images of strong females in the profession who can hold their own alongside their male counterparts. However, emphasis on the traditional femininity of the character or her sexuality obscure these more empowering images. Ultimately these character types work to draw attention to the gender of these characters, marking them as women and thus minimalizing the "threat" they pose to the male scientists of the show (and by extension male viewers). These portrayals not only limit viewer conceptions regarding the role of women in science, but also constrain possibilities for identification among female viewers. These depictions simultaneously work to inscribe rationality and detached objectivism as the ideal for scientific efforts. Given the traditional association of these traits with males, I argue that through the portrayal and treatment of female scientist characters, *BBT* subtly perpetuates an image of science as rightfully dominated by males, a message of particular concern given the wide viewership the show garners.

Before turning to my analysis of the female scientist characters on *BBT*, I briefly overview some of the relevant literature that traces the connection between mass media and public attitudes toward science as well as the depictions of women in science. I then examine the image of female scientists created by *BBT*, followed by an examination of some viewer responses to these characters. Finally, I end with a discussion of what these portrayals might imply about how Americans see the role of women in science.

Cultural Representations of Science

As Marcel LaFollette notes in her book *Making Science Our Own*, "As instruments of education and entertainment, fact and fiction, the mass media help to shape public beliefs and knowledge about all sorts of things, but they are most influential when describing places, people, and events outside the readers' everyday experience" (18). Mass media can play a particularly strong role in shaping public understanding of science since most citizens base their perceptions of science not primarily on first-hand knowledge of science or exposure to research and development processes but rather on education and mass media (LaFollette, *Making Science Our Own* 18; Nelkin 2). Additionally, research indicates that once outside the educational system, the majority of a citizen's exposure to science and technology (hereafter S&T) issues comes from media, with television serving as the primary source for exposure (National Science Board 7–7).

LaFollette demonstrates how images and messages about science within mass circulation magazines from 1910 to 1955 both influenced and reflected public perception of science: "Stereotypes in the mass media drew readers' attention to salient aspects of research and thereby guided and influenced political support for research" (*Making Science Our Own* 4). In more contemporary times, images of science have shifted from the glossy pages of mass market magazines to the bright glow of the television and computer screen (National Science Board 7–4). Americans report that 40 percent of their information about S&T comes from television, followed by 28 percent from the Internet and only 11 percent from newspapers and 11 percent from magazines (National Science Board 7–10). Many studies of science on television focused specifically on news coverage of scientific issues or science-focused educational programming, but images and messages about science in general entertainment television also carry significance for the viewing public (Gerbner et al., 41). Shows that heavily feature science, such as *BBT* or even the *C.S.I.* franchise and *House*, can also contribute to public exposure to science and shape how viewers see both science and scientists (Apsell; Nowotny 1117).

Media effects scholars have considered the relationship between popular television images of science broadly conceived and public attitudes toward science, as well as their understanding of the subject, from a variety of perspectives. In the 1980s Gerbner et al. conducted one of the earliest studies of science coverage in entertainment television. This cultivation study argued that despite the mainly positive (although infrequent) images of science and scientists on television, heavy television viewers tended to express a lack of faith in science institutions (Gerbner et al., 42). Given this finding the study concluded, "Television, on the whole, seems to make few friends for science but may confuse and alienate its potentially most likely students and supporters" (Gerbner et al., 41). The results of the Gerbner et al. study, although facing criticism since its publication, helped demonstrate the unexpected impact television viewing can have on attitudes toward science.

More recent research has developed updated media effects models for understanding the relationship between media portrayals of S&T and viewers' perceptions of science (Nisbet et al.; Dudo et al.). One study, by Nisbet et al., traced both direct and indirect effects of media use on perceptions of S&T. While use of newspapers, science television, and science magazines contributed to increasing belief in the benefits of science, general television viewing demonstrated a more ambiguous effect, increasing *both* belief in the promise of science and reservations about science (Nisbet et al., 601). A subsequent study updated Gerbner et al.'s cultivation study while taking into account the indirect effects television viewing has on scientific knowledge (Dudo et al.). While Dudo et al. did not find a strong direct effect between heavy television viewing and negative attitudes toward science, they did find support for displacement theory, establishing that television viewing has indirect effects on attitudes toward science because it negatively impacts scientific knowledge (768). They also found that portrayals of scientists had not changed much since the Gerbner et al. study—although images of scientists remained relatively infrequent in comparison with other professions, the portrayals tended to be positive.

Some studies have considered the influence of cultural images of scientists in the U.S. mass media more directly. Researchers use the "Draw a Scientist Test" (DAST) to determine how people envision scientists and how early that image develops (Chambers). From the DAST a dominant image emerges—depictions of the scientist as a white male, wearing glasses and a lab coat, often surrounded by laboratory equipment or technology dominate the images drawn by children participating in this test (Chambers 257). Administration of DAST across a variety of age groups shows the establishment of this stereotype as early as fourth or fifth grade (Chambers 259). This imagery doesn't just circulate among children. Such stereotypes about scientists have existed in Americans' minds for quite some time. Through her analysis of depictions of science during the first half of the 20th century, LaFollette identified certain repeated portrayals, such as the scientist as magician or the scientist as hero (*Making Science Our Own* 97–109). Such depictions framed the work of science as well as the people who conducted it, highlighting the wonder of what science discovered and the developments it enabled while also explaining scientists' motives for their research. As Lafollette further demonstrated, these portrayals fit within particular consistent narratives about how the scientific enterprise functioned. As LaFollette argued, "Many of our strongest beliefs about science come from what we think scientists are like, principally because those beliefs include assumptions about how the appearance, personality, and intellect of scientists relate to the importance and consequences of their work" (*Making Science Our Own* 66). That so often these depictions display males rather than females similarly shapes who we think can and should do the work of science.

The Elusive Female Scientist

Research has confirmed that this stereotypical image of the scientist gets perpetuated through television programing and feature films (Gerbner et al., 44; Long, Boiarsky, and Thayer 257–258) and that scientists in the media tend to be white males. Reviews of early 20th century magazine coverage of science personalities reveal the rarity of images of or stories about female scientists (LaFollette, "Eyes on the Stars" 262). When depicted, they tended to be portrayed as unusual—both as women and as scientists (LaFollette, "Eyes on the Stars" 262). Similarly, a review of DAST images revealed that children rarely drew female scientists, and then, only girls drew them (Chambers 261). Content analysis of science educational programming demonstrates that, encouragingly, female scientists receive the same treatment as their male counterparts; however, they receive significantly less screen time, possibly reinforcing perceptions of science as a masculine field (Long, Boiarsky, and Thayer 264–265). However, educational programing in the U.S. tends to be limited and draws smaller audiences. Images of scientists on the big screen offer the most likely source of citizen exposure. In a study of female scientist depictions in feature films, analysis revealed certain patterns in those depictions. Although scarcer than male scientist characters, female scientists often held leadership positions or at least a position in equal standing to their male colleagues (Steinke 44). However, female scientists faced challenges or questioning from their co-workers more often than male colleagues, and these films often depicted them struggling to handle both their professional life and their love life (Steinke 48–49). Female scientist characters were also generally quite attractive and if depicted as unattractive in the beginning of a film, that character typically received a makeover by the end of the film, transforming her into a more attractive person (Steinke 39). Researchers argue that these depictions of female scientists shape perceptions of what a life in science is like for women, potentially making it seem like a challenging or unappealing career choice (Long, Boiarsky, and Thayer 266–267; Steinke 54–55). As a result, these studies suggest a connection may exist between film portrayals of female scientists and the lack of girls entering science or engineering fields (Steinke 55).

Although the presence of female scientists in films, educational television, and other science-focused television programming has received attention from scholars, less attention has been paid to character depictions in serial television shows. While films may feature the greatest number of different female scientist characters, female scientist characters on television series also have the potential to significantly impact viewers, especially given their weekly appearance over the course of a season. This repetition creates opportunities for viewers to develop a deeper understanding of and identification with particular characters. As such, identifying and analyzing patterns of female scientist depictions within a particular series can reveal the influence these characters might have on viewers.

Character Types

Rhetorical scholar Celeste Condit's concept of "character types" provides a particularly useful concept for understanding some of the standardizations of female scientists that emerge within television shows. Condit used the concept in a study that traced images and discussions regarding abortion on popular fictional television shows in the '80s ("TV Articulates Abortion in America" 54). Condit defined character types as "universalized descriptions of particular agents, acts, scenes, purposes, or agencies" that have become "culturally accepted as accurate depictions" ("Democracy and Civil Rights" 4). For example, a fairly standardized image of a "Boy Scout" or "the South" comes to mind when those terms get used (Condit, "Democracy and Civil Rights" 4). Although somewhat similar to stereotypes, character-types do not assume a particular standardized portrayal is negative or avoidable; in other words, stereotypes represent a type of more narrowly defined character-type.

Condit argued that character-types serve as foundational elements in narratives. As such, character-types play a role in constructing and limiting narrative choices because in order to maintain narrative coherence only certain actions seem reasonable for particular character-types (Condit, "TV Articulates" 54). In fictional outlets, certain character-types come to be associated with certain narratives. In her study, Condit found that in maintaining narrative coherence for the character-types used, television shows ended up limiting the perspectives presented regarding abortion ("TV Articulates Abortion in America" 53). Condit argued the ways in which these shows constrained the discussion and excluded certain viewpoints could influence viewers' understanding and treatment of abortion in their own lives. In this way, character-types link the political and the fictional. As Condit noted, "The inter-textuality of politics and entertainment is based on the fact that each operates out of a common pool of character-types ("TV Articulates Abortion in America" 54). In other words, the character-types (and their accompanying narratives) deployed in the entertainment realm can influence action within the political realm and vice versa. Thus, the standard images of scientists created for television can create expectations among the public for how scientists should operate in the real world or even who should be a scientist.

In this essay I examine the character types of female scientists developed on *BBT* and explore the potential influence of those images on public perceptions of scientists, particularly the role of women in science, engineering, and technology fields. A rhetorical analysis of *BBT* demonstrates how the show inscribes powerful yet potentially problematic character types of female scientists through visual images and dialogue exchanges. While many of the characters' personality features drive the humor of the show, they also shape how audience members subsequently view scientists in the real world.

Women and Scientists on BBT

Although *BBT* did not immediately become a huge hit, with its quirky main characters and abundance of science fiction pop culture references, it did not take long for the show to build a significant following (Bennett). By the end of its fourth season, the show had won over a significant fan base among the coveted 18–49 year old demographic, and CBS renewed the show for three more seasons (Grunewald). However, not all viewers so readily embraced the show, in particular due to its treatment of women. Even some self-proclaimed fans of the show complained about the flatness of Penny's character (the main female character in the cast) and the overall absence of relatable female characters (Ball; Holmes; Polo). When the show added more main characters, it did so in a way that balanced out the main cast, which up to that point had consisted of four male characters who were either scientists or engineers and one female character who was an aspiring actress/waitress. With the addition of two recurring female characters—Amy Farrah Fowler and Bernadette—by the end of the third season, the show not only finally incorporated more women into the main cast, it incorporated women who were scientists.

Preceding Amy and Bernadette, a number of minor characters or one-episode female scientist guests appeared throughout the first three seasons and originally Amy and Bernadette also started as guest stars. However, the show eventually added Amy and Bernadette into the main cast and they began receiving significant airtime. They also represent the two female scientist character types featured prevalently on the show. As noted above, character types describe depictions that have become somewhat standardized and accepted as accurate portrayals of a particular person, place or thing (Condit, "Democracy and Civil Rights" 4; Condit, "TV Articulates Abortion in America" 54). An examination of the various female scientists portrayed on *BBT* reveal two main character types: the "hyper-feminized" female scientist, most strongly represented by Bernadette's character, and the "hyper-rational" female scientist, most strongly represented by Amy Farrah Fowler's character.

The Hyper-Feminized Female Scientist

The hyper-feminized character type of the show depicts the female scientist in a way that emphasizes her femininity—Bernadette represents the perfect example of this. She is first introduced in season three as one of Penny's friends from work and a potential love interest for Howard ("The Creepy Candy Coating Corollary"). A petite, cute girl with long blonde hair and bangs, Bernadette epitomizes the little girl look. Her voice is high-pitched and even a bit squeaky. She wears glasses and her wardrobe consists mainly of floral print dresses with full skirts topped off with a cardigan, tights and flats. Her outfits highlight her curvy figure, particularly emphasizing her small waist and ample chest. Overall Bernadette's appearance underscores her girl-next-door aura. This girl-next-door persona extends to Bernadette's personality as well. When Amy and Penny ask Bernadette to spy on Leonard's new girlfriend, she defends herself as a "good girl," claiming that she is not a good liar ("The Wildebeest Implementation"). All these features emphasize her femininity, making her an appealing and likable character.

The show further emphasizes Bernadette's feminine qualities by frequently portraying her as a highly nurturing person, often comforting other characters. When Sheldon gets stuck on a physics problem and hasn't slept for days, Bernadette steps in to "mother" him:

> BERNADETTE: Okay, Sheldon. What happens to our neuroreceptors when we don't get enough REM sleep?
> SHELDON: They lose their sensitivity to serotonin and norepinephrine.
> BERNADETTE: Which leads to...?
> SHELDON: Impaired cognitive function.
> BERNADETTE: Right, so march in there, brush your teeth and go to bed.
> SHELDON: (in a whining tone) But I don't want to go to bed.
> BERNADETTE: (sternly) I'm going to count to three. One....
> SHELDON: (reluctantly) Oh, all right.
> LEONARD: That was amazing how you handled him.
> BERNADETTE: I know how to deal with stubborn children. My mother used to run an illegal day care center in our basement.

During this exchange Bernadette takes on a very motherly persona (talking to Sheldon as if he were a child, counting to three), rather than engaging with Sheldon as a peer. The scene emphasizes Bernadette's nurturing, motherly characteristics rather than her intellectual ones, but given the tendency to emphasize femininity with this character type, the narrative fits the character (as opposed to an exchange where Bernadette would engage with Sheldon on a more intellectual level).

This motherly framing of Bernadette intensifies as the series continues and the relationship between Howard and Bernadette progresses. As the couple moves closer to marriage, a tension develops between them because Howard, who still lives with his mom, expects Bernadette to care for him in the same way, from cutting his meat to doing his laundry and bringing him breakfast in bed ("The Pulled Groin Extrapolation"). Although Bernadette initially expresses resistance, she seems to eventually give in to Howard's expectations, even working with Howard's mother to meet all his needs ("The Pulled Groin Extrapolation"). Bernadette begins to replace Howard's mother even more literally when she begins to yell in the same manner as his mother does. In one episode Sheldon mistakes Bernadette's voice for Howard's mother and in another episode Howard accidentally calls Bernadette "Ma" several times ("The Good Guy Fluctuation"; "The Countdown Reflection"). On the show, the voice of Howard's mother is iconic, as the character never actually appears on screen. Having Bernadette take on such a distinguishing feature of Howard's mother further frames her in the role of Howard's caretaker and support (especially since Howard lives with his mother up until marrying Bernadette). This larger narrative on the show portrays Bernadette as embracing this fairly traditional gender role.

In addition to highlighting the maternal, nurturing aspects of her character, the show also emphasizes Bernadette's femininity by portraying her as desirable. As a nurturing person, Bernadette frequently comforts Raj when he expresses feeling lonely. In one episode, after Bernadette reassures Raj that plenty of women might be interested in him, Raj tries to kiss her ("The Boyfriend Complexity"). Raj then develops a crush on Bernadette, writing poems about her and concocting elaborate fantasies where his best friend Howard dies or has to leave the country but gives Raj permission to look after Bernadette "sexually" ("The Thespian Catalyst"). In these fantasies, it is Bernadette herself that specifies that Raj must look after her sexual needs. In one fantasy she even comments that while most of her needs are normal, some are a little "messed up." These portrayals of Bernadette, although only imagined by Raj, frame Bernadette as an object of desire; as such she becomes the object of the male gaze (Mulvey 383), further emphasizing her femininity.

Overall, the narratives Bernadette participates in emphasize her femininity over her intelligence. On the show, viewers often hear Bernadette commenting on what might be considered very "girly" things, like Penny's cute shoes or nails, rather than referencing her professional life ("The 21-Second Excitation"; "The Gorilla Experiment"). This emphasis on Bernadette's femininity seems a purposeful character choice by the show's producers. For example, although Bernadette's voice is fairly high pitched, an interview with Melissa Rauch—the actress who plays Bernadette—reveals that she naturally speaks at a lower pitch (*The Big Bang Theory*; "Bernadette's Voice—The Show"). Despite the fact that Bernadette eventually earns her PhD in microbiology and lands a high-paying job with a major pharmaceutical company, the show minimizes her identity as a scientist. When first introduced on the show, it is as a waitress, and if she is shown working, she is typically at the Cheesecake Factory, not in her lab. This changes some once Bernadette begins working for the pharmaceutical company and quits working at the Cheesecake Factory; however, even then she typically sits at a desk rather than being in a lab, further minimizing her identity as a scientist. These placements of the character highlight certain details over others. In fact, one blogger misidentifies Bernadette as a waitress, failing to mention that she relied on her food service job to put her through graduate school (Blickenstaff). This misidentification of Bernadette's profession underscores the argument that the show downplays Bernadette's professional accomplishments for the sake of focusing on her feminine qualities.

When Bernadette does discuss her work as a microbiologist, it is often in a fairly nonchalant way that implies a sense of frivolity to what she does. She light-heartedly jokes about accidents at work, such as crossing Ebola with the common cold or accidentally dropping flesh-eating bacteria in the animal cages ("The Desperation Emanation"; "The 21-Second Excitation"). When not making light of workplace snafus, Bernadette de-emphasizes the significance of her research. In "The Gorilla Experiment" Bernadette expresses more excitement for an experiment Leonard is conducting than her own work, commenting, "The most exciting thing I get to work with is yeast." This same episode further emphasizes Bernadette's femininity over her intellect when Howard becomes jealous of her interest in Leonard's work. When Leonard invites Bernadette to observe his experiment, Howard sees it as a threat to his relationship rather than a reflection of Bernadette's intellectual interests. Howard assumes that Leonard's invitation indicates sexual interest, not intellectual camaraderie ("The Gorilla Experiment"). Howard's reaction enforces viewing Bernadette as an object of sexual desire rather than as a scientific colleague.

Such depictions portray Bernadette as, first and foremost, a woman who only secondarily happens to be a scientist. Not only that, but Bernadette fails to exhibit a strong sense of identification with her profession. In one episode she remarks that if she hadn't gone into science she would have been an ice dancer, and she continually makes light of the work she does, despite the highly complex nature of microbiology ("The Gorilla Experiment"). Thus, Bernadette may be a scientist, but through the narratives about her on the show, she is constructed as a "dumb blonde" scientist. By over emphasizing her femininity and undermining her intellectual achievements, the show depicts Bernadette as a character who shouldn't be taken too seriously, rather than as a character who might reframe the stereotypical image of scientists or inspire young women to consider scientific careers.

While Bernadette creates the strongest example of the hyper-feminized female scientists, some of the minor characters introduced on the show also demonstrate this character type. Ramona, the graduate student who becomes Sheldon's caretaker so that he can focus on his work, represents another hyper-feminized female scientist ("The Cooper-Nowitzki Theorem"). Similar to Bernadette, Ramona conveys innocence, with her hair in pigtails, her brightly colored hoodies, and her gushing admiration for Sheldon. Although she quickly conveys her intellectual aptitude through her ability to understand Sheldon's work, she takes on a very traditional female role in this episode. She does Sheldon's grocery shopping, gives him pedicures, and takes care of other tedious tasks so that he can concentrate on his research. At one point she tells Penny, "he's a gift to the whole world and we can't be selfish," justifying her support of Sheldon and his work through completing domestic tasks, even though, as a graduate student, she could potentially contribute intellectually to this work ("The Cooper-Nowitzki Theorem"). By the end of the episode, Ramona fully embraces a motherly persona, chastising Sheldon for spending time on comic books and video games rather than working out equations, and she even takes away his toys so that he won't be distracted. While at first Sheldon seems quite happy to have the attention, by the end of the episode he appears stifled by Ramona's attentiveness, but he doesn't know how to get rid of her. It is not until Ramona asks for credit on Sheldon's latest breakthrough that he demands she leave, implying that he does not view her as worthy of sharing credit with him, despite the support she provided that allowed Sheldon to achieve his breakthrough.[1] Ramona's character and Sheldon's subsequent treatment of her depict women as appropriate to provide a support system for male scientists but not to works as collaborators, and as such, the episode naturalizes a sense of science as appropriately dominated by men.

Dr. Elizabeth Plimpton, another one-episode character, also fits this hyper-feminized character type ("The Plimpton Stimulation"). Sheldon hosts Dr. Plimpton, a cosmological physicist visiting from Princeton, when she comes to Caltech. She is clearly highly intelligent, given Sheldon's respect for her. Leonard also refers to her as a "world-renowned scientist" and reveals that he highly admires her work. But throughout the episode her gender receives more attention than her professional accomplishments. In preparing for her visit, Sheldon makes sure to get feminine products for Dr. Plimpton, going so far as to ask Penny for her tampon brand preference and purchasing Activia yogurt because it is made specifically for women ("The Plimpton Stimulation"). When Dr. Elizabeth Plimpton arrives, her feminine qualities shine through. She dresses in bright, bold colors, mostly skirts with multiple layers of shirts and cardigans, often trimmed with lace or a flower. Like Bernadette she also has a high-pitched voice and comes across as very sweet and polite. Unlike some of the other hyper-feminized portrayals, rather than focusing on Dr. Plimpton's maternal nature, this episode highlights her femininity as a sexual being. In fact most of the action of the episode revolves around this aspect of her character. On her first night in town, she seduces Leonard when she enters his room in nothing but a robe and confesses that she was naked when she wrote part of her book (which Leonard is reading). She then proceeds to "demonstrate" her writing process for Leonard, dropping her robe. This scene literally undermines Dr. Plimpton's intellectual achievements by having her book (as a representative of her scholarly work) trumped by her feminine appeal. Throughout the remainder of the episode, Dr. Plimpton flirts with Sheldon's friends and makes comments laden with sexual innuendo. At the end of the episode, Leonard and Howard find her at Raj's apartment where she tries to seduce all of them by appearing in some sexy, silky bright pink and purple lingerie. This episode focuses on images of Dr. Plimpton as the "naughty" girl next door rather than providing viewers with a glimpse of what established her as a leader in her field or why Sheldon refers to her as "one of the great minds of the 21st century" ("The Plimpton Stimulation"). As such, this portrayal emphasizes her sexual identity as a woman rather than her professional identity as a scientist.

This character type of the "hyper feminized" female scientist implies that one is a woman first and a scientist second. Indeed its portrayal aligns with LaFollette's observations that depictions of female scientists in the early 20th century tended to emphasize the domesticity of these individuals ("Eyes on the Stars" 267). Such images frame female scientists as still possessing traditional female characteristics—nurturing, sweet, and attractive. At the same time, since character-types constrain narrative choices, making certain story lines implausible for particular characters, such depictions also work to constrain a character to a more traditional female role as the "weaker" sex, ultimately subordinate to men. Bernadette voices this explicitly in one episode when she reveals that she listens to NPR, rather than Howard, for intellectual stimulation. She states, "I'm much smarter than he is, but it's important to protect his manhood" ("The Alien Parasite Hypothesis"). This comment reinforces traditional male-female roles by having Bernadette consciously work to limit the threat her intelligence might pose to her husband by downplaying her aptitude. This portrayal not only may limit identification for viewers who have rejected more traditional concepts of gender roles but also may help perpetuate inequality in the work force by implying that even in the sciences, women are still viewed as the "weaker" sex or that they should minimize their intellectual capabilities so as to not threaten their male colleagues.

The Hyper-Rational Female Scientist

The other character type evident on *BBT*—the "hyper-rational" female scientist—frequently gets utilized to frame the characters on the show. As stated earlier, Amy Farrah Fowler represents the strongest and most frequently seen example of the character-type; however, this character type also describes a number of minor characters, including Leonard's mother and Leslie Winkle, a fellow Caltech physicist. This character type portrays female scientists as highly rational, intelligent, and unemotional. Characters fitting this type are also typically socially awkward, as they are oblivious to most social cues, and fairly homely in appearance and quite unfashionable. For example, viewers first meet Leslie Winkle when Leonard decides to ask her out on a date ("The Fuzzy Boots Corollary"). Leslie's hair is tied back and she is wearing a baggy hoodie and safety goggles, since she is working with lab equipment. She replies to Leonard's date request in a very matter of fact manner:

> LESLEY: Would you agree that the primary way we would evaluate either the success or failure of the date would be based on the bio-chemical reaction during the goodnight kiss?
> LEONARD: Heart rate, pheromones, etc., yes.
> LESLEY: Well, why don't we just stipulate that the date goes well and move to the key variable?
> LEONARD: You mean, kiss you now?
> LESLEY: Yes.
> LEONARD: Can you define the parameters of the kiss?
> LESLEY: Closed mouth but romantic. Mint?
> LEONARD: Thank you. *(Takes mint)*. Shall I count down from three?
> LESLEY: No, I think it needs to be spontaneous. *(They kiss).*

In her evaluation of their kiss, Leslie remarks on the technique and mentions the lack of arousal almost as an afterthought, as if the kiss were an objective empirical study rather than a social interaction. This exchange portrays Leslie as emotionally unattached, emphasizing her rational nature. Given that Leslie is the first female scientist featured on the show, her character conveys a lot about assumptions of what women in science look and act like.

Leonard's mother—Dr. Beverly Hofstadter—similarly falls into the hyper-rational character type. A psychotherapist with a degree in neuroscience, Leonard's mother is incredibly precise and analytical and has an almost robotic way of speaking. She wears glasses and her wardrobe consists of business suits in dark solid colors. In her first scene on the show, Penny runs into her in the apartment lobby as she stands looking at the elevator:

> PENNY: It's out of order.
> LEONARD'S MOTHER: Yes, I can read the sign. I'm just pondering the implications.
> PENNY: I think it implies that the elevator doesn't work.
> LEONARD'S MOTHER: Again, I can read the sign. But the sign and the tape are covered with a layer of dust, which indicates that the elevator has been non-functional for a significant amount of time. Which suggests either a remarkable passivity among the, I assume, 24 to 36 residents of this building—based on the number of mailboxes and given typical urban population density—or a shared delusion of functionality.
> PENNY: You must be Leonard's mother.
> LEONARD'S MOTHER: Oh, I don't know if I must be, but yes ["The Maternal Capacitance"].

This highly rational outlook gets highlighted further when Leonard's mother reveals that she only had sexual intercourse with her husband for the purposes of reproduction and that they each wrote an academic paper about the experience ("The Maternal Capacitance"). Sheldon finds this quite admirable. He expresses a high level of approval of Leonard's mother, treating her as an intellectual equal and allowing her to take a PET scan of his brain. In fact, as revealed during a later episode, Leonard's mother stays in contact with Sheldon after her visit, communicating with him more frequently than her own son ("The Maternal Congruence"). Again this character enforces an image of female scientists as highly rational and emotionally unavailable.

In some ways Leonard's mother offers a prototype for Amy Farrah Fowler, a character later introduced as essentially a female version of Sheldon. When Howard and Raj create an online dating profile for Sheldon, the site produces Amy Farrah Fowler as a match ("The Lunar Excitation"). When Sheldon meets Amy—after being blackmailed into it—he finds himself enjoying Amy's company despite himself:

AMY: Excuse me. I'm Amy Farrah Fowler. You're Sheldon Cooper.
SHELDON: Hello, Amy Farrah Fowler. I'm sorry to inform you that you have been taken in by unsupportable mathematics designed to prey on the gullible and the lonely. Additionally, I'm being blackmailed with a hidden dirty sock.
AMY: If that was slang, I'm unfamiliar with it. If it was literal, I share your aversion to soiled hosiery. In any case, I'm here because my mother and I have agreed that I will date at least once a year.
SHELDON: Interesting. My mother and I have the same agreement about church.
AMY: I don't object to the concept of a deity, but I'm baffled by the notion of one that takes attendance.
SHELDON: Well, then you might want to avoid East Texas.
AMY: Noted. Now, before this goes any further, you should know that all forms of physical contact up to and including coitus are off the table.
SHELDON: (with a slightly surprised but admiring look) May I buy you a beverage?
AMY: Tepid water, please ["The Lunar Excitation"].

Amy typically speaks in a fairly flat and almost robotic tone. She often misinterprets social cues or doesn't comprehend when she makes inappropriate comments, and she tends to interpret things literally. When Penny asks how her life is in one episode, Amy replies, "Like everybody else's. Subject to entropy, decay and eventual death. Thank you for asking" ("The Zazzy Substitution"). Amy's wardrobe typically consists of a variety of mismatched patterns and colors made up of a knee length, baggy skirt, dark tights, a solid color T-shirt, a floral patterned collared shirt, and a striped sweater vest or cardigan, topped off by a brightly colored coat and with her purse worn across her body. She wears her dark brown hair, long and straight, with just a small plain barrette to hold her bangs back. And, of course, she wears glasses. This wardrobe, largely inherited from her dead grandmother, clearly conveys that she is not into fashion and perhaps a little out of synch with the times.

While these ultra-rational female scientists may not be well versed in fashion trends, they do demonstrate high levels of intelligence. In one episode Leslie Winkle fixes a mistake in one of Sheldon's equations, causing him to lament the possibility of having to share a Nobel Prize with her ("The Hamburger Postulate"). Leonard's mother is described as highly successful, and it is revealed that she has a number of books on child rearing and family relationships ("The Maternal Capacitance"; "The Maternal Congruence"). And once Amy starts to hang out with Sheldon's friends, Sheldon claims Leonard doesn't like her because he is threatened intellectually ("The Zazzy Substitution"). While these women may be socially awkward and unstylish, they do exhibit high levels of intellectual achievement.

These ultra-rational female scientists seem to possess the ideal traits of scientists—highly intelligent, rational, and unemotional as well as a little socially awkward. In many ways the development of this character type offers great promise for re-crafting the dominant image of scientists as male. After all, these women can clearly hold their own alongside the best and brightest of their male colleagues and unlike the hyper-feminized character type, they more strongly emphasize their professional identity as scientists and express more pride in their achievements. However, the potential equal footing between these women and the male characters on the show gets undermined by shifting attention from their intellectual capabilities to their sexuality. For example, the majority of Leslie Winkle's appearances on the show revolve around her role as a sexual partner, first for Leonard, then Howard. After the first time Leonard and Leslie have sex, Leonard appears in her lab the next day, trying to cuddle with her. Leslie pulls away, explaining, "I don't know about your sex drive, but I'm probably good 'til New Year's" ("The Hamburger Postulate"). While Leslie remains emotionally detached from her sexual encounters, she still seeks out companions to fulfill those needs, however infrequently they occur. For Leslie, her sexual encounter with Leonard "scratched an itch" that once satisfied allowed her to return to things as normal, including her research. As such, Leslie's sexuality gets portrayed as a necessary evil of sorts, an element of her being that disrupts her typically hyper-rational mindset, but an element that must be addressed nonetheless.

Similarly, while on her first visit, Leonard's mother comes across as cold and unemotional. On her second visit though, she goes to a bar with Penny, in a storyline that reveals a whole new aspect of her personality. As she drinks, she literally sheds her ultra-rational persona, taking off her glasses, letting down her hair, and visibly loosening up with every shot she drinks ("The Maternal Congruence"). At one point she uncharacteristically remarks, "I'm seriously considering asking that busboy to ravish me in the alleyway while I eat cheesecake" ("The Maternal Congruence"). Toward the end of the episode, Leonard's mother spontaneously grabs Sheldon and kisses him vehemently. After un-planting her lips from him, she remarks that she would rather have the bus boy ("The Maternal Congruence"). With her actions, Leonard's mother not only acts on her sexual impulses, she expresses a preference for one male (the busboy) over another (Sheldon), confirming that she experiences sexual attraction. Considering that earlier in the episode Leonard's mother revealed that she hasn't had sex with her husband in eight years, this behavior seems quite unusual. As the narrative plays out, her sexual nature seems to get the better of her, despite her normally reserved and rational demeanor. The episode ends with Leonard's mother apologizing to Sheldon for her "inappropriate behavior," further enforcing a sense of her sexuality as a weakness ("The Maternal Congruence").

This pattern of ultra-rational females giving into their sexual natures *despite* their intellect continues with Amy Farrah Fowler. Although in her early appearances she seems as awkward and asexual as Sheldon, viewers begin to see the sexual side of Amy emerge. In one episode, Amy encounters one of Penny's hot ex-boyfriends and becomes so taken by him that she begins involuntarily saying, "Hoo" ("The Alien Parasite Hypothesis"). When her friends comment on the verbal tic, she declares, "I obviously have the flu coupled with sudden-onset Tourette's syndrome," seemingly oblivious to her own sexuality. Later in the episode, after an extensive diagnosis process with Sheldon that had them contemplating whether Amy had been infected by an alien parasite or was, perhaps, menopausal, Amy comes to recognize the real nature of her symptoms:

> AMY: I think we need to face the cold, hard truth; I was sexually aroused by Penny's friend Zack.
> SHELDON: Hang on. I don't know that we've given the alien parasite hypothesis a fair shake.
> AMY: Let's look at this logically. I have a stomach; I get hungry. I have genitals; I have the potential for sexual arousal.
> SHELDON: A cross we all must bear ["The Alien Parasite Hypothesis"].

By referring to sexual arousal as a "cross to bear," this exchange conveys the view that Amy's (or anyone's) sexual nature creates a burden. Sheldon makes it clear that—from his perspective—to act on that nature undermines one's intellectual capabilities. Later in the episode, after Amy decides not to pursue her sexual impulses, Sheldon remarks on his satisfaction that Amy ultimately chose her intellect over her base desires, further enforcing a view of sexuality as a weakness. However, after this episode Amy would not show this same restraint. Similar to the shift shown with Leonard's mother, as the show progresses, Amy's sexuality comes to play a more central role in her character, from Amy making innuendo-laden comments, often directed at Penny, to her acknowledging her desire for physical connection with Sheldon once they start dating. In "The Fish Guts Displacement," one of the key storylines highlights Amy's increased sexuality in juxtaposition with Sheldon's complete disinterest. When Amy gets sick, Sheldon reluctantly takes care of her. Amy begins getting frustrated with Sheldon's lack of empathy, but when he suggests using VapoRub, she perks up:

> AMY: Sheldon, this isn't helping. Why don't you just let me get some rest?
> SHELDON: How can you sleep? I'm not done making you feel better. I still have to put a cold rag on your head, sing to you, and apply VapoRub to your chest.
> AMY: You, you want to rub something on my chest?
> SHELDON: Yes. All over it.

AMY: Maybe we should start with that.
SHELDON: Now you're being a responsible patient. Now, you may notice some tingling.
AMY: Oh, I'm counting on it.

Amy jumps on the opportunity to have some physical connection with Sheldon, even if he remains oblivious to its sexual nature. Even after she has recovered, Amy continues to feign illness so she can continue to get this attention from Sheldon, implying that only under the ruse of illness will she be able to receive the intimacy she desires from Sheldon in their relationship. Bernadette finds out about Amy's deception and criticizes it, calling it something "lunatics do" ("The Fish Guts Displacement"). Amy acknowledges that she needs to tell Sheldon the truth, but ultimately, driven by her sexual needs, she continues to lie. When Sheldon finds out she has been lying, he demands that Amy be reprimanded. Even in this exchange, Amy's sexuality becomes a focus—when Sheldon suggests she be spanked (of course oblivious to the sexual overtones), Amy gladly accepts her punishment. While the earlier episode implied that giving in to one's sexual desires undermine intellectual abilities, this episode shows how they can come to overrule all reasoning and even honesty, as Amy resorts to deception in order to these needs satisfied, even if by a person who remains unaware of all the implications of their interactions. As such, the episode problematically implies that women can become so driven or overwhelmed by their sexual needs that they no longer can tell right from wrong nor have the power to resist or rise above this part of their nature.

Having sexual desires is not limited to women, and the show doesn't ignore the sexuality of the men on the show; however, the depictions of the male characters and the female characters differ significantly when it comes to sex. While the show often involves narratives revolving around Leonard, Howard, and Raj's sexual needs and experiences, these stories always emphasize this as a matter of defining their manhood. When they are successful, there is always a tone of triumph as the characters celebrate their ability to break out of their nerdy ways and get laid. For the men on the show, wanting sex is natural and having sex is a victory. But for Leslie, Leonard's mother, and Amy, having a sexual drive, or worse, acting on it, gets depicted as a weaknesses or character flaw.

Although the hyper-rational character type portrays female scientists as highly respectable in some regards, it also conveys the idea that there are limits to the rationality of any woman because eventually she, like Amy Farrah Fowler, will be distracted by her sexual nature. Thus, ultimately the show preserves Sheldon—with his detached objectivity, unemotional demeanor and extreme rationality—as the superior example of a scientist as he does not succumb to his base animal instincts or get overtaken by his emotional side. Through these narratives and the different depictions of the appropriateness of one's sexuality depending on one's sex, the character types and interactions featured on *BBT* undermine an image of the female scientist as an equal to her male counterparts. Such constructions imply that while women may assume the scientific persona for professional purposes, just like they may put on a lab coat when working in the laboratory, like the lab coat, the scientific persona is not innate to their nature. Ultimately only men inherently possess the traits required to be successful in the scientific realm—rationality, detached objectivism, and the power to control their sexual natures.

Interestingly enough, the show explicitly addressed the issue of women in science during an episode in the sixth season ("The Contractual Obligation Implementation"). The episode begins with Howard, Leonard, and Sheldon (quite reluctantly) brainstorming how to motivate more women to enter into science. This discussion starts due to a job requirement. With this framing, the show has already presented the problem of fewer women in science as an issue people (or at least men) don't care about unless forced to care about it. While Leonard claims to "believe in" the cause, a job contract obligation actually forces him to take action on the issue ("The Contractual Obligation Implementation").

Ultimately Sheldon suggests they talk to young girls to help motivate them to consider a career in science, so the three of them arrange to make an appearance at Howard's old school. However, the talk goes horribly. As Leonard goes into a tangent about his childhood dreams, Sheldon has a breakthrough:

> SHELDON: While I was listening to my colleagues waste your time, it occurred to me that it might be much more meaningful to hear about women in science from actual women in science, and, uh, I happen to know two brilliant examples who have agreed to speak to you on the phone right now. Uh, Dr. Rostenkowski, Dr. Fowler, are you there?
> AMY: *(voice)* We're here.
> SHELDON: Thank you for taking time out of your very busy schedule to enlighten these young women.
> AMY: It's our pleasure. I'm Dr. Fowler, and I'm a neuroscientist.
> BERNADETTE: And I'm Dr. Rostenkowski Wolowitz, and I'm a microbiologist.
> AMY: The world of science needs more women, but from a young age, we girls are encouraged to care more about the way we look than about the power of our minds.
> BERNADETTE: That's true. Every one of you has the capacity to be anything you want to be ["The Contractual Obligation Implementation"].

This scene contains a number of positive elements regarding its portrayal of female scientists. First, Sheldon refers to Amy and Bernadette as "brilliant," which is a very rare compliment from him. Having his character express praise and approval of these two women in science underscores treating female scientists equally and respecting their work. Additionally, this is one of the few times in the show that these characters are referenced as Dr. Fowler and Dr. Rostenkowski Wolowitz, which highlights their credentials and status. Third, the show presents a positive message of encouragement for girls to consider the sciences. However, the show undermines these positive elements because ultimately the scene plays as a joke. While Sheldon, Leonard, and Howard are at the school, Amy and Bernadette (along with Penny) skipped work to go to Disneyland and while there decided to get princess makeovers. Thus, as Amy and Bernadette dismiss the cultural assumption that beauty counts for more than brains, viewers see the two of them dressed as Cinderella and Snow White, presenting a visual contradiction to the argument they are making for the merits of women in science and beyond. While they tell this classroom of girls that looks don't matter, the characters themselves have given in to their desire to look as pretty as a princess. In one scene the show so clearly demonstrates the entirety of the argument I've been making here—that for every spark of possibility it offers for re-envisioning the role of women in science or motivating future trailblazers, it simultaneously erodes that message by contradicting it, often for the sake of making a joke.

Reception

While one can identify the development and use of these character types on the show, it is important to not grant too much agency to these television portrayals in terms of how they influence viewers' perceptions of female scientists. As Edward Schiappa argues in *Beyond Representational Correctness*, it is possible to find problems with any media portrayal and perhaps over-inscribe the impact any one representation creates. However, this does not mean critics should stop looking for problematic representations; rather it means claims should be tempered and if possible, evidence of audience impact should be gathered (Schiappa 87). Although not as empirical in nature as the type of audience response Schiappa recommends, a look at reception in the form of blog posts and article comments demonstrates that viewers have noticed some elements central to the character types outlined above. For example, viewers have noticed (and tend to dislike) the elevated pitch of Bernadette's voice ("Bernadette's Voice—The Show"). Viewers complain that they find it hard to believe that Bernadette works in microbiology or they argue that she doesn't add much to the show, while other viewers claim to like her precisely because she is so "cute" ("Bernadette—The Show"). Such comments indicate that Bernadette's "girly" persona tends to distract viewers from the fact that she is, indeed, a scientist. Viewers also recognize that Amy Farrah Fowler was introduced primarily as a character who could intellectually challenge Sheldon ("Bernadette's Voice—The Show"; "The Female Geeks Apology—The Show"). However, some viewers express mixed feelings regarding Amy's character; while they enjoy the Sheldon-like awkwardness she exhibits, they are less comfortable with some of her "toilet" humor ("What's Your Opinion of Amy Farrah Fowler?"; "I Seriously Hate Amy Farrah Fowler—The Show"). For these viewers, the emphasis on Amy's sexuality undermines her socially awkward, ultra-rational persona.

Some bloggers have discussed explicitly the role of sexuality in the portrayal of female scientists on *BBT*. One blogger notes that while the show incorporates some highly intelligent females that challenge the assumption that intellect is inherently a male trait, the focus on the sexuality of these characters limits the impact of that challenge (McIntosh). In a post written before the addition of Bernadette and Amy Farrah Fowler to the show, a blogger critiques the show for its over-reliance on a variety of stereotypes, arguing that in the *BBT* world, "Women who are scientists are sorta ugly and wear glasses and are not blond and are socially maladjusted and don't care about their appearance and—if they do have sex—they are kinda slutty about it and sleep around" (McIntosh). These observations draw attention to how the narratives developed for these characters limit identification with them for viewers, especially female fans.

Schiappa also argues that as much as critics may want to point out and break down every problematic representation on television or in film, it is also important to take note of those representations that break the mold, even if they fall short of perfection (165). For many viewers Leslie Winkle offers one such representation. Her ability to "outsmart" Sheldon and leave him speechless makes her a strong, highly intelligent character with whom viewers can identify. In fact, some viewers lament the loss of Leslie's character and express their hope that the writers will bring her back ("The Female Geeks Apology—The Show"; "Bring Back Leslie Winkle!—The Show"). One viewer even argues that Leslie should be viewed as a strong woman who treats the men on the show as sex objects rather than vice versa (Newitz). The possibilities viewers see for Leslie's character highlight the potential *BBT* has to change viewers' perspectives of the female scientist.

Additionally, at times Bernadette also pushes on the very gender role norms her character tends to enforce. Despite her traditional nature and her highly feminine persona on the show, Bernadette does occasionally break from this norm. By the end of the fourth season Bernadette earns her PhD, surpassing Howard's masters degree, and lands a high-paying job, making her the primary "breadwinner" in the relationship ("The Roommate Transmogrification"). She even asks Howard to sign a prenuptial agreement because she makes significantly more money than him (although this decision seems to originate with her father, and Bernadette seems less committed to it) ("The Vacation Solution"). In another episode Howard learns that she doesn't want to have children while he does ("The Shiny Trinket Maneuver"). While often in media women are portrayed as desiring children while men shy away, *BBT* breaks that mold to offer an alternative perspective. Bernadette's solution to this impasse in their relationship is to let Howard stay home with any children they have. These aspects of Bernadette's character provide discursive openings that provide viewers with opportunities for envisioning different narratives; however, they appear so infrequently that they don't carry enough force (yet) to outweigh the more traditional female role Bernadette typically assumes. Nevertheless, these alternative portrayals point to places where viewers might resist more traditional gender roles and adopt alternative perspectives on the role of women in science. At the same time, they underscore the untapped potential the show has to push back on these cultural assumptions through alternative discourses that offer a new vision of the female scientist.

Conclusion

The female scientist character types employed on *BBT* ultimately place the emphasis on "female" rather than "scientist." The "hyper-feminized" character type implies that femininity and traditionalism go hand in hand while the "ultra-rational" character type hints that an exaggerated sexuality can be used to compensate for social shortcomings. By relying on the repeated use of these character types, the show depicts female scientists as either constrained by traditional gender roles that lead them to emphasize their "innate" feminine nature or distracted by their sexual desires *despite* their rationality. In both cases such portrayals mark these characters as women first and scientists second. The show further enforced a perception of science as a male domain by not incorporating a female scientist as a full member of the main cast or even having any female scientist character who received significant airtime until the fourth season. The development of these female scientist character types throughout the series carries implications not only for viewers' perception of scientists and the role of women in the scientific enterprise, but also for gender roles more generally. Given the respect granted to science, conveying it as a man's world ruled by rationality and detached, unemotional objectivism with little room for women also promotes these as ideal traits more broadly, privileging characteristics typically associated with males. Additionally, female viewers of the show, whether in scientific professions or not, may adopt problematic ideas about being a woman. Although the two character types discussed here do not cover the full range of female character types used on *BBT*, they do represent the main female personalities utilized on the show. While such depictions may help remove any threat these characters might pose to the male scientists on the show (and by extension male viewers), they also entrench the idea that (the best) scientists are male and imply that a woman is always a woman first and only a scientist second, which is a troubling message to send all the viewers tuning in each week.

Note

1. This refusal to share credit may have less to do with the fact that Ramona is a female scientist and more to do with the fact that Sheldon's character is unlikely to share credit with anyone, but the fact that the show chose to have a female in this role means the scene can still be interpreted as devaluing female scientists.

Works Cited

Apsell, P. "Sex, Lies, and Science Television." *Communicating the Future: Best Practices for Communication of Science and Technology to the Public*. National Institute of Standards and Technology, 2002. Print.
Ball, Peter M. "Why I Have a Problem with the Big Bang Theory." *PeterMBall*. 16 Mar. 2011. Web. 29 Sept. 2012.
Bennett, Tara. "Geeks Embrace This 'Big Bang Theory' Too." TODAY.com. Web. 28 Sept. 2012.
"Bernadette—The Show." *The Big Bang Theory Forums* 28 Feb. 2012. Web. 30 Sept. 2012.
"Bernadette's Voice—The Show." *The Big Bang Theory Forums* 24 Sept. 2012. Web. 29 Sept. 2012.
The Big Bang Theory: The Complete Fifth Season [Blu-ray]. Warner Home Video, 2012. Film.
Blickenstaff, Jacob Clark. "The Big Bang Theory Effect." *NSTA Reports*. NSTA WebNews Digest. Web. 17 June 2011.
"Bring Back Leslie Winkle!—The Show." *The Big Bang Theory Forums*. 30 Sept. 2012. Web.
Cendrowski, Mark. "The 21-Second Excitation." *The Big Bang Theory*. CBS. 11 Nov. 2010. Television.
_____. "The Alien Parasite Hypothesis." *The Big Bang Theory*. CBS. 9 Nov. 2010. Television.
_____. "The Boyfriend Complexity." *The Big Bang Theory*. CBS. 18 Nov. 2010. Television.
_____. "The Contractual Obligation Implementation." *The Big Bang Theory*. CBS. 7 Mar. 2013. Television.
_____. "The Cooper-Nowitzki Theorem." *The Big Bang Theory*. CBS. 3 Nov. 2008. Television.
_____. "The Countdown Reflection." *The Big Bang Theory*. CBS. 10 May 2012. Television.
_____. "The Creepy Candy Coating Corollary." *The Big Bang Theory*. CBS. 19 Oct. 2009. Television.

_____. "The Desperation Emanation." *The Big Bang Theory*. CBS. 21 Oct. 2010. Television.
_____. "The Einstein Approximation." *The Big Bang Theory*. CBS. 1 Feb. 2010. Television.
_____. "The Fish Guts Displacement." *The Big Bang Theory*. CBS. 6 Dec. 2012. Television.
_____. "The Fuzzy Boots Corollary." *The Big Bang Theory*. CBS. 8 Oct. 2007. Television.
_____. "The Good Guy Fluctuation." *The Big Bang Theory*. CBS. 27 Oct. 2012. Television.
_____. "The Gorilla Experiment." *The Big Bang Theory*. CBS. 7 Dec. 2009. Television.
_____. "The Maternal Capacitance." *The Big Bang Theory*. CBS. 9 Feb. 2009. Television.
_____. "The Maternal Congruence." *The Big Bang Theory*. CBS. 14 Dec. 2009. Television.
_____. "The Plimpton Stimulation." *The Big Bang Theory*. CBS. 10 May 2010. Television.
_____. "The Pulled Groin Extrapolation." *The Big Bang Theory*. CBS. 29 Sept. 2011. Television.
_____. "The Roommate Transmogrification." *The Big Bang Theory*. CBS. 19 May 2011. Television.
_____. "The Shiny Trinket Maneuver." *The Big Bang Theory*. CBS. 12 Jan. 2012. Television.
_____. "The Thespian Catalyst. " *The Big Bang Theory*. CBS. 3 Feb. 2011. Television.
_____. "The Vacation Solution." *The Big Bang Theory*. CBS. 9 Feb. 2012. Television.
_____. "The Wildebeest Implementation." *The Big Bang Theory*. CBS. 5 May 2011. Television.
_____. "The Zazzy Substitution." *The Big Bang Theory*. CBS. 7 Oct. 2010. Television.
Chakos, Peter. "The Lunar Excitation." *The Big Bang Theory*. CBS. 24 May 2010. Television.
Chambers, David Wade. "Stereotypic Images of the Scientist: The Draw-a-scientist Test." *Science Education* 67.2 (1983): 255–265. *Wiley Online Library*. Web. 28 Sept. 2012.
Condit, Celest M. "Democracy and Civil Rights: The Universalizing Influence of Public Argumentation." *Communication Monographs* 54.1 (1987): 1–18. *Taylor and Francis+NEJM*. Web. 28 Sept. 2012.
_____. "TV Articulates Abortion in America: Competition and the Production in Cultural Repertoire." *The Journal of Communication Inquiry* 11.2 (1987): 47–59. Print.
Dudo, Anthony, et al. "Science on Television in the 21st Century Recent Trends in Portrayals and Their Contributions to Public Attitudes Toward Science." *Communication Research* 38.6 (2011): 754–77. crx.sagepub.com. Web. 28 Sept. 2012.
"The Female Geeks Apology—The Show." *The Big Bang Theory Forums* 17 May 2011. Web. 29 Sept. 2012.
Gerbner, George, et al. "Scientists on the TV Screen." *Society* 18.4 (1981): 41–4. *SpringerLink*. Web. 28 Sept. 2012.
Grunewald, Elizabeth. "Audiences Love Nerds: Big Bang Theory Renewed For 3 More Years." *The Escapist*. Web. 28 Sept. 2012.
Holmes, Linda. "How A Thorough De-Gazing Saved CBS's 'The Big Bang Theory': NPR." NPR.org. 6 Jan. 2010. Web. 30 Sept. 2012.
"I Seriously Hate Amy Farrah Fowler—The Show." *The Big Bang Theory Forums* 26 May 2011. Web. 30 Sept. 2012.
Kirby, David A. "Scientists on the Set: Science Consultants and the Communication of Science in Visual Fiction." *Public Understanding of Science* 12.3 (2003): 261–78. pus.sagepub.com. Web. 28 Sept. 2012.
LaFollette, Marcel C. "Eyes on the Stars: Images of Women Scientists in Popular Magazines." *Science, Technology, & Human Values* 13.3/4 (1988): 262–75. Print.
_____. *Making Science Our Own: Public Images of Science, 1910–1955*. Chicago: University of Chicago Press, 1990. Print.
Long, M., G. Boiarsky, and G. Thayer. "Gender and Racial Counter-stereotypes in Science Education Television: A Content Analysis." *Public Understanding of Science* 10.3 (2001): 255–69. pus.sagepub.com. Web. 28 Sept. 2012.
McIntosh, Heather. "Gendering Intelligence and Sexuality on The Big Bang Theory." *Flow* 14.1 (2011): n. pag.

Mulvey, Laura. "Visual Pleasure and Narrative Cinema." *Visual Culture: The Reader*. Ed. Jessica Evans and Stuart Hall. London: Sage, 1999. 381–89. Print.

National Science Board. *Science and Engineering Indicators 2010*. Arlington, VA: National Science Foundation, 2010. Print.

Nelkin, Dorothy. *Selling Science: How the Press Covers Science and Technology*. New York: W.H. Freeman, 1995. Print.

Newitz, Annalee. "Why the Women of the Big Bang Theory Are More Interesting Than the Men." *io9*. 22 Sept. 2011. Web. 29 Sept. 2012.

Nisbet, Matthew C., et al. "Knowledge, Reservations, or Promise? A Media Effects Model for Public Perceptions of Science and Technology." *Communication Research* 29.5 (2002): 584–608. crx.sagepub.com. Web. 28 Sept. 2012.

Nowotny, Helga. "High- and Low-Cost Realities for Science and Society." *Science* 308.5725 (2005): 1117–1118. www.sciencemag.org. Web. 29 Sept. 2012.

Polo, Susana. "Why the Big Bang Theory Is Good for Geeks, and Why I Hate the Big Bang Theory." 3 Mar. 2010. Web. 28 Sept. 2012.

Schiappa, Edward. *Beyond Representational Correctness: Rethinking Criticism of Popular Media*. Albany: State University of New York Press, 2008. Print.

Steinke, Jocelyn. "Gender Representations of Scientists." *Encyclopedia of Science and Technology Communication*. Ed. Susanna Hornig Priest. London: Sage, 2010: 323–26. Print.

Weyman, Andrew D. "The Hamburger Postulate." *The Big Bang Theory*. CBS. 22 Oct. 2007. Television.

"What's Your Opinion of Amy Farrah Fowler?—Page 2—The Show." *The Big Bang Theory Forums* 11 Sept. 2011. Web. 29 Sept. 2012.

The Big Theory on the (Not So) *Bang*in' Jewish Mother

Julia Spiegel

"Howard, get the door!" Mrs. Wolowitz shouts from an unseen room. "Really, is that what you do when someone knocks? I had no idea!" Howard sarcastically replies in "The Lizard-Spock Expansion," his voice increasing in irritation with each syllable. Howard is one of the four main characters on *The Big Bang Theory* (*BBT*), and one of his functions is to offer the audience a storyline with a Jewish mother character. This exchange between him and his mother is classic in the series and the viewer hears this and versions of this joke time and time again. Before diving in to the storyline of Howard and his mother, Mrs. Wolowitz, it is important to briefly explain the show in conversation. *The Big Bang Theory* presents the story of four brilliant young men as they navigate their way through "normal life" problems like finding and dating women, making robots, and enjoying *Star Trek* marathons. Leonard anchors the show, often functioning as the mouthpiece of sanity while his three best friends get into one absurd situation after another. Dr. Rajesh Koothrappali, Dr. Sheldon Cooper, and Howard Wolowitz—shamelessly teased by his three friends for the absence of a doctoral degree to his name, although he did earn his M.Eng., master's in engineering from MIT—provide the show's humor with their silly adventures and elaborate predicaments. Penny, the tall attractive blonde who lives next door, serves as a foil to the show's nerdy protagonists. She is an aspiring actress with very minimal knowledge on anything intellectual, particularly science—the occupation, hobby, and beloved pastime of the show's four main characters. Later in the series Dr. Amy Farrah Fowler and Dr. Bernadette Rostenkowski arrive on the show, the former as Sheldon's intellectual and socially awkward female counterpart, and the latter as Howard's (not Jewish) love interest. Bernadette and Howard's relationship is a very apt jumping off point for introducing the other woman in Howard's life: his mother. This is because Howard's relationship with Bernadette is highly informed by his relationship with his mother, which happens to be a very stereotypical Jewish mother/son paradigm. So Howard cannot simply engage in an adult romantic relationship; he is bound to his mother in adolescent ways, and she maintains an overbearing grip on him far past childhood. These circumstances, among other stereotypical qualities of the Jewish mother/son relationship, present challenge after challenge for Howard as he attempts to develop a serious relationship with Bernadette. Mrs. Wolowitz' characterization as an example of the Jewish mother stereotype will be at the forefront of this essay.

The Big Bang Theory, a show with four male characters at its center, seems to have a lot to say about the females that exist on the margin. The portrayal of Howard's mother, Mrs. Wolowitz, deserves particular attention for her clichéd representation of the Jewish mother figure. Through an analysis of the show's six seasons, comparing my findings to previous scholars' understanding of the Jewish mother stereotype, as well as an inclusion of gender theory and theory of stereotypes, I intend to place Mrs. Wolowitz in the larger history of representations of the Jewish mother, and explore the nature of this particular example found in *BBT.* Two central features of *BBT*'s Jewish mother cause her to be a stereotype. The first is the character's tie to earlier manifestations of this figure; indicating the continuity of representations of the Jewish mother over time. Mrs. Wolowitz, *BBT*'s Jewish mother, is indebted to earlier comediennes—for instance Belle Barth and Sophie Tucker as well as male creations of this figure such as those made famous by Philip Roth, Woody Allen, and Paul Mazursky—for her style of humor, a variety of comedy that continues to find success in contemporary media texts over a century after its establishment. The other component that places Mrs. Wolowitz within the definition of stereotype is her disembodiment throughout the series. The portrayal of Howard's mother is so reliant upon the familiar Jewish mother stereotype that the audience never needs to see her to know everything about her. In fact, the viewer never does see her, except when the writers teased the audience with a distant view of her a couple of times late in the series. The audience hears her from behind a bathroom door, or a dressing room curtain, or from a different room. Ultimately, the disembodiment of Mrs. Wolowitz proves the show's reliance on the Jewish mother stereotype and very little else for its comedic success. Additionally, in the case of Mrs. Wolowitz, the recursive nature of her presentation—whether in terms of the boundaries of the show itself or throughout time—denotes a problematic trend in contemporary portrayals of the Jewish mother. While the representation of the Jewish mother in *BBT* remains unquestionably within the parameters of a stereotype, here seems to be a shift in focus from earlier productions of the Jewish mother figure from ethnic or religious cues of otherness to ones pertaining to gender. One way this occurs is through the representation of Mrs. Wolowitz through the perspective of her son, Howard. The audience knows Mrs. Wolowitz as Howard knows her; only on rare occasions do we know something about her from her own perspective, and those moments serve as important windows of light into the intricacies of this particular example. This point does not mean to imply that previous portrayals of Jewish mothers are free of the (often) critical opinions of her son about her: the name of the stereotype denotes a mother/child relationship. It is, in fact, essential that the relationship of the Jewish mother to her children exist for the stereotype to exist. Later I will discuss how and why it mostly pertains to her relationship with her son.

This frame for thinking about the Jewish mother figure allows for consideration of *who* is creating the character in every example. It seems that female culture-makers had a large role in establishing the Jewish mother image and setting the foundation for certain attributes that have remained since its inception, but that the domain quickly switched over to male culture-makers, and Mrs. Wolowitz is one of the most current examples of the comedic representation of a Jewish mother made by men. Thus, while religious or cultural cues of otherness occur on occasion throughout the series, Mrs. Wolowitz is far more commonly understood by and teased for her attributes that pertain to her identity as a female. Examples of her gender description may come in the form of anywhere from her parenting techniques to her bathroom habits or her physical appearance. I will argue that Mrs. Wolowitz does not, in fact, bring anything new to the tradition of comedic Jewish mother representations, but that this example illuminates a paradigm shift in regard to the once more equal emphasis of ethnic, religious, and gender specific cues of otherness in the Jewish mother in popular culture, to one that now focuses the spotlight far more heavily on only gender.

> What is the difference between a Rottweiler and a Jewish Mother?
> Eventually, the Rottweiler lets go.

If Mrs. Wolowitz is a stereotype as this essay posits, then it is important to know a bit about how stereotypes function. Postcolonial theorist Homi Bhabha explains that a stereotype is "a complex, ambivalent, contradictory mode of representation, as anxious as it is assertive, and demands not only that we extend our critical and political objectives but that we change the object of analysis itself" (100). In other words, it would be a mistake to understand a stereotype as one fixed thought. Copious factors make it so that the stereotype, by definition, cannot be reduced to one stagnant image. One such factor is viewers' varying perspectives and interpretations of that representation, as well as the fact that *we make that stereotype by describing it*. Each description, either direct or indirect, recreates and molds the stereotype.

While Bhabha's thoughts on the structure of stereotypes help to understand the process behind it, historian Joyce Antler's *You Never Call! You Never Write! A History of the Jewish Mother* supplies the specifics about the Jewish mother figure. Antler points out a collection of more or less recurrent descriptions that accompany the Jewish mother figure throughout its history. Antler tracks the Jewish mother stereotype from its origin, through its transformations, to its treatment in popular culture, in memoirs, in personal stories, in academia and in politics, and the condition of the Jewish mother in current times. Describing the Jewish mother as "a universally recognized metaphor for nagging, whining, guilt-producing maternal intrusiveness" (2), Antler asks the questions: what are the reasons for the resilience and popularity of this image throughout the twentieth century and onto the twenty-first? And why has this stereotype been the punching bag for so many for so long (2)? Antler's work was published in 2007, the same year that *BBT* came out on CBS and introduced their Jewish mother character. The continuity of Antler's observations and the popular culture products demonstrates the sustained need to ask those questions she posited in her book. Without question Mrs. Wolowitz fits into the history of the Jewish mother that Antler gracefully draws for her readers. Her work sets the foundation for understanding representations that we see today in television and other media outlets. In addition, it serves as a timeline comparison: we can look at what came before and compare it to what is being created now. The Jewish mother figure has been known to hold a tight grip on her children, particularly her son. She has a knack for embarrassing him time and time again, and never letting up on her impeccable talent for guilting him.

Before exploring the how and why behind the Jewish mother, it seems appropriate to offer a brief sketch of the stereotype over the course of the last century. Susan Glenn, writing on theatre and early feminism in her book *Female Spectacle: The Theatrical Roots of Modern Feminism,* brings up an essential component—perhaps even the key—to the contour of the Jewish mother image: excessiveness. The important quality of excessiveness is that it can apply to any number of character traits. Put the word "excessively" or "overly" before the following adjectives and one has the generic Jewish mother stereotype: nurturing, guilt-producing, interfering, and sexually undesirable (Antler 2). A number of female performers working at the turn of the twentieth century blazed the trail for Jewish comediennes later on, and a portion of their work set the foundation for the contemporary Jewish mother image, namely, the idea of being physically or culturally "unfit" in comparison to the gentile masses.

Glenn explains that the turn of the twentieth century saw an avenue for female comediennes to find acceptance on the stage through what she calls "cultural girth" or excess (Glenn 46). Although Glenn's work focuses more on female performers who played central roles in creating their own public image, it provides an analytical foundation to a study of comedic female characters such as Mrs. Wolowitz because, as previously noted, excessiveness is at the heart of the characterization of the Jewish mother figure. Some of the oldest examples of Jewish mothers onstage, Sophie Tucker and Belle Barth, capitalized on their size for laughs, Sarah Blacher Cohen explains in her essay "The Unkosher Comediennes: From Sophie Tucker to Joan Rivers" (107–111). Excessiveness applied to a variety of facets of these early Jewish mother personas, largeness, of course, being the most evident and basic form of that. Both Tucker and Barth were heavy women, as one might think with the phrase "cultural girth." Nevertheless, largeness is not limited to physicality. Many of these performers were excessively naughty, or overly sexual, or too improper. In the case of Sophie Tucker, it was often her brazen sexual desires that were excessive, in addition to her appetite. A classic example of Sophie Tucker's utilization of her overweight form, her unapologetic onstage sexuality, and her Jewishness comes in a line from one of her famous routines: "I've put a little more meat on. So what, there's more schmaltz to sizzle when I turn the heat on" (Cohen 107). Schmaltz refers to rendered fat commonly used in Jewish cooking at the time.

While Tucker denied propriety with her unabashed musings on sex, she was also setting the stage for the classic Jewish mother figure in other ways, particularly one of her most famous routines called "My Yiddishe Mamme." Cohen writes on Tucker's unique combination of the Jewish mother speaking the words of a sex-starved woman in "The Unkosher Comediennes: From Sophie Tucker to Joan Rivers":

> Because of her girth, [Tucker] assumed the role of the Jewish mother figure. Indeed her most winning number was her tearful rendition of "My Yiddishe Mamme." Though Jews viewed sex not as a sin but as a virtuous act to be enjoyed within the framework of marriage, they still did not expect their food-pushing mammas to be starved for sex, let alone publicly announce their craving for sex... The incongruous spectacle of a large Jewish mother in heat initially produced shame in the audience, but since she so wittingly exaggerated her needs, their shame quickly dissolved into laughter [107–8].

Tucker had an admirable combination of personal characteristics and experiences that she wanted to emphasize in her onstage persona (at the forefront was her sexual appetite and romantic life more generally) and a utilization of already familiar traits that defined her for the audience (her largeness, and her use of Yiddish, both leading to her identification as a Jewish mother figure).

Tucker and Mrs. Wolowitz both share, for a brief moment, the storyline of the independent woman with a love life. In season six Mrs. Wolowitz finds a boyfriend: Howard's dentist, Dr. Schneider. Nevertheless, this storyline never becomes fully developed and it seems that it was more of a tangent for Mrs. Wolowitz.

A key distinction between Tucker and Mrs. Wolowitz is that Tucker had the power to turn the stereotype on its head and include her own story in her routine. She was able to talk and sing about her own life, including her sex life, and own her performance. That is why Tucker turned her audiences' shame to laughter, as Cohen wrote (107–8). And she was able to make her Jewish mother unique. She remains an important Jewish female performer and a trailblazer for the Jewish mother image, yet let us not forget her individualism as a performer, and her courage to challenge audiences' conceptions of the Jewish mother image. Cohen is right about Tucker's unique use of romantic and sexual language for a woman of her time and age, but I would also like to point out the Jewishness in her performance. Looking at Tucker's routines, we can see how *Yiddishisms* were far more prevalent in her time. For example, in a song about a woman who becomes pregnant before marriage, Tucker sings: "Mistah Siegel, Mistah Siegel, in my *boich is schoen a kiegel* (in my belly is already a noodle pudding). Mistah Siegel, make it legal for me" (Cohen 108). Tucker uses Yiddish for the funny line, and Cohen indicates that "her equation of the growing fetus inside her to the Yiddish *kiegel* or noodle pudding ludicrously converts the product of her sin into a gastronomic anomaly" (108–9).

Belle Barth, performing at around the same time as Tucker, shared a knack for offending audiences, although she is best remembered for her scatological humor (Cohen 110). Barth "put into practice Lenny Bruce's autobiography, *How to Talk Dirty and Influence People.* Only she employed more Yiddish to talk dirty than he, especially in her scatological humor of bodily excretions" (Cohen 111). Cohen argues that Barth employed Yiddish to replace the most vulgar word in the sentence as a way to intensify the offensiveness (111). For example, she would often say, "This drink tastes like *pishartz*" (urine) (111). Just as Tucker shares her physical girth with Mrs. Wolowitz, Barth and *BBT*'s Jewish mother have something in common: a tendency for discussing their bathroom habits. To take it one step further, Tucker's distinction from Mrs. Wolowitz is comprised of two facets: her use of Yiddish words and phrases in her act, and her brazen sexual appetite. Similarly, Barth departs from Mrs. Wolowitz in terms of her use of Yiddish as a way to emphasize the vulgarity, far more than what we hear on *BBT.*

"My mother's brisket is to die for"

Howard Wolowitz' storyline consists of his outrageous techniques for wooing women, although that all changes when he meets a nice *Shiksa* who went to Catholic day school and wears a cross necklace: Bernadette. They fall in love, which seems to create all kinds of trouble for Howard's overbearing, guilt-producing Jewish mother Mrs. Wolowitz. Howard has a dual function within the series, one of which is to provide the stereotype of the Jewish son to pull into existence and complete the stereotype of his mother. Going along with his role as the Jewish son on the show, Howard also provides the viewer with an understanding of Mrs. Wolowitz. Portrayed through conversations, often arguments, with her son, or descriptions by him, she is known to the audience as Howard knows her.

Mrs. Wolowitz is always yelling, usually at Howard, in the recognizable New York accent commonly associated with American Jews. Her dialogue generally consists of her troubles in the bathroom, the "up keep" of her unattractive body—which entails shaving her mustache, putting on her wig (which is not meant to be an indicator of her orthodoxy, rather, a sign of her withering femininity), and more—and lastly, her largeness (for instance in one episode she expresses her frustration at putting on her girdle). When she is not around, the talk about her most frequently alludes to Howard's childish dependence on her, or his arguably inappropriate involvement in her grooming routine (he cannot stay over at Bernadette's one night because he has to help his mother draw on her eyebrows and pin her hair up in the morning). As it has been stated, Mrs. Wolowitz easily conforms to all of the aspects of the Jewish mother stereotype: she nags and treats Howard like a child, she obsesses over him, and he in return depends on her as if he was still fifteen, and will not move out of her home. She is undoubtedly intended to be portrayed as unattractive and overweight, and her relationship with Howard regularly calls upon the stereotype of the oedipal dynamic between a Jewish mother and her son. She is excessive in all of these qualities.

I will now go through a series of moments in greater detail in which Mrs. Wolowitz' stereotypical qualities are illuminated. Calling back to Glenn's book *Female Spectacle: The Theatrical Roots of Modern Feminism* which deals with physical excessiveness and its early start in female comedy, it seems fitting to begin by examining Mrs. Wolowitz' all-too-well-known largeness and consequent undesirability. It is important to point out that physical girth is not meant to imply inevitable unattractiveness; rather, it is a comment on the writers' manipulation of normative ideas of beauty to accomplish their desired portrayal of Mrs. Wolowitz as not beautiful. Judith Butler's ideas in *Gender*

Trouble are valuable here: the normative imagination of gender is defined and reaffirmed through representations of counter-normative performances, and the converse is also true; "hence, one is one's gender to the extent that one is not the other gender" (30). This observation can also apply to reaffirming normative displays of either masculinity or femininity within one gender.

While Sophie Tucker embraced her girth to emphasize her sexual needs and attractiveness, Mrs. Wolowitz' size serves to highlight her utter lack of sexual appeal. In "The Hawking Excitation," Sheldon, indebted to Howard for the opportunity to meet Stephen Hawking, must take Mrs. Wolowitz shopping. Frustrated, Mrs. Wolowitz shouts from behind the dressing room curtain, "It's this dress! When I put my front in, the back pops out, and when I put my back in, the front pops out!" Sheldon, nearly nauseous from this all-too-graphic remark, now must enter the dressing room and help Mrs. Wolowitz. "We're going to have to work as a team, just grab a handful and start stuffing," Mrs. Wolowitz instructs. Her physical girth and sexual undesirability are well known to the *BBT* audience, despite never having seen her, and that is why this scene is successful. In "The Spaghetti Catalyst" Howard explains to Leonard that he cannot hang out because he has to pick up his mother from her water aerobics class. "Eighteen overweight women flapping their arm fat in a swimming pool. It's like the manatee tank at Sea World," he comments, pushing against conventional ideas of beauty to emphasize his mother's undesirability.

Tied to Mrs. Wolowitz' sexual unattractiveness is her openness about her bathroom habits. In "The Desperation Emanation" she calls to Howard to get the door (a joke that we can nearly rely on hearing every time a character visits their home), and Howard asks her why she cannot get it herself. She shouts, "You know I'm getting a bowel cleanse for my colonoscopy! I'm like an upside-down volcano here!" At this point Mrs. Wolowitz has already offered more information than anyone would like to know, but as Howard opens the door to encounter Leonard, Mrs. Wolowitz screams, "Holy Moses! How much liquid can be in one *tuchus*?" This style of humor stands in a long line of Jewish comediennes using bathroom jokes. Moreover, her use of Yiddish words—in this example the word *tuchus* which means buttocks—strengthens the fabric that weaves Mrs. Wolowitz together with her performing predecessors all the way back to Sophie Tucker and Belle Barth, although examples of Yiddish in *BBT* are fewer and watered down in comparison to the aforementioned performers.

Another theme that appears throughout the world of American Jewish humor regarding the Jewish mother figure is her arguably oedipal relationship with her son. Woody Allen, Paul Mazursky, and Philip Roth have all tread this terrain, among others. The following scene incorporates two central themes to the Jewish mother stereotype: her physical excessiveness, as I have mentioned, and the delicate line between mother and lover, a line that is crossed time and time again in the show for comedy. In "The Hot Troll Deviation" Howard is shown in his bed, adorned with red silk sheets and matching pajamas, and he begins to fantasize. Suddenly his mother asks from the other room if Howard has seen her girdle. "I can't find it and I am late to my Weight-Watchers meeting," she says. "Maybe it committed suicide. Leave it alone," Howard retorts, trying to quickly end the conversation and not let her ruin the mood. The fantasy continues. Bernadette appears on Howard's bed, and he asks her why the *Battlestar Gallactica* characters have left his fantasy and only she remains. "Because you really want to be with me," she explains, sensually. Immediately following Bernadette's line we hear Mrs. Wolowitz call again: "Howard, I found my girdle, it was in the dryer. I think it shrunk, I'm spilling out like the Pillsbury Doughboy here." That comment is enough to end the fantasy altogether. This exchange serves as a microcosm of Howard and his mothers' dynamic more broadly. Here, it is clearly intentional that Howard's mother interrupted his fantasy with a grotesquely descriptive story about her body, and yet even more significant is the person whom she interrupted: Bernadette. This perfectly summarizes what is to come: a constant tension between Howard's soon-to-be-girlfriend Bernadette and his mother.

Looking at the intertwining of two common motifs in the Jewish mother image (physical unfitness and implications of oedipal relations) perhaps it has already become evident that the various qualities that generate the Jewish mother stereotype play upon and interact with other facets. They are not separate entities; rather, each component works with the others to emphasize the core traits of the Jewish mother. One example is how Mrs. Wolowitz' physical excessiveness consistently serves as a vehicle for alluding to the possibly latent oedipal desires Howard and his mother harbor for each other.

"The Engagement Reaction" offers an apt example of the complex intertwining of the various thematic elements that create the Jewish mother stereotype. The episode begins with Leonard asking Howard how his mother thinks about him and Bernadette getting married. She doesn't know yet, Bernadette explains. "I was thinking of weaving it into her eulogy," Howard half jokes. Defensively, Howard asks Priya—Leonard's girlfriend at this point in the series, who also happens to be Raj's sister—if she has informed her Indian parents of her relationship with Leonard. She admits that she has yet to tell them but argues that it is different: Indian parents are really protective of their children. "Right, whereas Jewish mothers take a casual 'la-di-da' to their sons," Howard offers back, sarcastically. It seems important to note that the writers specifically chose the word "sons" rather than children, which is what Priya first says. The history of portrayals of the Jewish mother character is overwhelmingly composed by male comedians, writers, directors, and television personalities. Riv-Ellen Prell writes of the Jewish mother in *Fighting to Become Americans*: "Her excessive and dangerous nurturance held back her sons—the producers of this humor—from moving forward into adulthood" (150). The key idea here is that her "sons [are] the producers of this humor" (150), a claim that I agree with. Thus, it makes sense that she would be represented contingently, as a mother to her son. Going back to the beginning of this essay, this concept becomes highly relevant to the idea that Mrs. Wolowitz' representation leans strongly to the gender facet of the Jewish mother stereotype, or as it were, the "mother" in the "Jewish mother."

In the next scene Howard tells Leonard that his mother is currently lunching with Bernadette, so they can get to know each other. That sounds nice, Raj says to Howard. He replies, "I hope so, although if history is any indication then my mother will swallow her whole and spit her bones out like an owl." Leonard asks if Howard has met Bernadette's parents. "You mean Adolph and Ava?" Howard asks. There are many things at play here in this brief comment, which I will explain without delay. Of course Adolph—although with the contemporary tensions in the Middle East this might be changing—I would argue is the most anti–Jewish pairing of names, considering its historical implications. Also, yes, Howard *has* met her parents, the audience gathers from his use of their first names. This exchange serves to emphasize the protective nature of Howard's mother, compared to the more relaxed (the writers might also be implying healthier) parenting style of Bernadette's parents.

The exploration of the Jewish mother/son relationship continues in the next scene. Later, back at the house, Howard asks his mother (while she is in the bathroom) how the lunch went. She says it went well and that Bernadette is sweet, although she ordered eggplant lasagna, "like that's what a person orders at a Jewish deli." "That's good to hear, because I've got some news." "I hope it's good news, because I've got nothing but disappointment in here," she responds, referring to her performance in the bathroom. "Bernadette and I are getting married," Howard declares. A long pause follows, while Howard painfully awaits his mother's reaction, when suddenly we hear a loud thump. Mrs. Wolowitz has fainted.

At the hospital, waiting for news on Mrs. Wolowitz' condition, Howard tells the gang what happened. He picked up his unconscious mother and drove frantically to the hospital, he recounts. "Wait, you picked up your mother?" Penny questions. "Her own legs can barely do that." He implies to Bernadette that he believes his mother had a heart attack because she learned that he and

Bernadette were engaged. Realizing that this information hurts her, Howard tries to explain himself, "What you've got to keep in mind is that, ever since my dad left, I've been the whole world to my mother. I mean, she'd be threatened by any woman who can give me what she can't." "You mean sexual intercourse?" Bernadette asks. "Well when you say it like *that* you make it sound creepy," Howard responds. At this moment Raj and his sister Priya arrive and ask what happened to Howard's mom, Bernadette bursts into tears as she runs out of the room screaming: "Howard's mother had a heart attack because I have sex with him and she can't." While this scene might speak for itself, it should be noted that this moment does not shy away from the uncomfortable implications of the oedipal issues that many Jewish mothers and their sons present in other instances of popular culture. In fact, it speaks out loud the logical conclusion of the topic.

Just as soon as the writers leave no room for guessing whether Howard and his mother have something in common with Oedipus and his mother, they turn the tables on the audience. At the end of the episode Mrs. Wolowitz wakes up, and she asks to see "the little Catholic girl" first, which were her words. The doctor, with clear Jewish physical traits like a big nose and thinning hair, says to Howard, "You brought a Catholic girl home to your mother? Let me write you a prescription for Xanax." After visiting Mrs. Wolowitz in her room, Bernadette shouts at Howard: "You're a *putz*! Do you know what that means?" Howard, shocked at his fiancée's use of Yiddish and its harsh significance (in Yiddish *putz* is a vulgar term that has come to mean fool or idiot in contemporary American English), "Yes. Do you?" "Your mother just taught it to me. She thinks she got food poisoning from that deli and she just wanted to make sure I was okay." "And are you?" Howard timidly inquires. "No, because I am engaged to a *putz*! You let me believe I was the reason your mother had a heart attack." "Based on the available—"Howard tries to explain. "Shut up!" Bernadette bursts. and Howard asks where she is going. Suddenly, a new sound comes out of Bernadette's delicate, Catholic lips: "*To the toilet. Is that okay with you?*" It is almost exactly the same voice as that of Mrs. Wolowitz. Bernadette leaves and Howard turns to Raj and Leonard and says, "Is it just me or does she sound sexy when she's angry?" Bernadette almost literally, considering the fact that Mrs. Wolowitz only exists as a disembodied voice, has begun to take her place. This episode epitomizes the intertwined nature of the various components to the Jewish mother. It serves as a microcosm for the writers' overall utilization of Mrs. Wolowitz as a comedic tool. Within this one episode we have the potty humor, her physical excessiveness, a display of her tight grasp on Howard, the Yiddishisms, and the oedipal complex.

Additionally, this moment offers a very interesting example of the oedipal issue. As discussed, Howard is the one who assumes that his mother had a heart attack because of the news of his engagement to Bernadette, and he is the one to imply that his mother would be threatened by any woman that can give him what she cannot. Conversely, Mrs. Wolowitz proves to be happy that Bernadette will marry her son, in fact, Howard is lucky to have her, she says. In this example, it is clear that the idea of an oedipal relationship comes from Howard's perspective, not from his mother's. If this were not already enough proof, Howard says in response to Bernadette's "Jewish mother voice" that she sounds sexy when she is angry. In this example, Howard seems to be the perpetrator of the oedipal theme in the Jewish mother paradigm. Considering the trend of male produced Jewish mother figures, it seems probable that the oedipal theme often derives from the son's perspective, not the mother's.

While the oedipal complex boasts a long history of portrayals of the relationship between Jewish mothers and their sons in American popular culture, from Roth's Alex Portnoy to Woody Allen's short film *Oedipus Wrecks* or Paul Mazursky's *Next Stop: Greenwich Village*, I would suggest that a broader and more fundamental characteristic of the Jewish mother image throughout time is her overprotective and nagging nature, what Antler calls "parent-child struggles over autonomy" (9). While Howard regularly vocalizes his disdain for his mother, his dependence on her is abundantly clear. In "The Werewolf Transformation," Bernadette, concerned for her fiancée's well-being, decides to surprise Howard by visiting him in Houston, where he went for NASA training. Her good intentions are marred when she enters the hotel room and hears Howard's mother yelling from the bathroom. In this instance Howard's dependency is brought to its logical (albeit implausible) extreme. In another example Raj asks Howard what his mother will say if he gets a tattoo on his backside and Howard remarks, "She'll never see it. She takes my temperature orally now." Howard engages in the dynamic that perpetrates his childishness.

A humorous example of Howard's simultaneous resentment towards his mother for keeping him close and equal participation in the dependent relationship can be seen in "The Bus Pants Utilization." When Leonard asks the guys if they would like to participate in his experiment which could potentially land them scientific stardom, Howard's response is "A few extra bucks would be nice. I could finally move out of my mother's house." "Where would you go?" Raj asks. "I always dreamed of building a little place of my own, over the garage." In "The Benefactor Factor," Penny expresses her shock that Bernadette would let Howard wear a dickie to a fancy party, to which he replies defensively, "Excuse me, my girlfriend does not pick out my clothes ... my mother does."

One episode that truly illuminates the height of Howard's dependence on and desire to maintain proximity to his mother is "The Pulled Groin Extrapolation." Howard thinks he and Bernadette are going to move into his mother's house once they are married. This is news to Bernadette. Attempting to convince her of the idea, Howard says that if they have kids his mother can help out. "You know, when she does the 'Three Little Pigs' story she actually has hair on her chinny chin chin." "I'm not going to live with your mother," Bernadette announces to Howard, "not now. Not *ever*." "Wow, somebody obviously has mommy issues," Howard replies, playing on his obvious blindness to his own mommy problems.

Later in the episode, Bernadette stops by Howard's mother's home to apologize for making a fight out of it. Hoping to find a compromise, Howard suggests that they have a "trial run": Bernadette stays the weekend and sees how it goes. She asks if that is all right with his mother, to which he replies sure, sure, and turns back inside and yells, "Ma, do you mind if Bernadette stays here for the weekend?" "Frankly, after all your sleepovers with the little brown boy, a girl is a relief!" Mrs. Wolowitz responds. So they plan on Bernadette staying the weekend. Skip to later in the episode when Bernadette and Howard are arriving back from dinner, when they are in his room. "So dinner was nice," Howard offers. "Yeah, I guess," Bernadette replies hesitantly. "Does your mother always cut your meat?" she asks. "Only when it's fatty." Seeing Bernadette's discomfort Howard says, "Don't be jealous, babe. Someday you'll cut it for me," a comment in a long line of jokes suggesting the slow transition from mother to wife for Howard, with very little variation on the relationship.

Mrs. Wolowitz calls from upstairs, asking if Bernadette would like a toothpick. Howard shouts back, asking for some privacy. "Oh I know what that means, *hubba hubba,*" Mrs. Wolowitz playfully responds. "Oh god," Bernadette sighs, struggling with the whole situation. "Relax, it'll be fine," Howard says, beginning to kiss Bernadette. A moment later Mrs. Wolowitz calls down again, "Let me know when you're done canoodling, Mommy needs a foot rub." This juxtaposition of Howard's sex life (particularly with Bernadette) and his mother's intrusiveness, whether in regard to her graphic bathroom life or, in this case, her request for pampering, can be seen time and time again on the show. These moments serve only to accentuate the one thing that separates the role of Howard's girlfriend from the role of his mother, which is as Bernadette herself says in "The Engagement Reaction," the fact that she can have sex with him and his mother cannot.

In the next scene Bernadette enters Howard's room in her pajamas; it is clearly later in the same night. "Are you ready for bed?" Howard asks. "No, I need to brush my teeth but your mother has been in the bathroom for like, an hour," Bernadette complains. "Oh yeah, she sometimes has problems doing her business, hold on," Howard goes to the foot of the stairs and shouts, "Ma, give up! Tonight's not your night." Mrs. Wolowitz shouts back, "You don't know that, I just sat down." "C'mon, take a break, Bernadette needs to brush her teeth," Howard argues. "She can come in, I'm not embarrassed," his mother replies. Howard pops his head in his room and says, delighted, "Problem solved!" "No it's not! I'm not going in there." "Oh c'mon, honey, she's just sitting in their reading a magazine, you can't see anything. I go in all the time." As the viewer processes the unseemliness of that practice, Mrs. Wolowitz jumps in and yells, "Ha! The eagle has landed." Howard says in an official announcer voice: "And we have splashed down." He gets up and says, "Wait here, I'm going to go light a candle," "and then we make passionate love." Again, the viewer is confronted with an uncomfortable combination of Mrs. Wolowitz' bowel movements and Howard and Bernadette's romantic life.

As in "The Engagement Reaction," "The Pulled Groin Extrapolation" incorporates a number of the Jewish mother jokes that recycle throughout the series, ending amusingly similarly to the other episode. Bernadette brings Howard breakfast in bed. "Good morning, handsome." "Good morning, Mom," Howard responds, still with eyes closed. "It's *me,*" Bernadette coldly informs him. Realizing his sleepy mistake, Howard answers, "Yes it is, and you look so pretty in the morning." "Your mom and I made you breakfast," Bernadette says. "Oh wow, so you guys are getting along?" Howard enjoys the idea of his mother and his fiancée working together to make him a meal. "Yeah, I guess," Bernadette says, "we're very different people, Howard. So communication is a little tricky." Mrs. Wolowitz calls down, "Does he like the pancakes?" In her new vocal formation that sounds uncannily similar to her soon-to-be mother-in-law, Bernadette responds, "He didn't *try* them yet!" Howard: "Is there any butter?" Back in her sweet high-pitched voice, Bernadette explains that it is butter-flavored syrup. "So, what's the word?" Mrs. Wolowitz shouts. "He wants *buttah*!" Bernadette shouts back. To make the parallel even stronger, Howard's mother replies, "It's butter-flavored syrup!" "I just told him that!" Bernadette screeches. Hoping to deflate the tension Howard says that it is all right, he doesn't need butter. "If you want *buttah,* I'll get ya *buttah,*" Bernadette replies, nearly perfecting the classic Jewish mother voice with New York accent and topping it off with a thick layer of guilt. She leaves to get butter, and Howard says, "Well I guess I'll cut these by myself...." Referring back to the night before, when his mother cut his meat for him, and now illuminating his expectation for his fiancée to do the same with pancakes, an evidently less difficult food to slice.

While the Jewish mother often loses agency as she is taken into the hands of male culture-makers, she certainly has agency regarding the mutually dependent relationship with her son. Mrs. Wolowitz takes care of Howard as much as he takes care of her. Howard is certainly not the only participant in maintaining a mutually dependent, child/mother relationship for a man who is well beyond childhood. Nearly every time Mrs. Wolowitz appears she has a new food to offer Howard, or asks about his "little friends." She belittles him, asking if he is going to have a "sleep over," and if he would like her to pack him Fruit Loops to his trip to Russia (he unwillingly garners the nickname Fruit Loops because of this).

Weaving a Fabric Through Time

While girth served as a vehicle for comedic success, it did not thwart the high dose of sexuality found in a number of performers' routines of the time, particularly those of Tucker and Barth in the early twentieth century (Cohen 111). Belle Barth's comedy also relied heavily on bathroom humor, which is akin to—but not the same as—bodily humor. She called herself an "MD, a *maven* on *dreck*" (an expert on feces) (Cohen 111). Belle Barth, Sarah Blacher Cohen argues, "defies anal taboos and loosens her audiences' choked respectability so they can laugh at these shattered prohibitions" (111). Cohen's commentary on Barth could be extended to the humor of Mrs. Wolowitz. Cohen attributes the scatological humor to an aggression toward certain societal norms and restrictions, placing herself outside of the mainstream in two ways: in terms of respectability and also religious/ethnic identity.

> Jewish women comedians are brazen offenders of the faith. Their behavior violates the Torah's conception of *tzniut* or feminine modesty.... By invading the holy sphere of the Jewish male comic, they usurp his audience and so diminish his self-esteem.... But worst of all, the comediennes disbar themselves from performing Judaism's central commandment for women: the enforcement of the ritual of *kashrut*—keeping kosher, keeping clean. As creatures of unclean lips, they make dirty, they sully, they corrupt [105].

Mrs. Wolowitz follows in Barth's tradition of using foul language, soiling middle-class propriety with her inappropriate bathroom talk. Like Barth, Mrs. Wolowitz uses Yiddish in such moments, challenging mainstream political correctness. However, Mrs. Wolowitz departs from Cohen's analysis in a number of important ways. First, the moments in which her lips speak unclean words, breaking *kashrut*, are almost entirely removed of religious connotation. The ethnic identity remains, through use of Yiddish (albeit significantly less so than Barth), but the religious component seems to have evaporated. While the Yiddishisms remain, the Yiddish accent is replaced with a New York accent, reflecting a broader trend in portrayals of Jewish men and women over the course of the century, as they have become more Americanized. Howard and his mother live in Pasadena, not one of the five boroughs. Instead of focusing on religious themes, the writers of *BBT* characterize Mrs. Wolowitz more heavily through her bathroom habits and her physical girth.

The tension regarding gender roles manifests itself in "The Staircase Implementation" when they flashback to many years ago, and the boys stop by Howard's home. When his mother calls from a different room, a considerably lower, more masculine voice is heard. "Is that your dad?" Leonard asks Howard. "If she grows any more hair on her face, yes" is Howard's response. The Jewish mother figure has a long history of being depicted as dominating the family, often surpassing the father in terms of power and control over the children. Again, the makers of *BBT* mobilize the portrayal of the Jewish mother as domineering—over the father as well as the children—to comical extremes: in this joke she nearly turns into the father. Moreover, viewers of the show know well that Howard's father left him and his mother when he was eleven, a fact that permits Mrs. Wolowitz to almost literally subsume the role of father into her own identity. This detail works in the opposite way that Mrs. Wolowitz' disembodiment works: the writers rely on previous portrayals of the Jewish mother to be pervasive and excessive enough to augment their jokes about her without ever showing her body, whereas the Jewish father's passivity is so great that in fact he abandons his position as father when Howard is a young boy. Thus, neither parent is shown, one for the reason that she is already too present, and the other because he is too passive and unnecessary for the comedic success.

Does Mrs. Wolowitz' dirty bathroom humor and overly descriptive commentary about her large body illuminate the continuing need for Jews to poke fun at gentile respectability, and to separate themselves from the mainstream, like Cohen postulated? Does this style of humor work simply because it is older than Mrs. Wolowitz herself? I would postulate that these jokes would no longer function if the need to poke fun at mainstream political correctness and refinement had entirely disappeared. However, it seems that the analysis must be extended: in addition to the Jewish/gentile binary manifesting in the bursting of political correctness, we must recognize the tension between men and women at play here. A number of features of the Jewish mother image have endured quite a long time in American popular culture. Some attributes pertain to ostensibly ethnic or religious themes such as accents, Yiddishisms, faith and the Torah, while other qualities pertain to the gender camp, as it were: sexuality (or lack thereof), mothering techniques, and propriety. A closer view of Mrs. Wolowitz' portrayal illuminates the imbalance of Jewish and gender jokes (clearly the gender/female side of the stereotype receives more attention). An overweight, obnoxious, improper, nagging, older woman can hardly be placed in a zone of potential desirability. And if it were not already almost an impossibility to imagine Mrs. Wolowitz as an object of attraction, her personal accounts of her time in the bathroom close that door altogether. This is precisely what is being referenced by mentioning the distancing of Mrs. Wolowitz from a normative representation of feminine attractiveness. The Yiddishisms remain, but they seem almost secondary, hardly imperative to the success of the joke. What really is at play in the success of the Jewish mother stereotype as it is seen in *BBT* is the perversion of a normative imagination of feminine desirability, tagging on a surface Jewishness with the occasional use of Yiddish and a New York accent.

Concluding Thoughts

I would suggest that in the case of *BBT*, the writers simply make no attempt to cover the fact that Mrs. Wolowitz is nothing but a repetition, both within the broader history of the Jewish mother stereotype and throughout the course of the show as well. Bald recognition of the stereotype causes it to become evident that the character is implausible. People cannot repeat exactly or completely the norms of their time, in terms of gender or other social constructions, so when a character on television so reliably performs the same way over and over again it uncovers the absurdity of the representation. This, however, does not mean that Mrs. Wolowitz is not funny. In fact, perhaps it opens the door for her to be as comical as she is: the viewer—consciously or not—recognizes Mrs. Wolowitz as a stereotype and thus allows for her absurd one-dimensionality and complete lack of growth. Mrs. Wolowitz, unlike all other characters on *BBT*, undergoes no type of evolution, or development; she stays the same throughout the entire series.

For a character whose description is so focused around her body (which is clearly made out to be unpleasantly, excessively hefty, hair in all the wrong places, and varicose veins), it seems ironic that the audience never sees it. Indeed, central to Mrs. Wolowitz' depiction is her utter disembodiment (although her presence is undoubtedly known): she always speaks (or shouts) from behind the bathroom door or from a different room. While this component of *BBT*'s portrayal of Mrs. Wolowitz might appear at first to be a unique contribution to the depiction of the Jewish mother trope, I would suggest that it is, in fact, proof that the writers are doing nothing distinctive. Her disembodiment proves the power of the stereotype. We cannot know the intentions of the creators of *The Big Bang Theory*, but it is clear that they mobilized the Jewish mother stereotype for humor. Furthermore, the writers' decision to leave Mrs. Wolowitz offstage creates the effect that she only exists *in relation to her son*, either through his conversations with her or his comments about her. This effect only reinforces the clichés about the Jewish mother: that she indulges, nags, infantilizes, and *lives for* her children. The creators of *BBT* exploit the mother/son relationship to extremes for its humorous value.

Mrs. Wolowitz departs from her earlier counterparts in one significant way: the paradigm shift from what was once equal weight on both the "Jewish" facet and the "mother" component of the stereotype to what we now see as a different, less balanced equation—using all the same ingredients, just in different proportions—to generate the Jewish mother figure. (Perhaps it will be useful to consider this visually. I posit that once the Jewish mother figure was a more balanced combination of qualities pertaining to both a Jewish identity and a female identity, such that we can portray the figure in equal parts Jewish and Mother: the Jewish Mother. Now, I would suggest that the amount of attention given to the "Jewish" of the Jewish mother figure has decreased, while the "Mother" component has remained more or less the same, rendering the stereotype as the Jewish **Mother**.)

What are the implications of having a rehashed stereotype appear today on national television? Perhaps if the Jewish mother figure had developed on a different path, one that incorporated certain positive aspects in addition to the negative ones, the stereotype would be less harmful. It seems that if one were to take away the excessiveness of nearly all of Mrs. Wolowitz' attributes she would be quite an endearing character. This is not the case. Rather, the viewer is presented with a one-dimensional comedic tool that negatively represents a real demographic, a pattern that has had enough visibility that Antler set out to interview real-life Jewish mothers and compare them to their popular culture counterparts (this is also a part of her book *You Never Call! You Never Write!*).

Actually, it seems that mentions of Jewishness/religiosity are the only time descriptions of Howard's mother are positive or at least neutral, albeit superficial. For example, her Shabbos brisket is to die for. The writers play on the pair's quirky, albeit essentially, Jewish American practice of combining modernity with tradition, for instance their custom of lighting Shabbos candles on Friday night and then watching *Wheel of Fortune*, but it is not presented in a negative way. This comes in direct conflict with any mention of what would be the gender part of the stereotype: body, voice, and mothering techniques, which all receive highly negative portrayals. So, in this "new" formation of the Jewish mother, it seems that media makers are moving away from creating her negative/unpleasant characterization through religious references, but rather do so by manipulation of normative perceptions of gender.

While it is evident that Jewish women have capitalized on their unattractiveness for laughs, and non–Jewish and Jewish comediennes alike still do so today, there seems to be an added harshness whenever the jokes are written by someone else. Joan Rivers, a beautiful woman, volunteered herself as an object of deprecation, while Sophie Tucker, whose appearance did not align with conventional ideas of beauty for the time, disregarded normative perceptions and celebrated her body. What these women have in common, however, is their participation in the joke. With a character like Mrs. Wolowitz, her mere existence depends on the writers, the majority of which are male, who create and recreate her every episode (although she's pretty consistent, the viewer knows what he is going to get each time). Furthermore, although physical girth and unpleasant bathroom humor can be found over a century ago in Jewish female comedic performers' routines, they have to their credit the act of establishing, being part of creating a cultural/comedic tradition. Those women were active in the creation of their on-stage personas, playing almost the masculine role of creation and control of representation and jokes. They had agency. They were the minority in a male-dominated performing world (Cohen 105). Mrs. Wolowitz has no agency: she is a mere projection of earlier formations.

The writers of *BBT* can take no such credit. They are rehashing well-known comedic equations, but they are also simplifying the humor, and reducing it to purely gender-specific insults that have little to do with Judaism. Riv Ellen-Prell argues that the JAP stereotype actually has very little to do with Judaism, but is rather a projection of middle-class American anxiety of upward movement (*Fighting to Become Americans*). Is something similar happening here? Are we scapegoating again? What are we anxious about? Perhaps the recent movement towards gender studies, women's rights and progressive representations of women in popular culture is creating a push toward antiquated humor styles. *BBT* producer Lee Ahronson has been quoted to say, "Enough ladies ... I get it. You have periods ... we're approaching peak vagina on television, the point of labia saturation" (npr.org), speaking about new shows like *Whitney* and *2 Broke Girls* that explore feminine themes and highlight female protagonists. Perhaps Ahronson and his cohorts do not feel like it is incumbent upon them to produce interesting, realistic female characters because they feel that that box has already been checked.

Perhaps the reality is that culture-makers have some way to go before "Jewish female" can be championed as a worthwhile subject position, such that the identities "Jewish" and "woman" are not reduced to stereotypes, and heralded as identities that can be one of many that combine to create one individual, without undermining the uniqueness and pride that ought to go along with being both Jewish and a woman.

Works Cited

Allen, Woody. "Oedipus Wrecks." *New York Stories*. Dir. Woody Allen, Francis Ford Coppola, and Martin Scorsese. Buena Vista Pictures, 1989. Film.
Antler, Joyce. *You Never Call! You Never Write! A History of the Jewish Mother*. New York: Oxford University Press, 2007.
"The Benefactor Factor." *The Big Bang Theory*. CBS. WBBM, Chicago. 10 Feb. 2011. Television.
Bhabha, Homi. "The Other Question." *Location of Culture*. London: Routledge, 1994.
"The Bus Pants Utilization." *The Big Bang Theory*. CBS. WBBM, Chicago. 6 Jan. 2011. Television.
Butler, Judith. *Gender Trouble*. New York: Routledge, 1990. Rpt. 2008.
Cohen, Sarah Blacher, ed. "The Unkosher Comediennes." In *Jewish Wry: Essays on Jewish Humor*, 105–124. Bloomington: Indiana University Press, 1987.
"The Desperation Emanation." *The Big Bang Theory*. CBS. WBBM, Chicago. 21 Oct. 2010. Television.
"The Engagement Reaction." *The Big Bang Theory*. CBS. WBBM, Chicago. 12 May. 2011. Television.
Glenn, Susan A. "Mirth and Girth." In *Female Spectacle: The Theatrical Roots of Modern Feminism*. Cambridge: Harvard University Press, 2000.
"The Hawking Excitation." *The Big Bang Theory*. CBS. WBBM, Chicago. 5 Apr. 2012. Television.
Holmes, Linda. "A Comedy Showrunner's Lament And The Status of Lady Jokes." Web post. *NPR*. NPR/PBS, 3 Apr. 2012. Web. 5 Apr. 2012. http://www.npr.org/blogs/monkeysee/2012/04/03/149918490/a-comedy-showrunners-lament-and-the-status-of-lady-jokes.
"The Hot Troll Deviation." *The Big Bang Theory*. CBS. WBBM, Chicago. 14 Oct. 2010. Television.
"The Lizard-Spock Expansion." *The Big Bang Theory*. CBS. WBBM, Chicago. 17 Nov. 2008. Television.
Next Stop, Greenwich Village. Dir. Paul Mazursky. Twentieth Century Fox, 1976. DVD.
Prell, Riv-Ellen. *Fighting to Become Americans: Assimilation and the Trouble between Jewish Women and Jewish Men*. Boston: Beacon, 1999.
"The Pulled Groin Extrapolation." *The Big Bang Theory*. CBS. WBBM, Chicago. 29 Sep. 2011. Television.
Rocchio, Vincent F. "Introduction: Revisiting Racism and Cinema." *Reel Racism: Confronting Hollywood's Construction of Afro-American Culture*. Boulder: Westview Press, 2000.
Roth, Philip. *Portnoy's Complaint*. New York: Random House, 1967.
Sochen, June. "Fanny Brice and Sophie Tucker: Blending the Particular with the Universal."

In *From Hester Street to Hollywood: The Jewish-American Stage and Screen,* edited by Sarah Blacher Cohen. Bloomington: Indiana University Press, 1983.
"The Spaghetti Catalyst." *The Big Bang Theory.* CBS. WBBM, Chicago. 3 May. 2010. Television.
"The Staircase Implementation." *The Big Bang Theory.* CBS. WBBM, Chicago. 17 May. 2010. Television.
"The Werewolf Transformation." *The Big Bang Theory.* CBS. WBBM, Chicago. 23 Feb. 2012. Television.
"Writers." *The Big Bang Theory Fansite.* The Big Bang Theory Fan Site, n.d. Web. 31 Sept. 2012. http://the-big-bang-theory.com/crewsearch/joblist/W.

The Adolescent Quest

JANICE SHAW

This essay explores how *The Big Bang Theory* situates the traditional notion of the quest in a millennial context. The quest as a search for an unattainable and objectified patroness is reinscribed by the chivalrous knights being nerds, or characters who present a renegotiated contemporary image of adulthood and masculinity, and the patroness being an equally problematized "kidult" female. In this way, *The Big Bang Theory* is one of a number of contemporary television programs and films that challenges the notion of adulthood by interrogating the current social trend of young adults adopting "practices and attitudes associated with adolescence" (Blatterer 777).[1] The television series depicts a set of young adults who, in confounding the boundaries between adolescence and adulthood, conform to the terms "kidults" and "adultescents" as used in contemporary media.[2] In the process the series examines a model of masculinity in television and film that generates stereotypes of gendered behavior.

The Big Bang Theory contributes to a popular fictional genre that endorses conformity while it exploits it, consistent with Rebecca Feasey's claims about masculinity as it is constructed by popular television, that "contemporary programming forms a consensus as it investigates, negotiates and challenges the power, authority and patriarchal control of the hegemonic male" (*Masculinity* 4).[3] This examination of masculinity occurs in the series through the presentation of a subculture of "nerds" or, as such undergraduate men at MIT define themselves, "losers and loners who have given up bodily pleasures in general and sexual relations in particular" (Turkle 207).[4] The program exploits a set of cultural stereotypes about male intellectuals or nerds, especially those based in the science and math areas, as exhibiting social insecurity and an inability to accept "adult" responsibilities. In particular, the sexuality and the romantic relationships of the characters are presented in terms of adolescent insecurities and yearnings towards an idyllic and idealized object. The attitude of the male main characters (Leonard Hofstadter, Howard Wolowitz, Rajesh Koothrappali and Sheldon Cooper) towards women is an extension of their "nerdish" behavior, characterized by an adolescent involvement with games based on the quest;

they incorporate a chivalric code of honor into their aspirations for a relationship with an unattainable, objectified woman.

The Big Bang Theory incorporates a quest trope that operates to both present the nerd's search for ratification of their masculinity, and their desire for an accompanying sexual fulfillment. To do this, the show provides a hybrid of the standard situation comedy, which is normally based on one of two main factors: family, and sexual exploration (Hartley 66). *The Big Bang Theory* combines both of these aspects since the peer group replaces the family, and so it belongs to the types of sitcom John Hartley describes as "hybrids, joining family comportment (living together, couch-centric) and workplace (sexual exploration, flirt-centric)" (67). Since *The Big Bang Theory* incorporates elements of workplace as well as a pseudo-family, it appeals to Jane Feuer's "younger, hipper audience" because it is "ideologically more contentious" and "the workplace or 'friends' situation is distinct from the nuclear family setting" (69) in a way that challenges the traditional family structure, in accordance with a number of millennial programs.

The main premise of *The Big Bang Theory* is a standard device of situation comedy, that of introducing a disruption to a familiar and comfortable structure, thereby exploring and contrasting two different lifestyles, or what Feuer terms the "binary, dualistic structure so typical of the domestic sitcom" (70). In this case, a group of male twenty- to thirty-year-old physicists have their stable life thrown into disorder when a beautiful young woman rents the adjoining apartment to theirs, forcing an introduction of a "normal" female perspective and lifestyle into the cohesion of their group of geniuses, or in the terminology of popular culture, nerds.[5] Their friendship is based on shared attributes that include high intelligence, common employment as scientists, and a lifestyle based on aspects the viewer is invited to recognize as the stereotype of the nerd: an interest in computer gaming, science fiction and comic books, and collections of the associated merchandising.[6] The new tenant, Penny, immediately establishes a situation where she becomes both the idealized and distanced focus of the four men in the group and the symbol of real world normality, both in lifestyle and hetero-normative reality. The four men each find a quality in this character that appeals to or challenges their previously insular perspective. Ironically, the nerd girlfriends of the men who are introduced later in the series find similar qualities in Penny.

The Quest for "Grown-Up" Play

The lifestyle of the characters in *The Big Bang Theory* is representative of a generation for which, according to criminologist Keith Hayward,[7] "it is becoming ever-more difficult for young people to differentiate and dissociate themselves from the generation immediately ahead of them" (215). Hayward also claims that consumerism is a contributing factor in the identity millennial young adults display, since "the century-old opposition between the adolescent/youth stage and adulthood is being challenged by a late-modern capitalist culture now functioning artificially to extend the former" (215). While the main characters of *The Big Bang Theory* are physicists and aeronautical engineers, that is, real scientists, this depiction is invested with a child-like interest in popular and fictional science. Throughout, their scientific endeavors are depicted as an extension of play, and their goals are related to the quest motif that pervades the series. The presentation of male intellectuals as socially awkward and isolated from the larger community is intensified by the further stereotype of them inhabiting a subculture based on common interests in areas of popular science, such as computer games, science fiction and its merchandising. But while these interests are related both to the common depiction of the genius and the nerd, they also refer to the notion of adolescent interest in games and a social network based on play.

Rubik's cubes, *War of the Worlds* posters, and *Star Trek* officer's uniforms abound in their space, and are tellingly juxtaposed against whiteboards emblazoned with real-world science formulae as a symbol of the transgression of the boundaries between the existing and the virtual worlds in the characters' perspectives. Ironically, though, the real world of science and scientists beyond their university still marginalizes the characters. Even when Howard is accepted into the fraternity of elite physical and intellectual NASA corps by embarking on a space station mission in "The Decoupling Fluctuation" (Season 6, Episode 2), he rings his then-wife, Bernadette, with the plaintive, "The other astronauts are mean to me," in a manner reminiscent of a child at a new school or a summer camp, appealing to his mother for comfort. Those he is on the mission with include real-world astronaut Mike Massimono, aged fifty, and an actor playing a cosmonaut who is around the same age, both substantially older than Howard. The impression conveyed is that he is a boy among men. This is exacerbated by both his nickname as the sugary children's cereal Fruit Loops, and the role he plays as "Payload Specialist," which in this context is a euphemism for his job of technical expert in charge of the toilet he designed for the space station. Despite Howard's obvious pride in his achievement and feelings that he has attained cultural capital and acceptance in being on the space mission, he is never depicted as being a "real" astronaut.

This social incompetence is similar to a teenager's lack of confidence, and this is exacerbated by its adherence to and promulgation of a set of stereotypes about male scientists and academics generally, that they have an adolescent approach to life in general, and social relationships with women in particular. Lori Kendall categorizes "aspects of the nerd" as being "asocial and incompletely adult," as a result of "sartorial disregard, bad hygiene, and lack of social skills," as well as being predominantly male ("Nerd Within" 362). To support this, Kendall refers to the "nerdity test" available online:

> Although only one question on the nerdity test explicitly indicates gender, by and large, the test presents nerds as male. Nerds enjoy school and do well in it, especially math and science courses. The more types of computer experience, the higher the nerd score. Nerds have high IQs and possess large amounts of esoteric technical knowledge, but are socially inept. Nerds also collect objects connected with knowledge (atlases and maps; mathematical and scientific equipment such as telescopes and slide rules; etc.), and are avid science fiction fans. Section 10 of the text, concerning clothing and apparel, lays out several of the stock features of the nerd stereotype: uncoordinated clothing, pocket protectors, lack of personal hygiene, too-short pants ("high-water" pants or "floods"), and glasses, especially with ad hoc repairs (i.e., held together with tape or glue) ["Nerd Within" 353].

The Big Bang Theory capitalizes on this stereotype of the nerd, displaying most of these characteristics as part of the group dynamics, but while it is related to this formulation, it also relates strongly to the notion of an adolescent lifestyle. The male characters never cook unless it is in the form of an experiment or fun, such as Sheldon's Cylon toast, and the only meals are either take-away, or eaten in the Caltech cafeteria or the café where Penny works, the Cheesecake Factory. Their entertainment is based on what would be, from an adult perspective, playing with toys, such as going to the comic book store, electronic gaming, cosplay (or costume play, similar to the "dressing up" of children as a favorite book or game character) or flying kites. The characters seem to exist in a perpetual youth, surrounded by games and gaming devices, oblivious to their future in terms of what sociologists such as Harry Blatterer would consider the characteristics of adult life, in particular long-term commitment such as purchase of an apartment or house. The only time this seems to be of any concern is if they feel their collectibles will make them undesirable to women, a fear which is realized at various points when Leonard's one-time girlfriend, Priya, exasperatedly terms him her "boy-man," and when Penny sees his model of the capital city of Superman's home planet, Krypton, in "The Cooper-Hofstadter Polarization" (Season 1, Episode 9) he sadly acknowledges that "it seems a lot cooler when a girl isn't looking at it."

But the notion of collectibles being associated with being a nerd, and Penny's contrasting presentation as symbol of real world normality is problematized when, in "The Nerdvana Annihilation" (Season 1, Episode 14), Penny has an emotional outburst where she tells Leonard, in effect, to "grow up" after the boys jointly acquire a movie-prop time machine and it blocks her pathway to work. This is undercut by Sheldon pointing out Penny's hypocrisy, since she is equally guilty of the same consumerism through her collection of Care Bears and Hello Kitty attire. The show itself endorses the lifestyle of the characters, presenting it as limiting in terms of sexual relationships, but only as a result of the *types* of merchandise they collect and display, such as Sheldon's popular science t-shirts, Howard's Batman belt-buckles, and their collections based on *Star Trek* and superheroes merchandise, rather than on the consumer ethic itself, which is strongly linked to the identity of the characters as part of a millennial generation that defines itself by conspicuous consumerism.

"Dressing up"

The adolescent lifestyle of the four men extends and emphasizes the "sexual exploration" aspect of the show, in conjunction with introducing the trope of the quest: throughout, like adolescents, the men seek relationships with women as a confirmation of their masculinity, while paradoxically viewing women as a holy grail, or at least an impossible goal. This is most clearly displayed in the way Howard treats women as sexual objects, but all four of the male characters objectify women to some degree. Leonard's behavior is reminiscent of the knight to his patroness, Raj suffers from elective mutism in the presence of women as a result of regarding them as intimidating, and Sheldon distances himself even further by attempting to avoid physical or emotional involvement with females, while still relying on them as a nurturing agent. Tellingly, the role of each character is symbolized by their choice of costume for the Renaissance Faire in "The Codpiece Topology"(Season 2, Episode 2), where Leonard is dressed as a knight, Sheldon a medieval monk, Howard a court jester, and Raj a nobleman. The relationship of the nerd to women is exemplified in these figures, such that it is either the knight to a patroness like Leonard, the ridiculous figure inviting mockery such as Howard, the aloof and distant Raj or the celibate Sheldon.

The common conception of the nerd in terms of gender identity is both instated and explored through such symbolism as the characters' costumes and the games they play. For example, the presentation of both their homogeneity of perspective and the inclusiveness of the group is displayed in their choice of dress for Penny's Halloween party in "The Middle Earth Paradigm" (Season 1, Episode 6). The hybridization of the nerd figure in terms of problematic masculinity is depicted through Howard's parting injunction upon their acceptance of the invitation: "Gentlemen, to the sewing machines."

Importantly, they all appear in the same superhero costume of The Flash. The Flash is the ultimate symbol of escape: he has the ability to outrun and dodge the onslaughts of a hostile world. This, too, is a reference to the stereotype of the nerd or clever adolescent being bullied and ostracized at school. In "The Speckerman Recurrence" (Season 5, Episode 11), a former classmate who tormented Leonard throughout his schooldays makes contact with him, hoping to exploit his talents as a "gear jockey." In the course of the episode, the systematic abuse he suffered, not only from this character but other classmates as well, is revealed alongside the sub-plot of Penny realizing that she could have been considered a bully at her school. Again, Penny is cast in the role of normal character with a typical school experience, juxtaposed against the nerds' memories of their adolescence as recounted by Leonard, Howard and Sheldon. Interestingly, Raj, having come from a different culture and class due to his wealthy Indian background, provides a contrast to the typical Western-world experience of the genius adolescent being marginalized and bullied.[8] The inequality in a contest between the friends and a man such as Speckerman is encapsulated by Penny's comment "Terrific. High School Quarterback against four Mathletes," and the semi-serious suggestion by Sheldon that "as a symbolic gesture to all the bullies who tormented us for years, we open our home to Jimmy and once he's asleep we kill him."

As Sheldon states, they have spent their lives running away; the program reveals that little has changed from their adolescence, since they still run from bullies to the safe haven of the comic book store and to the group of like-minded others, represented by a mise-en-scène in their apartment dominated by science and science-fiction artifacts, and in particular *Star Trek* officers' uniforms. Such uniforms symbolize the quest for authority and power the characters are denied in real life. In addition, Raj's ambivalent sexual identity is conveyed by his preference for wearing a replica of the uniform worn by Uhura, a female *Star Trek* officer, further problematizing both the masculinity of the characters and their identification as adults.

The Adolescent Quest: The Search for Masculinity

The show makes clear that being marginalized has not ended with their school experiences, and that the male main characters still inhabit a sub-group that is not only defined by adolescent insecurities, but by adolescent yearning for acceptance, both culturally and sexually. Sheldon, especially, provides an example of teenage angst: self-centered and selfish, yet insecure and dependent, he is both needy in his relations with women, especially his mother, grandmother ("Meemaw") and the "girl who is a friend," Amy Farrah-Fowler, and yet reticent to commit. He is emotionally invested in the security of the nurturing presence of women, so that Penny has to sing "Soft Kitty" to him when he is ill in the same manner as his mother. This is intensified by his presentation as a child-like figure, unable to relate sexually to Amy or any other woman. Indeed, throughout, Sheldon is presented as infantilized and stultified in his emotional development, which translates into his relationship with women.

Sheldon is at the extreme end of a spectrum inhabited by the other four main male characters: Leonard is the most mature and normal in terms of relationships with women, exemplified by his ongoing quest for Penny, but Howard and Raj present elements that affect their interaction with both the world in general and women in particular. Howard has a maternal fixation that finally manifests itself in his marriage to Bernadette, a woman with an increasingly similar voice and behavior to his mother, so much so that on the eve of his marriage in "The Pulled Groin Extrapolation" (Season 5, Episode 3), he is involved in a number of Freudian slips by calling her "Mother." Raj's relationship with women is impeded by his inability to speak in their presence unless fortified by alcohol. Sheldon is the extreme case, whereby the elective distancing from women adopted by Raj becomes a total non-involvement. While he has a relationship with Amy Farrah Fowler, initiated in "The Lunar Excitation" (Season 3, Episode 23) as an experiment by Howard and Raj signing him into an online dating service, it appears to be an extension of his relationship with the computer that initiated it, as far as he is concerned, through its lack of emotional investment and sexual contact. It is also significant that much of their contact occurs through speaking on Skype and iPhone, rather than in person.

Sheldon's detachment and self-centered nature relates to his infantilization throughout the series. He is shown in a variety of episodes as being subject to his mother, most notably in "The Luminous Fish Effect" (Season 1, Episode 4), in which Mrs. Cooper directs him to ask for his job back at Caltech, after his naive bluntness to the new head of department, Dr. Gablehauser, results in him being suspended. In events ironically reminiscent of a mother marching to the school to sort out her child's problem with the principal, Mrs. Cooper's interaction with Gablehauser allows him to be reinstated. Sheldon's lack of adult tact and diplomacy in this situation culminate in his child-like questioning of his mother, "Will Dr. Gablehauser be my new daddy?" This infantilization is extended to his relationship with Leonard and Penny in a series of episodes that draw on stereotypes of married life. In "The Guitarist Amplification" (Season 3, Episode 7), Sheldon becomes the child worrying about the parents' quarrelling, obviously reverting back to similar childhood experiences. He retreats to the sanctuary of the comic book store, where he has "made himself a little nest," only to be bought off in the traditional manner of guilt-ridden parents by the bribe of a comic book and a new toy from the paternal Leonard. This is further presented in "The Spaghetti Catalyst" (Season 3, Episode 20), where Penny and Leonard become the estranged couple arguing over the child of the marriage. Interestingly, Leonard is the custodial parent here in an inversion of the normal mother's role, and Penny is the father-figure, taking the child to Disneyland on the weekend visitation and, despite warnings from the parent-in-residence, making the child ill with over-indulgence. This symbolism of Sheldon as an adult stultified in the adolescent phase culminates in "The Einstein Approximation" (Season 3, Episode 14) where he is referred to as "a special kid" by the security guard at an indoor playground, where he is eluding Leonard, the "parent" who has come to collect him, by burying himself in the ball-pit. Later, in "The Isolation Permutation" (Season 5, Episode 8), Leonard again acts as parent as he explains about Sheldon that "he had a late night last night, so I put him to bed early," but then laments, "The only problem is that he'll be up and wanting to play at sunup."

The Quest for Power: Masters of Technology and Computer Games

Penny functions within the series as the focus of real world quests, in the same manner as the traditional quest was provoked by a task set by the patroness, and undertaken in her honor. In this millennial context, though, the computer quest is more "real" to the characters than that inspired by Penny, and the idea of gaming, computer games and play relates to both the sexual relationships and the sexual identity of the characters. Much of the games the four males are engaged in are based on a quest motif, so much so that Leonard uses this idea to compel the others to accompany him on the various quests where he acts as knight errant on Penny's behalf. In the first episode of the series, "Pilot" (Season 1, Episode 1), Penny exploits Leonard's obvious infatuation for her to have him confront her previous boyfriend, Kurt, in an effort to regain her television. In the first attempt, Leonard and Sheldon return without their pants, a symbolic de-masculinizing that, again, relates to adolescent experiences. As Sheldon philosophically comments, "It wasn't my first pantsing and it won't be my last." In a later episode, "The Financial Permeability" (Season 2, Episode 14), where Leonard again undertakes a quest on Penny's behalf to obtain the money that Kurt owes her, the others accompany him only as a result of his taunts that they are happy to undertake virtual quests, but when an opportunity for a true quest is presented to them, they refuse it. That the real goal of Leonard's quest is to gain Penny's favor and to instate his masculinity and power is captioned by Sheldon's comment that "minstrels will sing songs in your honor." This relates strongly to the virtual quests and mock battles in computer games since, as Leo Baudry comments in his examination of the role of the chivalry as it impacts upon the changing nature of masculinity, there is "a legendary line" that linked "armour-clad heroes sallying forth to fight dragons and rescue fair maidens" (57). More importantly, "it was often primarily aristocratic women whose gaze directly inspired knights to great deeds and whose patronage supported the writers and artists who depicted them" (Baudry 58).

The representation of the relationship between the men and women as a sexual game further relates to the quest trope, as well as their presentation as adolescents. Throughout the series, the four men are displayed as playing games: board games based on science fiction series, computer games like *Age of Conan* that interact with other users online, electronic games with a pseudo-sports motif like Wii Sports, and role-play that involves dressing up as their favorite superhero or character. Like adolescents, they seek to identify with a role-model, often fictional, in terms of their identity as it relates to masculinity. Howard, in particular, adopts an avatar in his role-play that presents himself as he would wish to be: tall, muscular and empowered by armor and a sword. In particular, the hybrid nature of the nerd's identity is embodied by Raj, who has a female avatar. The paradoxical nature of the nerd involves a hybridized sexuality, since, as Kendall points out, "the nerd stereotype includes aspects of both hypermasculinity (intellect, rejection of sartorial display, lack of 'feminine' social and relational skills) and feminization (lack of sports ability, small body size, lack of sexual relationships with women)" ("Nerd Nation" 264). This is displayed in "The Rothman Disintegration" (Season 5, Episode 17) where Sheldon and Barry Kripke, a fellow scientist, both want Dr. Rothman's office upon his retirement. Realizing that Sheldon would have the advantage in a contest based on the conventional nerdish areas of *Star Trek* trivia and model trains, Raj asks what they are "equally bad at." Their reply, in unison, is "Sports." The farcical sequence that follows reinforces the popular notion of the nerd as inept, uncoordinated and emasculated, and culminates with Leonard's comment to Raj and Howard, "You know all those terrible things bullies used to do to us? ... I get it."

This hybridity calls into question the nature of the gender identity of the nerd, as it is portrayed in popular literature and television series such as *The Big Bang Theory*. Kendall, in her exploration of media representations of nerds, comments that while "nerds have an expected mastery of technology, which conveys masculinity," paradoxically, they have "low social skills and little or no sexual interaction, compromising their connection to hegemonic masculinity" ("Nerd Within" 356). Interestingly, Kendall found that it was not only in the portrayal of this sub-group that this paradox emerged, since in her exploration of a group of *BlueSky* (an online forum) participants, she found an equally contradictory response to the sub-group, since "they both embrace and distance themselves from that identity, reflecting the nerd's inclusion of both desirable and marginalized aspects" ("Nerd Within" 356).

This reinforces the motivation for the main male characters to excel at computer technology, in the process "protecting a form of hegemonic masculinity which continues to give primacy to aggressiveness and physicality" through the mastery of the machine (Kendall, White and Nerdy 519). Paradoxically, in order for an image of masculinity to be reinforced, it needs to be the right type of machine. While "in the cultural logic of late-twentieth-century America, masculinity bears a particular relation to technology," still "male-associated technologies tend to involve physical labor (lawnmowers and power drills), subduing nature through force (trucks and tractors), and physical violence (tanks and guns)" (Eglash 51). Sadly for characters such as Leonard, Sheldon, Raj and Howard, though, "the artificial spaces of mathematics and computing can be framed in opposition to manly identity," and so "the opposition between the more abstract technologies and normative masculinity keep nerd identity in its niche of diminished sexual presence" (Eglash 51–52), as demonstrated by Leonard's lament that the only time he hears from ex-girlfriends is when their hard drive crashes. The conjunction between the mastery of the computer and their primary use to play quest games further associates the main characters with adolescent play, and situates them not in terms of the masculine technological strength by the machine as pseudo-weapon, but more as an instrument of play: a computer games console.

The Quest for the Cool Kid

Penny's sexual attractiveness and the procession of her previous boyfriends symbolizes her as the object of desire for hegemonic masculinity. In *The Big Bang Theory*, like much presentation of nerds in popular discourse, the hybridized presentation of the nerd identity of the male main characters is emphasized by the contrast with the female, "normal" character, Penny. This dichotomy is in keeping with what Christine Quail refers to as "the hip/square dialectic," in which "the nerd is culturally placed in contrast with a more athletic, socially skilled, sexually aware individual—the cool kid or jock, who demonstrates a hegemonic heterosexual masculinity" (461). In this case, though, rather than the role model to be emulated, Penny, is both the "cool kid" and the embodiment of the desirable position in the same manner as Judith Butler states in *Gender Trouble,* that there is a ubiquitous enforcement of heteronormative values through a constant comparison to non-normative sexual orientations.

Indeed, while much of the first episodes of *The Big Bang Theory* concentrates on examples of the male nerd, with the introduction of Amy Farrah Fowler, Sheldon's girlfriend, the female nerd is explored. While Leonard, Sheldon, Raj and Howard conform to a traditional stereotype of the nerd as socially inept male who is dependent on the peer group for definition and emotional support, Amy is presented as an outsider even from the nerd subculture. Like the four friends, Amy is equally trapped in an adolescent phase, and this is most notably displayed through her relationship with Penny. While the males, Leonard especially, view Penny or any woman in sexual terms, Amy views her friendship as a token of acceptance into an arena of "cool kids" that she has been denied in adolescence. Even semantically, reference to Penny as "bestie" and "BFF," or the text-speak Best Friends Forever, indicate an adolescent crush on an admired social superior, reinforced by her continual comments on Penny's beauty and sexual attractiveness. "The Isolation Permutation" (Season 5, Episode 8), where Amy finds that Bernadette and Penny have been dress shopping for Bernadette's wedding, displays not only her adolescent fear of non-acceptance by the peer group, but the same experiences of marginalization that were exhibited by the males in other episodes. Her feelings of rejection culminate in her drinking from a wine bottle in a car park, because she declares that "this is where the cool kids hang out." Amy's social and even sexual identity, similar to the male nerds, is related to her adolescent desire for acceptance by the peer group. And also similar to the male nerds, Amy is strongly attracted to Penny, not due to homosexual tendencies so much as a desire to be linked to one she views as the idealized symbol of feminine appeal; consequently, Amy objectifies Penny in a similar manner to the males. This is symbolized by Amy commissioning a painting of herself and Penny in "The Rothman Disintegration" (Season 5, Episode 17), in an attempt to embody their relationship as "BFF," accompanied by her insistence that the portrait be displayed prominently in Penny's apartment. Significantly, she originally had them both painted nude.

While Penny may be the symbol of normality, she is also the focus of the quest for the nerd male characters to ratify both their masculine identity and allow them access to the dominant social discourse. At various points, each of the characters, even Sheldon, objectifies Penny, even if it is, as in Sheldon's case, to make another woman jealous. She symbolizes their adolescent desire to at once break free from the marginalized position of the nerd, and be accepted into the mainstream culture of sexual relationships, as well as be individualized by achieving a partnership with a woman admired and desired by others. Howard's ambivalence, for example, is shown in "The Vengeance Formulation" (Season 3, Episode 9), where he would rather have a fantasy life with a character from *Battlestar Galactica*, played by the actress Katee Sackhoff, than a real liaison with Bernadette. This adolescent confusion of ontological boundaries between the real and fantasy sexuality is further displayed where his avatar has virtual sex with Glacinda, the Troll in the online *World of Warcraft* game, in "The Hot Troll Deviation" (Season 4, Episode 4). That Howard did this in preference to a relationship with his real world girlfriend, so that he chooses to have virtual sex with a fictional character than real sex with Bernadette, is further related to the stereotype of the nerd immersing himself in online quests in opposition to a real world experience. The situation is summed up by Sheldon's statement in "The Fuzzy Boots Corollary" upon hearing that Leonard has finally decided to give up on his goal to have a relationship with Penny, "Well, at least now you can retrieve the black box from the twisted, smoldering wreckage that was once your fantasy of dating her and analyze the data so you don't crash into Geek mountain again."

In *Rethinking Chivalry and Courtly Love,* Jennifer Wollock considers the "wish fulfillment fantasies of courtly love" (7) apply to both males and females, but in *The Big Bang Theory,* the main aspect of the quest is applicable to the ideals of chivalry and courtly love through the fantasy of the males in their dealings with Penny. The embodiment of both the ideal woman and their own idealized avatars exist in the virtual world of the online games, which embody "the influence of heroes drawn from medieval romance" (13) in the "swords, sorcerers and comic book super heroes in various forms of shining armor" (13). The code of conduct of chivalry, associated with courtly love, is displayed in "The Weekend Vortex" (Season 5, Episode 19) when Leonard claims, "We're always the good guys. In *D and D*, we're lawful good. In *City of Heroes*, we're the heroes. In *Grand Theft Auto*, we pay the prostitutes promptly and never hit them with a bat." Interestingly, in *Dungeons and Dragons,* the lawful good are embodied in the knight in shining armor stereotype. The code of conduct according to chivalry is here transmuted into virtual world ethics that dictate sexual mores with a truly unattainable, idealized and objectified woman.

Conclusion

The Big Bang Theory reinforces a belief system already in place, not just simply about young adults, but about nerds. This set of stereotypes has long been utilized, even established, by literature that depicts highly intelligent males as a homogenized group, displaying attributes such as nervousness around women, emotional distance and lack of affect, and poor social skills generally. This is coupled with a non-involvement in sports or "manly" pursuits, and a corresponding obsession with sedentary activities such as computer and electronic gaming. It is intensified by what is portrayed as almost an obsessive interest in "adolescent" activities like the acquisition of toys and collectibles, comics, cosplay and watching science fiction or superhero films and television series. In gendered and sexual terms, as Quail argues, "nerds are assumed and shown to be white and male" and "the nerd has been constructed as an awkward and math-savvy social and sexual failure" (460). A series such as *The Big Bang Theory* exploits the familiarity of the viewer with such stereotypes, constructed by television series and films like *Beauty and the Geek*, and *Revenge of the Nerds.* But further, it sets up a duality between the beautiful, non-intellectual and, in most cases, distant woman and the social misfit, intellectual male. *The Big Bang Theory* exploits such a presentation by the way it "plays on disjunctions between discourses, modes of dress, behavior etc. in different classes or social groups" (Neale 24). It belongs to the type of comedy where, as Stephen Neale points out, "the spectator is maintained in a continuous and undisturbed mode of belief, against which the modes of belief of the characters in the discourses they inhabit/employ are measured" (24) as a result of the way the series interrogates and utilizes for comic effect the discourse and codes within the diegesis. It does this by constructing a contrast of the genius males with the assumed "normality" of the viewer by privileging the perspective of the "beauty," Penny. Throughout the series, Penny voices the "normal" reaction to the abnormal social expectations and reactions of the four nerds, Sheldon in particular.

The Big Bang Theory, then, exploits the current movement of millennial adults, the presumed viewing audience, to adopt an adolescent lifestyle. It does so by presenting the symbol of the adult/adolescent: the nerd. The nerd, as presented in fiction, is computer literate, smart, conversant with contemporary popular culture and immersed in merchandising, but at the same time adopts an approach to life that is uncommitted, lacking in responsibility, resistant to routine or nine to five employment, and idealistic. Above all, nerds are positioned as having an eccentric, hybridized gender construction. While the image of the nerd is of a white male, there is a consistently feminized aspect to the presentation: sensitive, precise, fussy, non-athletic and lacking in the sexually predatory techniques that are associated with masculinity. The characters in *The Big Bang Theory* engage with this stereotype prevalent in popular culture, even while much of the series is based upon their desire for a relationship with a hetero-normative woman, symbolized by Penny. Their adoration of her as the object of an unattainable, idealized woman contributes to this image, even as it draws on traditions of chivalry and courtly love.

Notes

1. These include the television series *Friends, Sex in the City, The IT Crowd* and *Charmed*, and films such as *About a Boy* and those that depict an adult trading places with an adolescent, which include *Freaky Friday, 18 Again* and *Vice Versa*.
2. Rachel Falconer explores what she terms as "a cult of 'the inner child' or the 'kiddult'" as it was "permeating adult cultural life on many levels in the late 1990s" (32) in Britain in *The Crossover Novel*. Here she cites the earliest use of the term "kidult" by Peter Martin in 1985 in a *New York Times* article, and explores other subsequent usage.
3. Robert W. Connell created the term "hegemonic masculinity" in reference to white, heterosexual males that dominated their social environment through characteristics of aggression and competitiveness. Other sociologists have also extended his definition, such as Michael Kimmel who defines such males as "a man in power, a man *with* power, and a man of power" (184).
4. Sherry Turkle conducted a series of interviews with undergraduate computer science students at MIT, who, interestingly, define themselves in terms related to the notion of knights as defenders of the faith; the hackers view themselves as "holders of an esoteric knowledge, defenders of the purity of computation seen not as a means to an end but as an artist's material whose internal aesthetic must be protected" (207).
5. Despite earlier an earlier usage in a Dr. Seuss book, the term "nerd" in its current meaning as an intellectual, marginalized by his or her dress and behavior was not common until its frequent presentation in the 1970s American situation comedy *Happy Days*.
6. The scientist characters work at the real-world California Institute of Technology, which disrupts the boundary between fiction and reality within the show. This disruption is furthered by the appearance of real-world physicists, astronauts and famous figures in the comic book genre, such as Stephen Hawking, George Smoot, Mike Massimono and Stan Lee. These guest appearances, like the real formulae and problems written on the whiteboards within the characters' rooms, function to position the nerds within the "real" world of scientists.
7. Keith Hayward is a criminologist who asserts that the contemporary capitalist culture is eroding the perceived differences between adolescence and adulthood (213). He also makes the point that life stage dissolution is occurring for young adults in both preceding and succeeding generations, so that "the *bi-directional* processes of 'adultification' and 'infantilisation'" are occurring simultaneously (215).
8. *The Big Bang Theory* draws from a stereotypical fictional portrayal of nerds in such films and television series as the *Revenge of the Nerds* films, *Broadcast News*, *Numb3rs* and a host of others.

Works Cited

Baudry, Leo. *From Chivalry to Terrorism: War and the Changing Nature of Masculinity*. New York: Vintage, 2005. Print.

Bennett, Tony, Susan Boyd-Bowman, Colin Mercer and Janet Woollacott, eds. *Popular Television and Film*. London: British Film Institute, 1981. Print.
Blatterer, Harry. "Contemporary Adulthood: Reconceptualizing an Uncontested Category." *Current Sociology* 55 (2007): 771–92. Print.
Butler, Judith. *Gender Trouble: Feminism and the Subversion of Identity*. New York: Routledge, 1990. Print.
"The Codpiece Topology." *The Big Bang Theory*. CBS. 29 Sept. 2008. Television.
Connell, R.W. *Masculinities*. Berkeley: University of California Press, 1995. Print.
"The Cooper-Hofstadter Polarization." *The Big Bang Theory*. CBS. 17 Mar. 2008. Television.
Crawford, Kate. "Adult Responsibility in Insecure Times: The Post-crash World Necessitates a Redefinition of Adulthood." *Soundings* 41 (2009): 45–55. Print.
Creeber, Glen, ed. *The Television Genre Book*. London: British Film Institute, 2001. Print.
"The Decoupling Fluctuation." *The Big Bang Theory*. CBS. 4 Oct. 2012. Television.
Eglash, Ron. "Race, Sex, and Nerds: From Black Geeks to Asian American Hipsters." *Social Text* 20 (2002): 49–64. Print.
"The Einstein Approximation." *The Big Bang Theory*. CBS. 1 Feb. 2010. Television.
Falconer, Rachel. *The Crossover Novel: Contemporary Children's Fiction and its Adult Readership*. New York: Routledge, 2009. Print.
Feasey, Rebecca. "Anxiety, Helplessness and 'Adultescence': Examining the Appeal of Teen Drama for the Young Adult Audience." *European Journal of Cultural Studies* 12 (2009): 431–46. Print.
_____. *Masculinity and Popular Television*. Edinburgh: Edinburgh University Press, 2008. Print.
Feuer, Jane. "Situation Comedy, Part 2." *The Television Genre Book*. Ed. Glen Creeber. London: British Film Institute, 2001. 67–70. Print.
"The Financial Permeability." *The Big Bang Theory*. CBS. 2 Feb. 2009. Television.
"The Fuzzy Boots Corollary." *The Big Bang Theory*. CBS. 8 Oct. 2007. Television
"The Guitarist Amplification." *The Big Bang Theory*. CBS. 9 Nov. 2009. Television.
"The Hamburger Postulate." *The Big Bang Theory* .CBS. 22 Oct. 2007. Television.
Hartley, John. "Situation Comedy, Part 1." *The Television Genre Book*. Ed. Glen Creeber. London: British Film Institute, 2001. 65–67. Print.
Hayward, Keith. "Pantomime Justice: A Cultural Criminological Analysis of 'Life Stage Dissolution.'" *Crime Media Culture* 8 (2012): 213–29. Print.
"The Hot Troll Deviation." *The Big Bang Theory*. CBS. 14 Oct. 2010. Television
"The Isolation Permutation." *The Big Bang Theory*. CBS. 3 Nov. 2011. Television.
Kendall, Lori. "Nerd Nation: Images of Nerds in US Popular Culture." *International Journal of Cultural Studies* 2 (1999): 260–83. Print.
_____. "The Nerd Within: Mass Media and the Negotiation of Identity among Computer-Using Men." *Journal of Men's Studies* 3 (1999): 353–67. Print.
_____. "'White and Nerdy': Computers, Race, and the Nerd Stereotype." *The Journal of Popular Culture* 44 (2011): 505–24. Print.
Kimmel, Michael. "Masculinity and Homophobia: Fear, Shame, and Silence in the Construction of Gender Identity." *Feminism and Masculinities*. Ed. Peter Murphy. Oxford: Oxford University Press, 2004. 182–99. Print.
"The Luminous Fish Effect." *The Big Bang Theory*. CBS. 15 Oct. 2007. Television.
"The Lunar Excitation." *The Big Bang Theory*. CBS. 24 May 2010. Television.
"The Middle Earth Paradigm." *The Big Bang Theory*. CBS. 29 Oct. 2007. Television.
Murphy, Peter, ed. *Feminism and Masculinities*. Oxford: Oxford University Press, 2004. Print.
Neale, Stephen. "Genre and Cinema." *Popular Television and Film*. Ed. Tony Bennett, Susan Boyd-Bowman, Colin Mercer and Janet Woolacott. London: British Film Institute, 1981. 6–25. Print.

"The Nerdvana Annihilation." *The Big Bang Theory*. CBS. 28 Apr. 2008. Television.
"Pilot." *The Big Bang Theory*. CBS. 24 Sept. 2007. Television.
"The Pulled Groin Extrapolation." *The Big Bang Theory*. CBS. 29 Sept. 2011. Television.
Quail, Christine. "Nerds, Geeks and the Hip/Square Dialectic in Contemporary Television." *Television and New Media* 12 (2011): 460–82. Print.
"The Rothman Disintegration." *The Big Bang Theory*. CBS. 16 Feb. 2012. Television.
"The Spaghetti Catalyst." *The Big Bang Theory*. CBS. 3 May 2010. Television.
"The Speckerman Recurrence." *The Big Bang Theory*. CBS. 8 Dec. 2011. Television.
Turkle, Sherry. *The Second Self: Computers and the Human Spirit*. New York: Simon & Schuster, 1984. Print.
"The Vengeance Formulation." *The Big Bang Theory*. CBS. 23 Nov. 2009. Television.
"The Weekend Vortex." *The Big Bang Theory*. CBS. 8 Mar. 2012. Television.
Wollock, Jennifer G. *Rethinking Chivalry and Courtly Love*. Santa Barbara: Praeger, 2011. Print.

Disciplining Heterosexuality
Interrogating the Heterosexual Ideal

Andrea McClanahan

In the first episode of *The Big Bang Theory*, three of the main characters—Dr. Leonard Hofstadter, Howard Walowitz, and Dr. Rajesh Koothrappali (Raj)—are awestruck by the hot blonde girl—Penny—who just moved into the apartment across the hall from Dr. Sheldon Cooper and Leonard ("Pilot"). The audience quickly becomes aware that the struggle of Leonard to "get the girl" will be a common theme throughout the series. It is also evident that Howard and Rajesh are smitten with Penny, showing them as clearly heterosexual. However, in the second episode, Howard and Raj do something unexpected. Raj is late returning to Sheldon and Leonard's apartment. He begins explaining that he was "chatting up" Penny:

> Raj: Then she hugged me.
> Howard: She hugged you? How'd she hug you?
> Raj: [puts his arms around Howard's waist and holds him]
> Howard: Is that her perfume I smell? [smells Raj]
> Raj: Intoxicating, isn't it?
> Howard: [closes his eyes and moves his hands up Raj's back] ["The Big Bran Hypothesis"].

Throughout the conversation, Leonard and Sheldon look at each other wondering what is happening between their two friends, thus signaling that the exchange is crossing the boundaries of masculinity. Additionally, laughter ensues as Howard rubs Raj's back showing the audience that this act of physical closeness between two males is supposed to be funny.

From the beginning of *The Big Bang Theory*, the hegemonic ideals of masculinity, femininity, and sexuality are called into question. However, the questions of idealized gendered performance are hidden beneath an overarching heterosexual desire three of the four characters have from the beginning of the series for a romantic relationship. Sheldon, the character who does not express an interest in having a heterosexual relationship at the beginning of the series appearing asexual to the audience, begins to recognize the benefits of such a pairing at the conclusion of season three in "The Lunar Excitation" when he meets Dr. Amy Farrah Fowler. Simply, *The Big Bang Theory* utilizes the heterosexual imaginary, the idea that individuals must desire a heterosexual relationship and the belief that a heterosexual romantic relationship brings with it a sense of well-being (Ingraham, *White Weddings*), in order to conceal the disruptions of masculinity, femininity, and heterosexuality from the audience as anything other than comic relief. By using the guise of the heterosexual imaginary, *The Big Bang Theory* helps to make the challenges to hegemonic ideals of gender and sexuality more acceptable.

In this essay, I explore the constructions of gender and sexuality in *The Big Bang Theory*—specifically the challenges to hegemonic ideals of masculinity, femininity and heterosexuality. There are numerous studies focused on the construction of gender and sexuality in television programs (Cooper and Pease; Ivory, Gibson, and Ivory; Kim et al.; Lauzen, Dozier, and Horan; Markle; Miller; Quail; Shugart). Often when researchers look at the challenges to heterosexuality, they focus on homosexuality as the opposite. However, Chrys Ingraham asserts, "we pose heterosexuality as the good, normal, and natural form of sexual expression and frame it in opposition to its socially constructed opposite, homosexuality" (*Thinking Straight* 2). However, when there are no homosexual characters on a show, disrupting gendered expectations offer another "opposite" to the performance of heterosexuality. "Researchers have challenged the insistence of placing individuals in a fixed manner into one of three groups: heterosexual, bisexual, or homosexual. In sum, certain researchers question whether there are sexual identity categories with fixed essences or whether these are social constructions which support heterosexism and the nuclear family structure" (Dworkin and Wachs 11). The characters in *The Big Bang Theory* are constructed to challenge traditional notions of heterosexuality, masculinity and femininity thus questioning the fixed boundaries regarding sexuality and gender typically imposed upon individuals.

The Big Bang Theory provides an interesting text for analysis for two reasons. First, *The Big Bang Theory* was not an instant television success story. It took three tries for the pilot to be picked up and for the show to be produced (Stelter). In 2010, just three years after the show premiered in the United States, *The Big Bang Theory* was the second highest rated comedy show (Bissell). In January 2013, one episode garnered 20 million viewers and "has been regularly finishing at number one on the Nielsen list" (Hoerburger 44). The second reason why *The Big Bang Theory* requires in-depth analysis is because of the construction of the main characters in the television series. At first glance, *The Big Bang Theory* appears to follow a familiar narrative—a man longing after a sexy blonde female. However, the obvious difference *The Big Bang Theory* presents compared to other television sitcoms is the focus on nerds and the construction of nerdiness among the four main characters. Rob Hoerburger explains that *The Big Bang Theory* is different because "here [is] a popular prime-time sitcom in which five of the seven main characters [are] Ph.D.s and another [has] 'only' a master's from M.I.T., a hit show that regularly reference[s] bosons and derivatives and string theory, a show in which there [are] running gags about Madame Curie and Schrodinger's cat" (44). The four main male characters are not what we traditionally see in television sitcoms—"these are not especially pretty people" (Hoerburger 44).

The Big Bang Theory uses heterosexuality, specifically the heterosexual imaginary, to make challenges to hegemonic ideals of masculinity and femininity more culturally digestible or acceptable to a mass audience. On the surface, the show promotes heterosexuality and the heterosexual imaginary but, at the same time, challenges hegemonic masculinity and, in later seasons, hegemonic femininity to expand gender boundaries. Through this analysis, I aim to answer the following questions: first, how is the heterosexual imaginary promoted in *The Big Bang Theory* to create a surface appearance of compliance with what is considered the norm of heterosexuality? Second, how are sexual scripts and hegemonic ideals of masculinity and femininity constructed to disrupt heterosexuality and the heterosexual imaginary? Finally, how are characters that present the largest challenges to heterosexuality and hegemonic ideals of gender disciplined for such resistance?

I consider *The Big Bang Theory* unique in its continuous challenges to expectations of gender performativity and feel the show works to expand gender boundaries within the confines of heterosexuality. More importantly, I believe *The Big Bang Theory* resonates with the general population as most males and females do not "fit" into the ideal images of masculinity and femininity. In order to make images that are antithetical to the ideal images of masculinity and femininity more acceptable for the audience, two characters—Amy and Raj—are used as the most extreme challenges to ideals of gender performance and, more importantly, challenge the constructs of heterosexuality. This allows the audience to question the sexuality of the two characters. To deal with their extreme resistance, the characters are punished by themselves as well as those around them. Hoerburger argues, "You might laugh at the characters, pity them or love them, but you don't want to *be* them (especially because you might already be them)" (44).

Theoretical Background

In exploring *The Big Bang Theory,* I approach gender and sexuality as a performance (Butler). Butler postulates, "Gender is not to culture as sex is to nature; gender is also the discursive/cultural means by which 'sexed nature' or 'a natural sex' is produced and established as 'prediscursive,' prior to culture, a politically neutral surface *on which* culture acts" (357). I view gender as something acted out in response to cultural expectations and norms. Falling into the area of performance and gender are the concepts of heterosexual imaginary, sexual scripts, and the ideas of power and discipline.

First, heterosexual imaginary relies on the idea of imagination. Imagination is defined as "the set of symbols and meanings we use when trying to communicate to ourselves or others a *possible,* yet non-existent, situation" (Bachen and Illouz 280). The goal of narratives is often to create a culturally digestible imaginary—one that people can see as a possibility. This includes the idea of the heterosexual imaginary.

Media promotion of heterosexuality as normal is not new (Cooper and Pease; Ingraham, *Thinking Straight;* Ingraham, *White Weddings;* Ivory, Gibson, and Ivory; Watson and Shaw). The construction of heterosexuality as normal—or heteronormativity as "the view that institutionalize heterosexuality constitutes the standard for legitimate and expected social and sexual relations" (Ingraham, *White Weddings* 17)—is a result of the heterosexual imaginary. At first, the notion of the heterosexual imaginary does not seem negative. However,

> through the use of the heterosexual imaginary, we hold the institution of heterosexuality as timeless, devoid of historical variation, and as "just the way it is" while creating social practices that reinforce the illusion that as long as this is "the way it is" all will be right in the world. Romancing—creating an illusory—heterosexuality is central to the heterosexual imaginary [Ingraham, *White Weddings* 16].

Heterosexuality is created as what is "good" and variations on heterosexuality—whether bisexuality, homosexuality or other ways of performing heterosexuality outside of hegemonic masculinity and femininity—are called into question and considered deviant. Further, Ingraham argues, "in American society, we frequently refer to heterosexuality as something that is naturally occurring, overlooking the myriad [of] ways we have *learned* to practice heterosexuality, have given meaning to it, and allow it to organize the division of labor and distribution of wealth" (*Thinking Straight* 1).

The lessons of the heterosexual imaginary and how we "learn to practice heterosexuality" (Ingraham, *Thinking Straight* 1) are displayed through sexual scripts. Scripting theory explicates that individuals learn about sexuality through the scripts that are available—including those presented in the media (Gagnon and Simon; Simon and Gagnon).

> Sexual scripts are guidelines for how we are supposed to feel and act as sexual persons. They are shaped by the communities and societies in which we participate and therefore are socially constructed (they emerge from communities and societies). In this way sexual scripts can be said to reflect social norms and practices accepted in particular social contexts [Shaw and Lee 163].

From an early age, individuals learn what is expected for masculine behaviors and feminine behaviors. Men are "directive, venturesome, enterprising, and pursuing engaging occupations and recreational activities. In contrast, women are usually shown as acting in dependent, unambitious and emotional ways" (Bussey and Bandura 701). Women are expected to perform the feminine and men are expected to perform the masculine. There are very few variations within the hegemonic ideals of masculinity and femininity.

While David Gauntlett asserts "there can be no 'real' or 'authentic' male or female performance" (25), he further explains that "the mass media conspicuously circulates certain kinds of male and female performance as preferable, thereby making the gender categories more 'real'" (139). These accepted gendered performances feed into the promotion of the heterosexual imaginary. Ingraham argues "ascribed behaviors for women and men—gender—actually organize the institution of heterosexuality" (*Thinking Straight*, 4). Considering that performances of hegemonic masculinity and femininity promote heterosexuality, one can assume that disrupting these sexual scripts will then lead to a disruption in the heterosexual imaginary.

The heterosexual imaginary, performances of heterosexuality and scripting theory connect to Foucault's ideas of discipline. In his book *Discipline and Punish: The Birth of the Prison*, Foucault writes about the dispersion of power, discipline and punishment. He moves the disciplinarian from being defined as a homogeneous external, or one locatable disciplinarian that imposes discipline upon a person, to the heterogeneous external, or the possibility of multiple disciplinarians to impose punishment. He also writes of the psychological and internal punishment of the self through the mind and soul. Consequently, humans act as their own agents of discipline in enacting the standards set by the dominant group—in this case, performing socially constructed gendered behaviors.

Foucault recognizes collusion with the dominant paradigm as a natural order of society. "The individual is no doubt the fictitious atom of an 'ideological' representation of society; but he [sic] is also a reality fabricated by this specific technology of power that I have called 'discipline'" (194). Further, Foucault explains, "power produces; it produces reality; it produces domains of objects and rituals of truth" (194). In this case, power produces the idealized forms of femininity, masculinity and sexuality.

When someone attempts to migrate from the expected behaviors of a socially constructing organizing mechanism—including gender and sexuality—discipline is enacted.

> One way in which power is exercised in a repressive manner is through the politicking of deviant acts. Deviant acts and identities are defined in contrast to what is deemed normal. Deviant acts and identities require surveillance and policing so that what is "normal" could not exist without some form of deviance which set the boundaries and limits on normality [Dworkin and Wachs 4].

In this essay, I explore how discipline is manifested for those individuals performing gender and sexuality that is in opposition to the hegemonic ideals and how this reaffirms heterosexuality and the heterosexual imaginary.

Method

In order to uncover how the heterosexual imaginary is produced and disrupted through sexual scripts and power, I complete a narrative textual analysis of various episodes throughout the first five seasons of *The Big Bang Theory*. Brown explains, "Narrative is an iconic social representation of moral action, an expression and preparation" (157). In other words, narrative helps to communicate to an audience the overarching expectations of society. Further, "narrative enables us to understand the actions of others and endow them with meaning, because it is through narratives that we live and understand our own existence" (165). By interrogating media narratives we can begin to understand how these narrative forms work to create ideas (or ideals) about heterosexuality. Dissecting representations present in media narratives is important because

> media images help shape our view of the world and our deepest values: what we consider good or bad, positive or negative, moral or evil. Media stories provide the symbols, myths and resources through which we constitute a common culture.... Media spectacles demonstrate who has the power and who is powerless.... They dramatize and legitimate the power of the forces that be and show the powerless that they must stay in their places or be destroyed.... Ideologies make inequalities and subordination appear natural and just and thus induce consent to relations of domination [Kellner 5].

The media creates powerful narratives that circulate acceptable ways of being. Textual criticism helps critics understand the obvious as well as the hidden narratives within a text. Leff explicates, "Textual criticism (or 'close reading') centers on the effort to interpret the intentional dynamics of a text" (223). A close reading provides insight into the meanings within a text and how these meanings are enacted. "Texts are like lumps of clay waiting for a reader to fashion them and give them structure" (Sless 121). "A text must present some semblance of the structure of an individual's social world—either as they believe it to be, how they hope it will be, or how they allow it to occur" (Manning 172–173). By creating narratives that, on the surface, reflect what is expected, other hidden narratives that challenge expectations are able to be consumed.

Analysis

In the remainder of the essay, I focus on (a) analyzing *The Big Bang Theory* for the ways in which the heterosexual imaginary is reinforced, (b) uncovering the sexual scripts enacted by several characters that demonstrate a queering of masculinity and femininity, and (c) exposing how those individuals who enact femininity or masculinity that is antithetical to our accepted sexual scripts are disciplined to reaffirm heterosexuality and the heterosexual imaginary.

The Heterosexual Imaginary Is Alive and Well in The Big Bang Theory

The heterosexual imaginary is evident in *The Big Bang Theory*. All of the main characters either enter into heterosexual relationships or express their desire to be involved in one. The overarching narrative of the nerdy guy, Leonard, trying to get the hot girl, Penny, is just one of the demonstrated heterosexual relationships within the series.

First, *The Big Bang Theory* largely supports the narrative of the heterosexual imaginary through showing the main characters entering into heterosexual relationships. Leonard is a key example of this as he longs for a romantic relationship with Penny. While the relationship between Leonard and Penny is not always perfect, the idea that they would be happier paired instead of alone is depicted. Leonard and Penny have an on-again off-again relationship throughout the first five seasons of the television series. The first season focuses on Leonard trying to attract Penny and the season ends with the two going out on their first date ("The Tangerine Factor"). Unfortunately, their first date is not as successful as Leonard had hoped and Leonard spends the entire second season mooning over Penny. At the end of the second season, the audience sees Penny upset about Leonard going away on a three month expedition to the North Pole—showing the audience that Penny's feelings for Leonard have changed from friendship to romance ("The Monopolar Expedition"). Leonard and Penny almost make it through the entire third season together except Leonard tells Penny "I love you" and she does not say it back. This leads to the ending of their romantic relationship ("The Wheaton Reoccurrence"). While not in a romantic relationship during season four, the two flirt and occasionally kiss one another. It becomes clear to the audience when Leonard starts dating Priya, Raj's sister, that Penny is jealous and still has feelings for Leonard ("The Toast Derivation"). However, Leonard and Penny remain friends until the middle of season five when the two reunite by having sex ("The Recombination Hypothesis"). Leonard and Penny's relationship is the key narrative story line supporting the heterosexual imaginary. From the beginning, the audience has been aware of Leonard's attraction to Penny and roots for him and Penny to be in a successful romantic heterosexual relationship.

Even when Leonard is not romantically involved with Penny, Leonard enters into relationships with other women showing that he has a strong desire to be successful in a heterosexual relationship. In the first season, Leonard dates Leslie Winkle ("The Codpiece Topology"; "The Hamburger Postulate"). In season two, Leonard meets and has a short relationship with Dr. Stephanie Barnett ("The Lizard-Spock Expansion"; "The Varabedian Conundrum"; "The White Asparagus Triangulation"). Finally, in season four he becomes romantically involved with Raj's sister, Priya ("The Cohabitation Formulation"; "The Irish Pub Formulation"). Leonard's continual quest for a romantic relationship—mainly with Penny—presents a familiar narrative to which the audience can relate. *The Big Bang Theory* is about the boy getting the girl—in this case, Leonard getting Penny. It is this narrative and the quest for the heterosexual imaginary that allows the show to appear as fitting into the cultural standards of gender and sexuality.

Leonard is not the only character involved in an ongoing heterosexual relationship. Howard also desires participation in the heterosexual imaginary which masks his challenges to hegemonic masculinity. Howard is the main flirt of the group and invokes "The Girlfriend Pact" in season three. "The Girlfriend Pact" is an agreement Leonard and Howard made saying that if one of them had a girlfriend and the other did not the person in the relationship would set the other one up with a female friend of the girlfriend. Howard forces Leonard to set him up on a date with one of Penny's friends. The date results in the most successful heterosexual relationship on *The Big Bang Theory*—Howard and Bernadette ("The Creepy Candy Coating Corollary"). While Howard and Bernadette have ups and downs in their relationship, the two solidify their relationship by marrying each other at the end of season five ("The Countdown Reflection").

Perhaps the most surprising pairing in *The Big Bang Theory* is Sheldon and Amy. In the beginning of the series, Sheldon is seen as eschewing heterosexual relationships claiming that they just get in the way of more important things in life. However, Raj and Howard secretly create an online dating profile for Sheldon and he ends up meeting Amy ("The Lunar Excitation"). Sheldon scoffs at the idea that Raj and Howard could have found him a compatible mate. The following is the first exchange between Amy and Sheldon:

> AMY: Excuse me. I'm Amy Farrah Fowler. You're Sheldon Cooper.
> SHELDON: Hello, Amy Farrah Fowler. I'm sorry to inform you that you have been taken in by unsupportable mathematics designed to prey on the gullible and the lonely. Additionally, I'm being blackmailed with a hidden dirty sock.
> AMY: If that was slang, I'm unfamiliar with it. If it was literal, I share your aversion to soiled hosiery. In any case, I'm here because my mother and I agreed that I will date at least once a year.
> SHELDON: Interesting, my mother and I have the same agreement about church.
> AMY: I don't object to the concept of a deity but I'm baffled by the notion of one that takes attendance.
> SHELDON: Well then you might want to avoid east Texas.
> AMY: Noted. Now before this goes any further you should know that all forms of physical contact up to and including coitus are off the table.
> SHELDON: May I buy you a beverage?
> AMY: Tepid water please ["The Lunar Excitation"].

While Amy and Sheldon agree to the terms of their relationship from the very beginning (no physical contact), overtime, largely to appease Amy, the two develop a more intimate relationship. Eventually, Sheldon does become jealous of Amy dating other men and finally agrees to call Amy his girlfriend ("The Flaming Spittoon Acquisition"). It is important to note that Sheldon does not do this willingly—Amy challenges Sheldon by going on a date with Stuart, the manager of the comic book store. Sheldon crashes Amy's date with Stuart by showing up to the movie theater and sitting next to Amy. I believe it is only when Sheldon realizes he may lose Amy and the possibility of experiencing the heterosexual imaginary that he succumbs to Amy's request to call her his "girlfriend." Amy demonstrates to Sheldon in the movie theater that she could choose Stuart instead of Sheldon when she moves her body over next to Stuart as soon as Sheldon challenges Amy's request to call her his girlfriend. As soon as Amy moves close to Stuart, Sheldon quickly responds with frustration, saying, "Amy, will you be my girlfriend?" ("The Flaming Spittoon Acquisition"). This act of adherence to the heterosexual imaginary makes Sheldon's challenges to hegemonic masculinity more acceptable.

Even when the main characters in the show are not involved in committed romantic relationships, they are consistently making comments about wanting to have a girlfriend or, at the very least, are having sexual relations with various women. Howard has sex with Penny's friend, Christy, who is visiting from Nebraska ("The Dumpling Paradox"). Raj has sex with a woman during Penny's Halloween party ("The Middle Earth Paradigm"). In "The Desperation Emanation," Leonard has a terrible date with Joy, one of Bernadette's friends, but agrees to go out on a second date with her because he may get to have sex. One of the key themes of the show is for the men to figure out how to obtain girlfriends and be successful in heterosexual romantic relationships. This theme clearly promotes the heterosexual imaginary.

The Creation of Deviants Through Queering Masculinity and Femininity

Understanding how the heterosexual imaginary is promoted in *The Big Bang Theory* is the first step in trying to comprehend how the series works to question the heterosexual imaginary through offering alternative sexual scripts for the characters. Specifically, I argue *The Big Bang Theory* dislocates hegemonic masculinity and femininity through queering masculinity and femininity. Chris Barker explains, "Hegemony implies a situation where a 'historical block' of powerful groups exercises social authority and leadership over subordinate groups through the winning of consent" (10). In the case of *The Big Bang Theory*, the ideas of hegemonic masculinity and femininity are called into question. "Women are gendered as passive, vulnerable, and nurturing, while males are supposed to be aggressive, emotionally self-contained (meaning non-expressive), and less nurturing" (Heasley 112). The construction of almost all of the characters in the series works in opposition to the hegemonic ideals—essentially queering masculinity and femininity for the viewer. I use the term queer here to mean "a person who is a nonconformist in challenging existing constructions and identities" (Shaw and Lee 109).

Queering masculinity and femininity in *The Big Bang Theory* presents an interesting opposition to heterosexuality. Typically, television sitcoms offer the audience a clear deviant—the homosexual character—in which to reinforce heterosexuality. In *The Big Bang Theory* there are no homosexual characters but many of the characters do not fit with the expected behaviors of males and females in heterosexual relationships, sometimes questioning their sexual orientation. Offering alternatives to heterosexual characteristics and challenges to the hegemonic ideals of masculinity and femininity help "resist, dismantle, or circumnavigate hegemonic systems of sexual oppression and normalization" (Hanson 4).

The four main male characters all represent, to some extent, queer-straight males. Queer-straight males are those who disrupt heteronormative constructions of masculinity, and in the process, disrupt what it means to be straight, as well as gay. Many straight men experience and demonstrate "queer masculinity" defined as ways of being masculine outside heteronormative constructions of masculinity that disrupt, or have the potential to disrupt, traditional images of the hegemonic heterosexual masculine [Heasley 110].

The performance of queer-straight masculinity by the four main male characters helps to disrupt the hegemonic ideals of masculinity.

Of the four main characters in the show, Sheldon is the closest to demonstrating hegemonic masculinity through his ambition, arrogance, and non-expressiveness. Specifically, Sheldon exemplifies autonomy. Friedman explains,

> The term "autonomy" is largely a term of philosophic art, yet it encompasses an array of notions familiar to ordinary people, notions such as being "true to myself," doing it "my way," standing up for "what I believe," thinking "for myself," and, in gender-egalitarian reformulation, being one's "own person" [3].

While many of the qualities of autonomy may sound masculine, Sheldon takes autonomy to the extreme and steps outside of the boundaries of masculinity by being completely uninterested in sex as shown in the episode "The Isolation Permutation," where Amy has to negotiate cuddling with Sheldon. Hegemonic masculinity as performed in heterosexual relationships often involves an eagerness to have sex (Connell). Sheldon breaks the boundaries of hegemonic masculinity by falling more into an asexual role when it comes to physical relationships. Yet, Sheldon also recognizes that he must appear to be interested in sexual relations. In "The Cooper/Kripke Inversion," Sheldon lies to his coworker about having a sexual relationship with Amy. Penny inquires as to the reason for Sheldon's lie.

PENNY: I don't understand. Why didn't you just tell Kripke the truth?
SHELDON: Because the truth made me look bad. Whereas a ridiculous bald-face lie made me look good. [Turning to Leonard] Anyway, if Kripke asks, tell him my coitus with Amy is frequent, intense and whimsically inventive.

Penny continues to inquire about Sheldon's sexual relationship with Amy, going as far as to ask him if he "is ever going to sleep with Amy." Sheldon simply responds with "Well, word around the university is I'm giving her sexual organs a proper jostling" ("The Cooper/Kripke Inverion"). Sheldon clearly recognizes that by adhering to more of an asexual relationship he does not follow the ideals of hegemonic masculinity. In order to be revered by his peers, he realizes that he needs to fabricate actions that fit within the expectations of masculinity thus recognizing the need for surface adherence to hegemonic ideals of masculinity.

Further, when Sheldon interacts with others who follow the hegemonic ideals of masculinity more closely, Sheldon shows more of a departure from what is expected. For instance, in "The Creepy Candy Coating Corollary," Sheldon plays a competitive card game with Wil Wheaton—a person who Sheldon feels wronged him when he was younger. During the game, Sheldon is intent on beating Wheaton, until Wheaton tells Sheldon the story of his grandmother dying. Sheldon feels badly for Wheaton and throws the game—even though he clearly could have won. After Sheldon lets Wheaton win, he discovers that Wheaton lied and that his grandmother did not die. Sheldon, in this case, lets his emotional attachment to his own "Mee Maw" (grandmother) distract him from his overall goal of winning the game. This situation shows that Sheldon, while interested in winning most of the time, allows his emotions to sway him away from complete adherence to hegemonic masculinity and the desire to win.

Sheldon is also upfront about his physical incapacity to perform masculinity. When he witnesses Leonard embark on a situation that could lead to a physical confrontation, he says to Leonard, "Let me remind you that while my moral support is absolute, in a physical confrontation I will be less than useless" ("The Middle Earth Paradigm"). Again, Sheldon recognizes his limitations when it comes to performing the ideals of hegemonic masculinity.

Leonard also presents a diversion from the norms of hegemonic masculinity through his appearance—he is shorter than the majority of the other males on the show (Howard is the exception) and is not muscular—and through his emotional disclosures to Penny. Leonard is shown as being the more sensitive person in his and Penny's relationship. He reveals to Penny that he loves her and demonstrates his heartbreak at her not saying it back in ways that would be expected for a female but not for a male. He mopes around the apartment and challenges Penny when she mentions she "loves" something else. Leonard is crushed at the possibility of his relationship not working out with Penny ("The Wheaton Reoccurence"). While he does queer masculinity in some respects, he is also the character that tries the hardest to demonstrate his masculinity when it is called into question. For example, often when Leonard feels like "less of a man," it is around Penny. In "The Cornhusker Vortex," he attempts to learn all about football in hopes of fitting in with Penny's friends when they are at her apartment to watch a football game. Throughout the episode, Leonard attempts to demonstrate his masculinity through an interest in sports, but after a while he gives up and goes to fly kites with his friends. Another instance of Leonard attempting to assert his masculinity is in "The Middle-Earth Paradigm" when he attends a Halloween party at Penny's apartment. At the party, Penny's ex-boyfriend, Kurt, shows up. Kurt is the picture-perfect image of hegemonic masculinity in terms of his height and muscular build. Leonard explains to Sheldon:

> LEONARD: Look if this were fifteen hundred years ago, by virtue of his size and strength, he would be entitled to his choice of female partner.
> SHELDON: And male partners, animal partners, primordial partners. Pretty much anything that tickled his fancy.
> LEONARD: Yes. But our society has undergone a paradigm shift and in the information age, Sheldon, you and I are the alpha males. We shouldn't have to back down.
> SHELDON: Hm. Why don't you text him that and see if he backs down?
> LEONARD: No. I'm going to assert my dominance face to face.
> SHELDON: Face to face? Are you going to wait for him to sit down or are you going to stand on a coffee table? ["The Middle Earth Paradigm"].

Leonard desperately tries not to back down and tries to confront Kurt using his intelligence. Unfortunately, Kurt resorts to showing off his physical strength by picking Leonard up off of the floor and only putting him down when Penny tells him to. Leonard leaves the apartment humiliated. Leonard is the character who tries the hardest to fit into what is expected of masculinity and is seen as failing in many respects. The recognition of Leonard's struggles to fit into what is ideal for masculinity sheds light on the extreme nature and, to some extent, the absurdity of our idealization of what is considered "manly." While Kurt may embody hegemonic masculinity, he is not likeable and appears as a brut. On the other hand, Leonard who does not represent hegemonic masculinity, is likeable and sincere. The juxtaposition of these two characters allows the audience an opportunity to critically view hegemonic masculinity.

Just like Leonard, Howard demonstrates several characteristics of hegemonic masculinity mainly through his sexual desires. Howard is shown as animalistic in nature, being only concerned with having sex with whichever woman is available at the time. However, Howard is not completely within the confines of hegemonic masculinity. He queers straight masculinity in three ways. The first is through his wardrobe. Out of all of the men on the show, Howard is the most interestingly attired. He usually wears skinny jeans in bright colors and has a large collection of belt buckles. Heasley defines men who "allow themselves to develop and display an aesthetic, such as stylish haircuts and clothes, having facials and pedicures" as stylistic straight-queers (121). Howard represents a stylistic straight-queer through his display of a unique aesthetic. While all of the characters have distinct wardrobes, Howard's clothing stands out to the audience because they are not choices you would see males who embrace hegemonic masculinity making. For instance, Sheldon wears superhero t-shirts but this is a clothing choice that appears masculine or, at least, within the realm of "normal" masculinity. Howard wearing dickies, skinny jeans, and flashy belt buckles portrays something other than what is expected for males.

The second way that Howard is seen as not conforming to hegemonic masculinity is through the constant reminders he receives from Sheldon and the others about his lack of a doctoral degree. Regardless of how many times Howard tries to defend his credentials, the criticism of his educational standing being no higher than a master's degree remains. In the episode "The Roommate Transmogrification," Bernadette, Howard's fiancé, announces that her dissertation was accepted and she will earn her doctoral degree. The episode causes Howard to question his masculinity because his significant other has a doctorate and he does not. His friends all criticize him having a lower educational status than his girlfriend.

> LEONARD: Howard, tell us how you will feel when you get married and you will be referred to as "Dr. and Mr. Wolowitz"?
> SHELDON: Unless he takes Bernadette's last name and considering her advanced status that could open some doors for him.
> HOWARD: Please, this isn't about me. [turning to Bernadette] I'm proud of you.
> BERNADETTE: Well you'll really be proud of this. I was head hunted by a big pharmaceutical company and they're going to pay me a butt load of money.
> HOWARD: What?
> LEONARD: Bernadette, that's great. [looking at Howard] Howard, do you make a butt load?
> HOWARD: Better than what you've got a butt load of.
> LEONARD: Hey if I roll down the windows in the car, everything's peachy. If you do it, you're still not a doctor.

While Howard's storyline included working for NASA and going into space during the end of season five and the beginning of season six, Howard is still seen as not being equal to his male counterparts or his wife in terms of his educational status. In "The Holographic Excitation" Howard continually reminds his friends of his time in space. Eventually, Bernadette and his friends tell him that he needs to stop talking about his time in space. While his constant talk about his accomplishments annoys his friends, it is clear Howard is doing it in an attempt to establish himself as being at the same level of his male counterparts and his wife. Howard remarks continuously that he is only one who has gone to space, thus indicating that he has an experience that is even better than their accomplishments of doctoral degrees.

Finally, Howard's relationship with Raj contributes to his queering of straight masculinity—though not as much for Howard as for Raj. As mentioned in the beginning of this chapter, Howard and Raj often cross the boundaries between what is expected for male friendships. For instance, in "The Infestation Hypothesis," Howard creates a kissing machine for Leonard to use with his long distance girlfriend Priya. The kissing machine has two controls—one for each person to place his/her mouth and tongue so that they can kiss passionately from a distance. Howard demonstrates the machine and tries to get Leonard to participate. Leonard refuses but Raj says, "I'll try it." Then, Howard and Raj start kissing each other through the kissing machine. Howard even tries to teach Raj how to do it, saying, "Really get your tongue in there to activate the motion sensor." After a few awkward moments of the two kissing—with Leonard looking at the two with a confused look and a laugh track playing—Howard pulls away exclaiming, "You just bit my tongue." Raj replies, "I nibbled. I was being playful." Howard responds, "Why do you have to make everything weird?" After Raj apologizes, they go back to practicing on the kissing machine. While Howard does queer straight masculinity through his interactions with Raj, he seems to recognize more easily when these interactions are 'weird' and go against the expected behaviors of hegemonic masculinity.

The person who demonstrates queer-straight masculinity the most in *The Big Bang Theory* is Raj. From the beginning of the series, with the scene between him and Howard where he is shown holding Howard to let him smell Penny's perfume that has rubbed off on him, the audience is aware of Raj's more feminine behaviors. Raj is seen as being familiar with feminine things. For instance, in "The Isolation Permutation," Raj mentions that he likes cap sleeves for bridesmaid's dresses—showing he is knowledgeable about clothing design. He calls himself a "brown Martha Stewart" and makes statements like "Tyra Banks says the most important thing in your makeup bag is a good night's sleep" and "A minute on the lips, a lifetime on the hips" ("The Roommate Transmogrification"). All of his comments that show him expressing more feminine knowledge are accompanied by a laugh track—indicating to the audience that he is stepping outside of hegemonic masculinity.

Ambivalences in Raj's sexuality are also evaluated within the series. In "The Thespian Catalyst" he is overwhelmed by his crush on Bernadette which leads him to say he is "definitely not gay." However, Leonard's mother, Beverly Hofstadter, calls Raj and Howard's relationship into question labeling it an "ersatz homosexual marriage" ("The Maternal Capacitance"; "The Maternal Congruence"). His sexuality is ultimately a subject of humor in the show. In "The Roommate Transmogrification," the exchange below demonstrates how writers have played on his queer-straight masculinity. Penny walks into Sheldon's apartment and finds out that Raj has moved into Leonard's bedroom.

PENNY: What happened to Leonard?
SHELDON: Same thing that happened to homo-erectus. He was replaced by a superior species.
RAJ: I'm the new homo in town.

Additionally, throughout seasons four and five of *The Big Bang* Theory, Raj constantly mentions feeling left out of the group because he is the only one of his friends without a girlfriend. He even asks Penny, "What's wrong with me?" in an attempt to figure out why women are not attracted to him ("The Roommate Transmogrification"). He also questions Bernadette about whether he has a chance with Penny and she yells, "Of course you do. You're a cutie pie. Any girl would be lucky to have you" ("The Skank Reflex Analysis"). Raj's performance of queer-straight masculinity includes feminine behaviors, open questioning of his sexuality, and his inability to be in a heterosexual relationship.

Along with the male characters on the show, several of the female characters demonstrate behaviors that could be considered queer-straight femininity. The difference with the female characters on the show is that the females who break the boundaries of hegemonic femininity do so in contrast to Penny—the one person on the show who, for the most part, demonstrates hegemonic femininity. The males who queer masculinity do so in contrast to what people "think" is appropriate for masculine behaviors or by using guest characters like Penny's ex-boyfriend Kurt as a point of comparison. The series begins by only having individuals in guest roles showing alternatives to hegemonic femininity. However, Bernadette and Amy become continuing characters in *The Big Bang Theory* making the disruption of the hegemonic femininity—or the idealized form of femininity—more prominent.

While Bernadette appears to be completely feminine—she takes great care with her appearance, is caring, and is the relationship expert when it comes to her relationship with Howard—she, as mentioned earlier, has a higher educational degree than Howard. Hegemonic femininity does not traditionally involve success—especially success that is greater than a romantic other. Additionally, in season five, Bernadette expresses very clearly that she has no desire to have children—something that is outside of the norm for a female performing heterosexuality. In the episode "The Shiny Trinket Maneuver," Howard attempts to convince Bernadette that deep down she really does want children.

BERNADETTE: I just don't like children.
HOWARD: Yeah. We all got that. Don't you think it will be different when the child is ours?
BERNADETTE: Right. When it's our kid that's ruined my body and kept me up all night and I've got no career and no future and nothing to be happy about for the next 20 years. Sure, that'll be completely different.

Bernadette's clear disdain for children represents a disruption of hegemonic femininity because traditional images of femininity show women who want to be mothers and bear children. Even after discussing the issue with Howard, Bernadette is not convinced that she wants to have children. Bernadette challenges what is expected for females in our culture—allowing an expansion of gender roles for women. Bernadette and Howard's relationship is not the romantic heterosexual ideal.

The female character who disrupts hegemonic femininity the most is Amy Farrah Fowler. Amy is extremely intelligent and, at least in the beginning stages of her character on the show, is fairly unexpressive in her discussions with others and uninterested in a romantic relationship that may involve physical intimacy ("The Desperation Emanation"; "The Lunar Excitation"). She also appears, in the beginning, uninterested in feminine things like makeup or clothing. Even when Sheldon buys her a present after not taking her newest scholarly publication seriously, she starts to open the present while speaking about how jewelry is not that exciting. However, after she opens the present, she is exuberant because Sheldon has given her a tiara. She runs to Penny telling her, "Put it on me. Put it on me. Put it on me!" After placing the tiara on her head, Penny says, "You look beautiful." Amy responds, "Of course I do. I'm a princess and this is my tiara" ("The Shiny Trinket Maneuver"). There are other instances where Amy seems completely uninterested in feminine things—disrupting hegemonic femininity—but then changes her mind as she starts to experience the feminine side of things.

The most outward way in which Amy unsettles hegemonic femininity is through her expressions of attraction to Penny. Even though Amy is heterosexual—much like Raj—her sexuality is called into question. Amy is shown as desiring Penny—through her discussions of lesbian experimentation ("The 21-Second Excitation") and her statements about Penny's beauty ("The Isolation Permutation"). Amy complicates heterosexuality and hegemonic femininity through her excitement at the possibility of going to a Korean Spa where she, Penny and Bernadette can bathe naked together. She sees Penny as perfect and in her expressions of these feelings, she queers femininity. For instance, when speaking to Leonard about the list he created for Penny about the habits he did not like of hers, Amy responds,

> AMY: What is baffling me is what you could have possibly put on the list. Hair too golden? Laugh too musical? World too much a better place for her mere presence in it?
> SHELDON: How about constantly talks with food in her mouth?
> AMY: Her heart's full of love. No one cares what's in her mouth ["The Beta-Test Initiation"].

In the episode "The Isolation Permutation," Penny makes a comment to Sheldon about him looking at her and Amy responds, "Who didn't? Your skin is like alabaster. Do you even have pores?" Later in the same episode, Amy says to Bernadette, "You do look beautiful. Not Penny beautiful, but beautiful." Further, she makes clear statements that demonstrate how she is disrupting heterosexuality. For example, after giving Penny a three thousand dollar painting of the two of them, she explains,

> AMY: I'm going to let you in on a little secret. Originally, we were painted nude. But I had him add clothes because I thought it was an unnecessary challenge to our heterosexuality. But if you ever change your mind all it would take is some warm soapy water and a couple of sponges.
> PENNY: You're talking about the painting, right?
> AMY: Sure ["The Rothman Disintegration"].

Like Raj's transgressions from hegemonic masculinity that call into question his sexuality, Amy's expressions of attraction that hint at homosexuality are accompanied by a laugh track—signaling to the audience that these actions are not normal. Cooper and Pease explain, "Social critiques ... often are articulated within comic narratives, in which hegemonic ideals can be safely questioned by lampooning them because the humorous context allows audience members to participate with mockery without feeling threatened or alienated" (301). Amy's hints at homosexuality are comedic relief that allow a disruption of hegemonic femininity.

Punishing the Deviants Back into the Heterosexual Imaginary

While the majority of the characters in *The Big Bang Theory* work to queer femininity and masculinity, the two characters that disrupt hegemonic ideals the most are Amy and Raj. In order to deal with their extreme challenges to gender and sexuality, they are punished in the narratives through their relationships—or lack thereof—with others. I argue that the punishing of Amy and Raj is necessary because it makes the other characters who challenge hegemonic ideals of masculinity and femininity while striving to fulfill the heterosexual imaginary more acceptable to the audience. Amy and Raj challenge ideal conceptualizations of gender and sexuality too much—making the audience question the sexuality of the two characters. Hoerburger writes, "In Raj and Amy, *The Big Bang Theory* could very well have two bona fide bisexuals among its characters" (44). Interestingly, Amy and Raj are punished more by themselves than by their friends. As Foucault noted in his explanations of power, the disciplinarian does not have to be external. Instead, punishment can be enacted internally through psychological punishment.

These self-inflicted punishments serve as a reaffirmation of heterosexuality as the norm.

Amy is punished for her behaviors that work to queer femininity through her relationship with Sheldon. While one could argue that Sheldon is an external disciplinarian—Sheldon is unaware of what he is "supposed" to do in order to be involved in a successful heterosexual romantic relationship. Amy continues to agree to Sheldon's disinterest in her as a sexual partner even as she recognizes her need for physical contact. When Sheldon finds her on a date with Stuart—the man who works in the comic book store—he finally agrees to call her his girlfriend. However, in order to be his girlfriend, she has to sign a relationship agreement which clearly dictates the terms of their relationship. It is clear to the audience that some of the terms are unreasonable, but Amy is quick to sign the contract. There are other instances where Amy makes it clear to Sheldon that she is interested in moving their relationship to a more intimate level. In "The Isolation Permutation," Sheldon goes over to Amy's apartment to see why she is not answering her cell phone or responding to his Facebook messages. After hearing why she is depressed, Amy confronts Sheldon:

> AMY: At this moment, I find myself craving human intimacy and physical contact.
> SHELDON: Oh boy. You know ours is a relationship of the mind.
> AMY: Proposal: One wild night of torrid love making that soothes my soul and inflames my loins.
> SHELDON: Counterproposal: I will gently stroke your head and repeat, "Awe, who's a good Amy?"
> AMY: How about this? French kissing. Seven minutes in heaven culminating in second base.
> SHELDON: Neck massage. Then, you get me that beverage.
> AMY: We cuddle. Final offer.
> SHELDON: Very well.
> AMY: [moves closer to Sheldon]
> SHELDON: Oh boy.

Clearly, Amy is starting to wish her relationship was more in line with what is expected in heterosexual romantic relationships. Yet, she remains with a man who refuses to provide what she needs. Later in "The Isolation Permutation," Sheldon and Leonard go to pick up Amy from the parking lot of a liquor store. Amy asks, "Sheldon, what would it take for you to go into that liquor store, buy a bottle of Hooch, and take me across the street to that motel and have your way with me?" Sheldon doesn't answer except to say to Amy and Leonard, "I'm begging both of you. Please, let's go."

The development of Amy's character through seasons four and five on *The Big Bang Theory*, show her increased desire for a more intimate romantic relationship with Sheldon as well as her physical attraction to Penny. While Amy wishes for something more with Sheldon, he is incapable of providing much to her in the realm of physical intimacy. Sheldon does not understand the point of physical intimacy and has a difficult time understanding emotional intimacy—though he does recognize that certain individuals need it in their lives. Yet, Amy stays with Sheldon and agrees to conditions on their relationship that do not necessarily benefit her—other than being called a "girlfriend" instead of just "a friend who is a girl" ("The Flaming Spittoon Acquisition"). This is Amy's punishment. She is punished—whether through her own decision to stay with Sheldon or through her treatment by Sheldon. Amy's sexuality is questionable because of her verbal statements and nonverbal actions signaling her attraction to Penny. Because of her questionable sexuality, she is punished through her relationship with Sheldon.

Raj is the other character—and perhaps the more obvious character—that is disciplined in *The Big Bang Theory* for his disruptions of hegemonic masculinity. Raj experiences selective mutism when around females. I argue that his selective mutism is punishment for his noncompliance to hegemonic masculinity that leads to the audience questioning his sexuality. He is able to express his emotions which cross into what is expected of those performing femininity when he is surrounded by men but is unable to express anything when he is around women.

Raj's selective mutism obviously influences his ability to be in a successful heterosexual romantic relationship. He attempts to overcome his selective mutism through taking pills for his social anxiety ("The Wildebeest Implementation") and drinking ("The Grasshopper Experimentation"; "The Psychic Vortex"; "The Roommate Transmogrification"). The audience discovers early on that the only time Raj is able to speak to women is when he is drinking and this becomes a continuing story line in *The Big Bang Theory*.

While Raj has sexual relations with various women and occasional dates, there are only two situations where Raj thinks he is in a successful heterosexual romantic relationship. The first relationship, shown in "The Wiggly Finger Catalyst," is a result of Penny setting Raj up on a date with a deaf woman. Raj quickly discovers that he can say whatever he needs to around her because she cannot hear him. However, she takes advantage of him—having him pay off her credit cards and buy her a car and a ruby necklace. The two end their relationship when Raj chooses love over money and his parents cut him off from his inheritance.

The second time Raj thinks he is in a romantic relationship is with his iPhone's personal assistant, Siri. When Raj first gets his iPhone, he begins talking to Siri and Howard remarks, "Look at that! There's finally a woman in your life that you can talk to."

RAJ: [to Siri] Are you single?
SIRI: I don't have a marital status if that is what you are asking.
RAJ: You're right. That's too personal. We hardly know each other. How about a cup of coffee?
SIRI: I found six coffee shops. Three of them are fairly close to you.
RAJ: [to his friends] I will see you gentlemen later.

Raj begins to speak to Siri about his personal life.

RAJ: Why don't women like me?
SIRI: Let me check on that. How about a web search for "why don't women like me?"
RAJ: No need. I've already done that.

At one point, when Siri asks, "Would you like me to call you Raj?" Raj replies, "I'd like you to call me 'Sexy.'" From that point on, Siri calls Raj "Sexy." Eventually, Raj invites Bernadette and Howard over for dinner. When they arrive, Raj asks, "What should we put Siri in for dinner? Leopard, sparkles, or to paraphrase Coco Chanel, you can never go wrong with a little black case." Finally, the relationship comes to an end when Raj has a nightmare about meeting the "real" Siri. In his dream, he goes to visit Siri in her office.

SIRI: Hello Sexy. What can I help you with?
RAJ: [unable to speak]
SIRI: If you'd like to make love to me, just tell me.
RAJ: [opens mouth to speak] Crrr. Crrrr.
SIRI: I'm sorry I don't understand crrr, crrrr ["The Beta-Test Initiation"].

Raj wakes up from his nightmare yelling, "No!" Raj recognizes in his nightmare, that even if he were to meet Siri in person, he would be unable to have a successful relationship with her because he is unable to speak to women and to express his needs and desires.

The audience is consistently treated to the humor of Raj's selective mutism but his inability to speak to any girls without being drunk or on anxiety medication is also quite sad. Even after spending a night with Penny, Raj is unable to speak to her. She responds by saying, "Really? You still can't talk to me?" ("The Roommate Transmogrification").While Raj shows a strong desire to be involved in a heterosexual romantic relationship throughout the series, he is unable to be successful in his pursuit of a romantic relationship because he is being punished by selective mutism.[1]

Conclusion

The Big Bang Theory provides a rich cultural narrative for analysis and allows us to see how the heterosexual imaginary is continuously reinforced through the television sitcom. While *The Big Bang Theory* does not offer the expected opposite to the heterosexual characters—a homosexual character—the queering of masculinity through all of the main male characters and the queering of femininity through two of the female characters allows the reaffirmation of heterosexuality as the norm. Recognizing gendered heterosexual performances that work to disrupt the heterosexual imaginary is important especially in a show where the heterosexual imaginary seems so pervasive. Further, understanding how characters who demonstrate the most variations from hegemonic femininity and masculinity are disciplined can help viewers recognize how punishment creates a means of reinforcing heterosexuality and the heterosexual imaginary.

As researchers explore cultural narratives such as media representations, the issues of gender and sexuality will continue to push forward from the texts. Ingraham argues that researchers have "overlooked the ways in which ascribed behaviors for women and men—gender—actually organize the institution of heterosexuality" (*Thinking Straight* 4). This chapter strives to contribute to the research showing how gendered behaviors—particularly those that break the boundaries of hegemonic masculinity and femininity—still work to promote heterosexuality as the preferred performance regarding sexuality. "Stories of the unusual or the odd serve to secure the 'normal,' the center, making all who occupy this space feel comforted by their compliance" (Ingraham, *White Weddings* 109). *The Big Bang Theory* has done a lot in terms of showing the audience alternative performances to hegemonic masculinity and femininity as well as challenging idealized representations of sexuality. While *The Big Bang Theory* largely reinforces the heterosexual imaginary, I believe that through the exclusion of a main character that demonstrates hegemonic masculinity and through queering straight masculinity and femininity, the boundaries of what is acceptable as gendered performance have been expanded.

Note

1. In the final episode of season six, "The Bon Voyage Reaction," Raj is seen speaking to Penny about his break-up with Lucy, the girl he had been dating during the second half of season six. After a few minutes of speaking, Raj realizes he is able to speak to Penny without consuming alcohol. The final scene of the episode shows Raj venting to Penny, Bernadette and Amy about his feelings—clearly sharing too much information. His dialogue to the women continues as the credits roll for the episode.

Works Cited

"The Alien Parasite Hypothesis." *The Big Bang Theory: Season Four*. Prod. Chuck Lorre and Bill Prady. Warner Brothers, 2011. DVD.

Bachen, C. M., and E. Illouz. "Imagining Romance: Young People's Cultural Models of Romance and Love." *Critical Studies in Mass Communication* 13.4 (Dec. 1996): 279–308.
Bednarek, M. "Constructing Nerdiness: Characterisation in 'The Big Bang Theory.'" *Multilingua* 31 (2012): 119–129.
Bissell, T. "A Simple Medium; Chuck Lorre and the Rules of the Network Sitcom." *The New Yorker*, Dec. 6, 2010, p. 34.
Brown, R. H. *Society as Text: Essays on Rhetoric, Reason and Reality*. Chicago: University of Chicago Press, 1987.
Butler, J. *Gender Trouble: Feminism and the Subversion of Identity*. New York: Routledge, 1990.
Cooper, B., and E. C. Pease. "Don't Want No Short People 'Round Here: Confronting Heterosexism's Intolerance through Comic and Disruptive Narratives in 'Ally McBeal.'" *Western Journal of Communication* 66.3 (Summer 2002): 300–318.
Corcoran, F. "Television as Ideological Apparatus: The Power and the Pleasure." *Critical Studies in Mass Communication* 1.2 (1984): 131–145.
Davies, B. "Women's Subjectivity and Feminist Stories." In C. Ellis and M. G. Flaherty, eds., *Investigating Subjectivity: Research on Lived Experience* (pp. 53–76). Thousand Oaks: Sage, 1992.
Dworkin, S. L., and F. L. Waches. "Disciplining the Body: HIV-Positive Male Athletes, Media Surveillance, and the Policing of Sexuality." *Sociology of Sport Journal* 15.1 (March 1998): 1–20.
Foucault, M. *Disciplinine and Punish*. A. Sheridan, trans. New York: Vintage, 1995.
Friedman, M. *Autonomy, Gender, Politics*. New York: Oxford University Press, 2003.
Gagnon, J. H., and W. Simon. *Sexual Conduct: The Social Sources of Human Sexuality*. Chicago: Aldine, 1973.
Gauntlett, D. *Media, Gender and Identity*. New York: Routledge, 2001.
Gross, L. "The Paradoxical Politics of Media Representation." *Critical Studies in Media Communication* 18.1 (2001): 114–120.
Heasley, R. "Crossing the Borders of Gendered Sexuality: Queer Masculinities of Straight Men." In C. Ingraham, *Thinking Straight: The Power, The Promise and The Paradox of Heterosexuality* (pp. 109–129). New York: Routledge, 2005.
Ingraham, C. *Thinking Straight: The Power, the Promise, and the Paradox of Heterosexuality*. New York: Routledge, 2005.
Ingraham, C. *White Weddings: Romancing Heterosexuality in Popular Culture*. New York: Routledge, 1995.
Ivolry, A. H., R. Gibson, and J. D. Ivory. "Gendered Relationships on Television: Portrayals of Same-Sex and Heterosexual Couples." *Mass Communication and Society* 12.2 (2009): 170–192.
Kellner, D. *Media Culture: Cultural Studies, Identity and Politics Between the Modern and Postmodern*. New York: Routledge, 1995.
Kim, J. L., C. L. Sorsoli, K. Collins, B. A. Zylbergold, D. Schooler, and D. L. Tolman. "From Sex to Sexuality: Exposing the Heterosexual Script on Primetime Network Television." *Journal of Sex Research* 44.2 (May 2007): 145–157.
Lauzen, M. M., D. M. Dozier, and N. Horan. "Constructing Gender Stereotypes Through Social Roles in Prime-Time Television." *Journal of Broadcasting and Electronic Media* 52.2 (June 2008): 200–214.
Leff, M. "Textual Criticism: The Legacy of G.P. Mohrmann." *Quarterly Journal of Speech* 72.4 (1986): 377–389.
Leff, M. "Things Made by Words: Reflections on Textual Criticism." *Quarterly Journal of Speech* 78.2 (1992): 223–231.
Markle, G. "'Can Women Have Sex Like a Man?' Sexual Scripts in 'Sex and the City.'" *Sexuality & Culture* 1 (2008): 45–57.

Miller, D. "Masculinity in Popular Sitcoms, 1955–1960 and 2000–2005." *Culture, Society and Masculinities* 3.2 (2011): 141–159.
Monro, S. *Gender Politics*. Ann Arbor: Pluto Press, 2005.
Quail, C. "Nerds, Geeks, and the Hip/Square Dialectic in Contemporary Television." *Television and New Media* 12.5 (2011): 460–492.
Reiss, B., and R. Grossmark. *Heterosexual Masculinities: Contemporary Perspectives from Psychoanalytic Gender Theory*. New York: Routledge, 2009.
Shaw, S. M., and J. Lee. *Women's Voices, Feminist Visions: Classic and Contemporary Readings*, 5th ed. New York: McGraw Hill, 2012.
Shugart, H. A. "Reinventing Privilege: The New (Gay) Man in Contemporary Popular Media." *Critical Studies in Media Communication* 20.1 (March 2003): 67–91.
Simon, W., and J. H. Gagnon. "Sexual Scripts: Permanence and Change." *Archives of Sexual Behavior* 15.2 (April 1986): 97–120.
Sless, D. *In Search of Semiotics*. London: Croom Helm, 1986.
Stetler, B. "Few TV Shows Survive a Ruthless Proving Ground." *New York Times*, May 14, 2012, p. B4.
Watson, E., and M. E. Shaw. *Performing American Masculinities: The 21st Century Man in Popular Culture*. Bloomington: Indiana University Press, 2011.
"The Weekend Vortex." *The Big Bang Theory: Season Five*. Prod. Chuck Lorre and Bill Prady. Warner Brothers, 2009. DVD.
"The White Asparagus Triangulation." *The Big Bang Theory: Season Two*. Prod. Chuck Lorre and Bill Prady. Warner Brothers, 2009. DVD.
"The Wiggly Finger Catalyst." *The Big Bang Theory: Season Five*. Prod. Chuck Lorre and Bill Prady. Warner Brothers, 2012. DVD.
"The Wildebeest Implementation." *The Big Bang Theory: Season Four*. Prod. Chuck Lorre and Bill Prady. Warner Brothers, 2011. DVD.

The Mutual Exclusivity Proposition
Female Intellectualism and Sexuality

ALISSA BURGER

In early seasons of the CBS sitcom *The Big Bang Theory*, women were featured as love interests—best epitomized by Leonard's infatuation and eventual romantic relationship with Penny (played by Kaley Cuoco)—though rarely as intellectual equals. Leonard, Howard, and Raj sought out women, often unsuccessfully, for relationships and sexual intimacy, but did not regularly work with them side by side, with the exception of their colleague and occasional love interest Leslie Winkle (played by actress Sara Gilbert). While the lack of female scientist characters was commented upon by critics and fans alike, there was a logical explanation for their absence: the number of women working in the sciences remains significantly lower than that of their male counterparts for a variety of reasons, including social stigma against intelligent women, as well as the perception of science, technology, engineering, and math (STEM) fields as "male" (Hill, Corbett, and St. Rose xiv–xv). As physicist and series consultant David Saltzberg explains of early seasons of *The Big Bang Theory*, "the [female-male] ration is actually higher on the show than it is in my part of the field, which is pretty bad" (qtd. in Heyman 741). Female scientists early in the series include experimental physicist Leslie Winkle, who appears sporadically over the course of the series, and cosmological physicist Elizabeth Plimpton (played by Judy Greer), a one-episode guest star. However, in the third season, two regular female characters were introduced: microbiologist Bernadette Rostenkowski (played by Melissa Rauch), Howard's girlfriend and later wife, and neurobiologist Amy Farrah Fowler (played by Mayim Bialik, who in real life has Ph.D. in neuroscience from UCLA), the match chosen for Sheldon by an online dating website.

In each of these cases, Leslie, Elizabeth, Bernadette, and Amy are considered love interests, to varying degrees, as well as colleagues and fellow scientists, creating a dynamic negotiation between professional performance and romantic gender roles in their interactions with their male counterparts. Each of these women is highly intelligent and successful in her field, though these representations of intelligence are frequently complicated by social ineptitude or unsuccessfully negotiated romantic roles. As Sherrie A. Inness points out in her introduction to the edited collection *Geek Chic: Smart Women in Popular Culture*, "mainstream American society has a deeply rooted fear of brilliant women" (2), which is especially significant because "in a mass culture that remains ambivalent about women's intelligence, the manner in which women are portrayed in popular culture influences and shapes how society views intelligence" (4). The same can be said of representations of female scientists, which are of particular importance given the low numbers of women in STEM fields. In her article "Cultural Representations of Gender and Science: Portrayals of Female Scientists and Engineers in Popular Films," Jocelyn Steinke argues that "a better understanding of cultural representations of women, specifically a better understanding of the portrayals of female scientists and engineers in the media, may enhance the efficacy of efforts to promote the greater representation of girls in science, engineering, and technology" (29).

With the significance of representations of women in general, and representations of female scientists specifically in mind, what kind of female characters does *The Big Bang Theory* offer its viewers? The female scientists of *Big Bang* are all involved in highly specialized and respected fields: Leslie and Elizabeth are physicists, tackling the same theoretical and cosmological constructs as Leonard and Sheldon, while Bernadette and Amy both do biological research, with Bernadette focusing on microbiology and Amy on neurobiology.[1] They also seem to be very successful in their fields: Bernadette lands a high-paying pharmaceutical job almost immediately upon completion of her doctoral program ("The Roommate Transmogrification"), and Amy's sole authored article is the cover story in a prestigious journal ("The Shiny Trinket Maneuver"). In addition, these women refuse to eschew their sexuality and each works to balance their professional and romantic lives rather than privileging one over the other, though it is notable that these relationships are solely comprised of their romantic relationships with their partners, at this point in the series, with little discussion of having children or starting families, neutralizing—at least temporarily—the added element of motherhood as another potential facet of their gendered identities.

However, as previously mentioned, that negotiation often proves contentious and not altogether successful, with Leslie and Elizabeth characterized as sexually aberrant through their promiscuity and multiple sexual partners, Amy failing to meet traditional feminine standards in her appearance and behavior, and Bernadette slipping back and forth between the roles of an accomplished scientist and a stereotypical blonde bimbo, as well as resisting the traditional heterosexual family roles of wife and mother. In addition, when it comes to the women's professional success, their achievements at times make their male counterparts uncomfortable, with Howard feeling emasculated by the fact that Bernadette's job is much higher-paying and more prestigious than his own, and Sheldon dismissing Amy's work in biology as dealing with only "yucky, squishy things" ("The Shiny Trinket Maneuver"). Finally, in terms of acceptable feminine appearance and behavior, it is inevitable that each finds herself measured against and frequently found wanting in comparison to Penny, Leonard and Sheldon's next-door neighbor, waitress, aspiring actress, and Leonard's on-again off-again love interest.

Therefore, while at first glance *The Big Bang Theory* offers a wide range of female scientists from different specialized and sophisticated fields, it also reflects a pronounced anxiety regarding both intelligent and sexual women and the perceived mutual exclusivity of these characteristics. As Inness explains, women in popular culture tend to fall into one of two categories: either sexually attractive and "dumb" or awkward, unattractive, and intelligent (1–3). This dichotomy is especially notable because, as David Anderegg explains in his book *Nerds: How Dorks, Dweebs, Techies, and Trekkies Can Save America (and Why They Might Be Our Last Hope)*, "the nerd/geek stereotype ... is complex and not immediately visible" (18) with this either/or categorization that "beauty and brains are mutually exclusive" (13) and often accepted as simply matter of fact. Along with physical appearance, attributes of gender performativity and acceptable feminine roles are also played out through this dichotomy, with the less intelligent, beautiful women often deferential to their male counterparts, viewed as sexual objects, and "ladylike" in behavior, while their intelligent opposites frequently challenge men, bumble through gender-coded social interactions with little chance of success, and are generally considered unfeminine and thus, undesirable.[2] A close consideration of the four female scientists so far featured in *The Big Bang Theory*— Leslie Winkle, Elizabeth Plimpton, Bernadette Rostenkowski, and Amy Farrah Fowler—will highlight the ongoing negotiation of female intellectualism and sexuality in *The Big Bang Theory* and its engagement with the struggle over popular culture representations of brilliant women in general and female scientists in particular.[3]

The first female scientist featured in *The Big Bang Theory* is experimental physicist Leslie Winkle, and her appearance is commented upon by Penny, who admiringly calls her a "girl scientist," to which Leslie quips, "Yep. Come for the breasts, stay for the brains" ("The Hamburger Postulate"). After initially rejecting Leonard's romantic advances in an earlier episode, Leslie becomes straightforward and sexually aggressive, bluntly telling him of her sexual availability and interest in him with a no-nonsense "so how 'bout it?" ("The Hamburger Postulate"). Even in the midst of their sexual liaison, however, Leslie's intelligence remains foregrounded, as she "spends part of their tryst correcting an equation" (Heyman 741) on Sheldon's equation board in the apartment. Leslie proactively balances her sexuality and her intelligence, forgoing extended, emotionally intimate relationships in favor of casual sex, allowing her to fulfill her erotic needs while still remaining focused on her career, a choice that Leonard struggles with after their initial sexual encounter, which he has perceived to be the start of ongoing relationship and which Leslie has seen as an end in and of itself.

While Leslie embraces her sexuality, this mastery does not carry over to the gender roles that establish traditional femininity. Later in the series, Leslie reaches out to Leonard once again, telling him that she has decided to give up casual sex to pursue a more conventional romantic relationship.[4] As she tells him in a less than flattering romantic overture, "I just figured it's time to slow things down and who better to slow things down with than you?" ("The Codpiece Topology"). She lectures Leonard on the proper courtship procedures, including appropriate first-date activities, the necessary amount of time he needs to wait before calling her after their date, and that he shouldn't expect sex on their first date. While Leonard and Leslie develop this relationship, her embrace of the traditional feminine gender role is clearly self-reflexively performative, and both her posture and voice change dramatically as she tilts her head coyly and chirps, "Call me" ("The Codpiece Topology"). In addition, she takes this gender role performance and her newfound commitment to a conventional heterosexual romantic relationship to the extreme, talking about marriage, children, and Leonard's genetic traits during their first date. However, the relationship fails not because of sexual incompatibility, but because of an insurmountable intellectual difference of opinion, between string theory and loop quantum gravity, a debate on which Leslie will not waver, establishing this dissonance as "a deal-breaker" ("The Codpiece Topology"). As a result, Leslie returns to a primary intellectual role, unable to balance the dynamics of these two opposing personas and unwilling to sacrifice her deeply held scientific beliefs to create harmony—and a possible long-term romantic future—with Leonard.

After the failure of Leonard and Leslie's relationship, she enters into a relationship with Howard, though in the intervening time, she seems to have given up some of her commitment to the traditional feminine gender role, extending her relationship with Howard beyond an isolated instance of casual sex but remaining emotionally unattached, plying Howard with promises of lab equipment and trips rather than reciprocated feelings or trust. While Howard initially has no qualms about this quid pro quo relationship, when Leslie begins to take the upper-hand, withholding access to scientific perks when he tells her he'd rather not be her date to a wedding, he becomes uncomfortable, wishing their relationship was based more on emotional equality and respect rather than a structured series of give-and-take exchanges. However, as Leslie responds, "if I weren't controlling you with new equipment and research trips, then I'd be uncomfortable.... Because then we'd be in like a real relationship with feelings and all that crap" ("The Cushion Saturation"). In her romantic encounters with Leonard and Howard, Leslie struggles to balance her intelligence, sexuality, and intimate relationships, which ends up being a complex, contentious, and ultimately irreconcilable issue, at least within these two relationships. At this point in the series, Leslie is firmly established as a well-respected scientist and colleague,[5] in control of her pleasure and sexuality, but remaining outside the bounds of traditional feminine identity.

Elizabeth Plimpton is another female scientist character who aggressively claims her own sexuality, though in doing so, is perceived as unstable and, like Leslie, sexually aberrant. A well-known and highly-respected quantum cosmologist interviewing for a position at the university, Elizabeth stays with Sheldon and Leonard while she's in town. After Sheldon has gone to sleep, sexually attractive and aggressive Elizabeth appears unsolicited in Leonard's room and disrobes while reciting a passage from her book, stunning Leonard with both her intellect and her unabashed nudity. Much as in his previous relationship with Leslie, Leonard assumes this sexual encounter marks the start of an ongoing relationship. However, even as she and Leonard engage in morning after banter, Elizabeth shifts her romantic attentions to Raj, and then when Howard and Leonard show up at Raj's apartment, proposes erotic role playing and group sex with all of them. She has sex with Leonard and, presumably, later with Raj as well, after the others have left. Her appearance is limited to this isolated episode ("The Plimpton Simulation"), and she has not, as of the end of the sixth season, returned. As with Leslie, while Elizabeth is a world-renowned expert in her field, clearly brilliant, and in control of her own sexuality and the satisfaction of her erotic desires, she does not fulfill the traditional feminine role, leaving the men baffled, unsure of how to respond to her, and, in spite of her attractiveness and sexual availability, put off by her.

With the introduction of regular characters Bernadette Rostenkowski and Amy Farrah Fowler in the third season, *The Big Bang Theory* developed a wider range of female scientists, who are also more complex characters than their predecessors. Bernadette is arguably the most feminine of the female scientists featured: petite, with long blonde hair, large breasts, and a high-pitched voice. While she's in school, Bernadette works with Penny waitressing at The Cheesecake Factory, arguably bridging the gap between Penny's life and the guys' specialized, scientific world. According to Melissa Rauch, the actress who plays Bernadette, she also "occupies the middle ground between Amy's nerd and Penny's girlie girl" (qtd. in Deerwester), a mid-point on the continuum between some of the other diametrically-opposed smart or sexy women. Bernadette's traditional femininity and sexual desirability are also established by her previous romantic relationships, when Howard is intimidated after meeting Bernadette's ex-boyfriend, who is tall, well-muscled, and good looking ("The Love Car Displacement"). In terms of her sexuality, Bernadette also adopts a more traditionally feminine role, in contrast to Leslie and Elizabeth, waiting for Howard to initiate their first sexual encounter rather than being the aggressor, even though she wants to take their relationship to the next level of intimacy ("The Hot Troll Deviation").

However, as with Leslie and Elizabeth, Bernadette's negotiation of her intellectualism and sexuality is contentious. While Bernadette is clearly intelligent, as seen in her successful graduate work and the lucrative job she lands almost instantly upon completing her doctoral work, at times she falls into the "blonde bimbo" stereotype, with many of Howard's jokes going over her head. Their first date gets off to a rocky start because of this inability to communicate, such as when Howard quips that as a microbiologist, she can study him, since he is "a tiny living thing" ("The Creepy Candy Coating Corollary"), an analogy that befuddles her.[6] She is quite literal-minded, which often leads her to explain Howard's meaning, in essence "decoding" it for others who already understand, though are not amused by, what he is trying to say. For example, when Howard takes Bernadette to see the university and his lab, he uses the popular euphemism that he wanted to give her "a tour of the old salt mines," at which she giggles and tells Leonard that "he doesn't mean salt mines. He means where he works" ("The Gorilla Experiment"). She also attempts to run interference between Penny and Howard, when Penny gets annoyed with Howard for his condescension to their "girly" interests, such as shoes.

BERNADETTE: Don't take him too seriously. A lot of what he says is intended as humor.
PENNY: Yeah, well I don't think it's very funny.
BERNADETTE: Me neither. But he just lights up when I laugh ["The Gorilla Experiment"].

Later, in a girls-only discussion, Bernadette more overtly explains, "I'm much smarter than [Howard] is. But it's important to protect his manhood" ("The

Alien Parasite Hypothesis"). Though she has a higher-level degree—finishing her doctorate while Howard, as an engineer, has his masters'—and is competitive in the sophisticated field of microbiology, early in their relationship she routinely defers to him, generally taking a submissive role to Howard's presumed intellect and humor. However, this becomes a point of ongoing negotiation as the series, and their relationship, progresses, with Bernadette taking control of their shared finances,[7] insisting that Howard pitch in with domestic chores,[8] and making a bargain with him that she's willing to overcome her aversion to motherhood and have children, as long as he's willing to be the stay-at-home parent while she continues her career ("The Shiny Trinket Maneuver").

Further compromising her intelligence, it is also hinted throughout the series that she may not be the most responsible scientist, such as when she tells Howard and Leonard that she and her labmates "made a pinky swear never to admit we'd crossed Ebola with the common cold" ("The Desperation Emanation") and when her lab is quarantined because she and the other scientists had done "Jell-O shots out of petri dishes that used to contain yellow fever" ("The Justice League Recombination"). While scientific ethics are not a central concern of the series, obviously this type of experimentation has the potential for catastrophic destruction—a threat which is compounded by the apparently light-hearted and lackadaisical attitude of Bernadette and her colleagues, bordering on the potentially super-villainesque. The guys express some reservations about this testing when it comes up, though no one seems to take it all that seriously, with Bernadette's irresponsible and potentially dangerous lab activities becoming a humorous and repeated occurrence over the course of the series.[9] Even when she is not personally compromising laboratory safety or ethics, she seems to have a knack for capitalizing on a scientifically unsuccessful situation. For example, in one episode, she provides Amy with potentially dangerous, experimental cold medicine from her lab ("The Fish Guts Displacement") and in another, when her pharmaceutical company discovers their new drug has uncontrollable anal leakage as a side effect and she proposes they brand it as a drug for constipation, rather than scrapping it as a failed experiment ("The Spoiler Alert Segmentation"). In many ways, this lack of scientific integrity or responsibility calls into question her intelligence, both scientific and moral, despite the formal validation of her degree and her high-paying job.

Finally, though she and Howard are in an extended heterosexual relationship, progressing from dating to engagement and finally, at the end of the fifth season, marriage, Bernadette does not like children and expresses serious reservations about motherhood and starting a family.[10] After a disastrous birthday party at which Howard puts on a magic show with Bernadette as his short-tempered and confrontational assistant, she tells him, "I know it makes me sound like a bad person, but I just don't like children" ("The Shiny Trinket Manuever"). Significantly, it seems to never have crossed Howard's mind that Bernadette may not want children; in fact, he convinces her to be his assistant for the magic show by pointing out that it will be good practice for eventual motherhood. Despite the resounding failure of the magic show, Howard continues to try appealing to her presumably biologically-encoded maternal instinct with the belief that her aversion to children will magically disappear when the child in question is their own. But Bernadette sarcastically retorts, "when it's our kid that's ruined my body and kept me up all night and I've got no career and no future and nothing to be happy about for the next twenty years, sure, that'll be completely different" ("The Shiny Trinket Maneuver"). Bernadette understands the social stigma associated with women who are childless by choice ("I know it makes me sounds like a bad person, but ...") and appreciates the importance of children and family to Howard, but she refuses to cave to traditional feminine expectations or buy into the romanticized idealization of motherhood—instead continuing to privilege her career and her intellectual pursuits. However, she and Howard are able to come to a compromise, where Howard will be a stay-at-home dad, while Bernadette continues her career; as she tells him, "You watch Barney and pull Cheerios out of their noses and go on play dates, and I'll work and have conversations with people my own age and enjoy my life" ("The Shiny Trinket Maneuver"). This initially gives Howard pause, especially coupled with the likewise potentially emasculating fact that Bernadette's earning potential is dramatically higher than his own, though after perfunctory consideration these seem to be sacrifices he is willing to make for the children and family he wants, creating the possibility of a reversal of traditional gender roles as they build their lives together.[11] Her aversion to children and motherhood also seem to be mellowing as well, as she and Howard begin their married life in the sixth season. When she and Howard watch Raj's dog, Cinnamon, the dog becomes a child proxy of sorts. After an outing in the park together, Bernadette tells Howard that "there were a few moments today when I almost felt like we were a little family. I never thought of myself as a mom but when the three of us were out there having fun, I felt like maybe someday we could do it" ("The Proton Resurgence"). While she is still far from catching a case of "baby fever," this openness is tempered by her anxiety when she and Howard lose Cinnamon. Over time, she is beginning to seem less resistant to the idea of starting a family and assuming a maternal role, though it is still couched in the time-frame indeterminate of "someday."[12]

While Bernadette balances her intelligence and femininity, albeit with varying degrees of success, Amy Farrah Fowler more closely fits the image of a typical nerd; in fact, she is the female character most closely aligned with stereotypical characteristics of the male scientist. As Robert A. Jones explains in his article "How Many Female Scientists Do You Know?," "stereotypes of male scientists have been identified in popular culture ... [including that] they are frequently outsiders, their difference from ordinary people [is] signaled by eccentricity of appearance or behaviour, and they tend to be obsessive about their work, lacking a normal emotional range" (84). Amy's masculine attributes are highlighted over the course of the series, especially in her early appearances. She confesses to having penis envy, though for convenience rather than sexual pleasure ("The Love Car Displacement"). In addition, as she tells Bernadette, that when she was a child, she "did two years of Cub Scouts before they found out I was a girl" ("The Wildebeest Implementation"). In appearance, behavior, and past experience, she often finds herself excluded from traditionally feminine groupings, by both her male and female peer groups. For example, when Penny plans to capitalize on her beauty and femininity to sway the university's tenure committee in Leonard's favor, Raj criticizes Leonard, Sheldon, and Amy all in one fell swoop—the men for their underhanded competitiveness and Amy for her lack of femininity—as he says "you two should be ashamed of yourselves, using women to advance your cause with sexuality ... and whatever Amy plans on doing" ("The Tenure Turbulence"). Critiques of Amy's femininity and sexuality, or notable lack thereof, fare little better when she's talking with her fellow women, like when an irate Bernadette quips, "Gosh, Amy, I'm sensing a little hostility. Is it maybe because like Sheldon's work, your sex life is also theoretical?" ("The Parking Spot Escalation"). As a result of this wholesale questioning of her femininity and sexuality, while Leslie, Elizabeth, and Bernadette have several pronounced female characteristics, including their physical appearance and their embrace of their sexuality, Amy can be viewed more as a female version of Sheldon, with her femininity often questioned, in terms of both her appearance and her gender performance. However, as the series progresses and Amy spends increasing amounts of time with Penny and Bernadette, she begins picking up on social gender cues and trying to be more traditionally feminine, though these attempts are rarely successful.

Amy first enters the series when Howard and Raj sign Sheldon up for online dating, unbeknownst to him ("The Lunar Excitation"). Although Amy and Sheldon's individual social awkwardness would likely have prevented them meeting otherwise, once Sheldon and Amy have met, they find themselves to be very compatible, in terms of both intellect and personality. However, they are both initially against a romantic relationship, with Sheldon repeatedly characterizing Amy as a female friend but "not my girlfriend" ("The Robotic Manipulation"). Their relationship is largely an intellectual one and is structured by a well-defined "relationship agreement" outlined by Sheldon, which precludes physical contact and limits their potential levels of intimacy ("The Flaming Spittoon Acquisition"). Despite these limitations, however, they develop intense camaraderie, often to the exclusion of others, creating a strong pair-bond between them. As Mayim Bialik, who plays Amy, explains, "these are two people who know a lot of things other people will never understand" (qtd. in Deerwester), which leads them to develop games that they deem Leonard not advanced enough to play as well as Amy's dismissal of Howard's potential to understand her work since, as she tells him, "You only have a masters degree" ("The Zazzy Subsitution"). In their pairing, they are quite isolated from others and happy to be.

In spite of this compatibility, unlike Bernadette's deference to Howard, Amy refuses to sublimate her intelligence to spare Sheldon's ego. Her professional preeminence in neurobiology is a central part of her personal identity—one that she is not willing to compromise under any circumstances—and the majority of Amy and Sheldon's arguments center around these intellectual differences of opinion. They temporarily break up when Amy asserts that neurobiology is a more scientifically significant field than physics ("The Zazzy Substitution"), Sheldon has to work to win back her affection when he is dismissive of her professional accomplishments ("The Shiny Trinket Maneuver"), and they argue when Sheldon uses his vacation to come work in Amy's lab and is resistant to respect and defer to her expertise in an area of which he has little knowledge ("The Vacation Solution"). She is often willing to accept their unconventional relationship barriers, including his resistance to validate their relationship by calling her his "girlfriend" and his refusal to incorporate physical or sexual intimacy into their relationship, though as will become apparent, she get increasingly frustrated and begins to lose patience with these boundaries as their relationship progresses. But despite this compromise in other areas of their relationship, she will not downplay her own intelligence or her strong opinions in order to please Sheldon, assuage his ego, or validate his masculinity or—from his perspective—his superior intelligence.

Amy's appearance also sets her apart from the more traditional female scientists, and even more dramatically, from Penny. Amy's clothing is conservative and though she wears skirts, they fall at or below the knee, paired with thick tights and clunky shoes. As Bialik reflects, style gurus "would not approve of Amy's wardrobe" (qtd. In Deerwester). As she explains, "[t]hey'd say there's nothing right about what she does. It fits wrong, the tights are wrong, the shoes are wrong, even the way (she) stands is wrong" (qtd. in Deerwester).[13] Amy's clothing works to conceal her feminine figure rather than to accentuate it and, much like her male counterparts, she dresses in multiple, shapeless layers. However, as her friendship with Penny and her incorporation into a larger female peer group develops, she attempts to incorporate more feminine elements into her appearance, though these remain awkwardly performative rather than effectively assimilated.[14] After going shopping for shoes with Penny and Bernadette, Amy shows up at the apartment building in a pair of ultra-feminine, bright yellow high heels, hobbling ungracefully. Encountering Leonard, she asks him, "Did you know that women wear high heels to make the buttocks and breasts more prominent?" and poses awkwardly to demonstrate her point, before admonishing him to "try not to ogle my caboose as I walk away" ("The Wildebeest Implementation"). While she grasps the theory of physical attractiveness being played out here, she is unable to effectively put it into practice, coming across as odd and laughable rather than sexy. She dons more feminine attire when she accompanies Leonard to a wedding ("The Pulled Groin Extrapolation"), and later as Bernadette's maid of honor ("The Isolation Permutation," "The Countdown Reflection"), again highlighting the performativity of feminine dress, especially in the larger structure of heterosexual courtship rituals. Finally, after being initially dismissive of a retributive gift of jewelry from Sheldon, she becomes overwhelmingly ecstatic to discover he has given her a tiara, exclaiming, "I'm a princess and this is my tiara!" as she jumps about erratically, unable to contain her physical excitement ("The Shiny Trinket Maneuver"). Amy arguably wants to embody a girly, feminine appearance and her near-hysteria at the presentation of a tiara would suggest that on some level, likely cultural rather than personal, she has bought into the idea of the feminine princess as a gender ideal, seizing this isolated moment to claim this coveted identity that is otherwise denied her.[15]

As Amy becomes more traditionally feminine in both dress and behavior over the course of the series, she also attempts to restructure the parameters of her relationship with Sheldon, vying for a more intimate physical and sexual connection, though Sheldon is resistant. When Amy feels rejected and emotionally vulnerable after being left out of wedding plans by Bernadette and Penny, she turns to Sheldon for "human intimacy and physical contact" ("The Isolation Permutation"). After a spirited negotiation, Amy convinces Sheldon to cuddle with her, much to his discomfort and annoyance. This rebuff does not deter Amy, however, and she continues to strive for a greater degree of physical and sexual intimacy in her relationship with Sheldon, later challenging him with the query, "What would it take for you to go into that liquor store, buy a bottle of hooch, take me across the street to that motel, and have your way with me?" ("The Isolation Permutation"). While she continues in her persistence for a sexual relationship, she later takes a neurobiological approach to deepening the intimacy in her relationship with Sheldon, forgoing overt sexual aggression and instead appealing to Sheldon with emotional cues from his childhood and adolescence to get him to associate these feelings of nostalgic happiness and well-being with her as well ("The Launch Acceleration"). She also resorts to more covert trickery to gain physical intimacy with Sheldon, such as when she pretends to be sick so that he will take care of her, catering to her needs, rubbing VapoRub onto her chest, and bathing her; when he discovers her ruse, she tells him that though she got better shortly after he started caring for her, the intimacy it has fostered between them has "just been so nice" that she wasn't willing to give it up quite yet ("The Fish Guts Displacement").[16] Interestingly, while Sheldon continues to be resistant to defining theirs as a romantic coupling and balks at Amy's attempts to extend the level of intimacy in their relationship, he also objects to her seeing other men, such as when Stuart (played by Kevin Sussman), the owner of the comic book store the guys frequent, asks Amy out on a date—a conflict that results in Sheldon finally giving in to formally calling Amy his "girlfriend" ("The Flaming Spittoon Acquisition"). Once their relationship is semiotically formalized, however, it still continues to develop along its own unique trajectory. For example, for a romantic Valentine's Day gift, Sheldon presents Amy with paperwork officially naming her his emergency contact, a gesture which nearly moves Amy to tears as she tells him, "This is the most beautiful gift you could have ever given me" ("The Tangible Affection Proof"). In addition, when the others tease Sheldon and Amy about the lack of physical intimacy in their relationship, Sheldon compromises with a Dungeons & Dragons-mediated sexual encounter via role playing which seems, at least for the time being, a suitable, if unorthodox, simulacrum for Amy ("The Love Spell Potential").

Much like the other female scientists featured, Amy takes ownership of her own sexuality, though she does so in unconventional ways. As Amy tells Sheldon on their first date, she has repeatedly been a test subject in an experiment where the pleasure centers of the brain were stimulated, resulting in orgasm ("The Robotic Manipulation"). She also has an electric toothbrush for masturbation that she has named Gerard ("The Toast Derivation"). However, when she feels sexual arousal in response to an actual human male, she is unable to understand the connection; instead, after considering her myriad of physiological responses, she comes to the conclusion that "I obviously have the flu coupled with sudden-onset Tourettes Syndrome" ("The Alien Parasite Hypothesis"). Similar to her intellectual understanding of fashion cues that she is unable to fully embody, such as her awkward wearing of high heels, Amy understands the neurobiological and physiological facts of arousal and orgasm and has no problem enacting these on her own, from a scientific perspective. However, when put into the everyday practice of attraction, arousal, and sexual intercourse between individuals, she is flummoxed. While she finally comes to terms with her sexual arousal, she chooses to abstain from sexual intercourse anyway, remaining committed to her unconventional sexuality and awaiting the possibility of a physical, or even someday sexual, relationship with Sheldon, which at least seems to be a marginally viable possibility. When questioned about whether his relationship with Amy might someday become more conventionally intimate, he tells Penny that "it's a possibility" ("The Cooper/Kripke Inversion") and tells Amy that "I haven't ruled it out" ("The Love Spell Potential"), both of which are significantly more open and ambiguous than his previous, unquestioned aversion to physical and sexual contact under any circumstances.

Furthering her unconventional sexuality, Amy also demonstrates a quasi-queer fixation with Penny and her interactions with Penny frequently shift between friendly, amorous, and almost lecherous. Amy frequently and effusively compliments Penny's appearance, at times making Penny visibly uncomfortable. As a *Huffington Post* article recapping the Season 5 episode "The Rothman Disintegration," sums up Amy's relationship with Penny, Amy "has declared them best friends, heaps uncomfortable amounts of praise upon her at any given moment, and even goes so far as to declare her essentially perfect. She is blissfully confident that Penny feels much the same way" ("'The Big Bang Theory': Amy's Gift to Penny"). In addition, much as Bernadette laughs at Howard's jokes regardless of whether or not she understands them, Amy flatters Penny's sense of humor, quipping "golly, Penny, your whimsy is boundless" ("The Wildebeest Implementation").[17] Sheldon keeps Amy at arm's length regarding emotional, physical, and sexual intimacy within their relationship and Amy at times seems to transfer this unfulfilled desire to Penny. Amy repeatedly refers to Penny as her "bestie" and "BFF," often pushing this closeness past the bounds of Penny's comfort level; for example, she insists that she and Penny "are perfectly comfortable sharing a bed" when the group goes to a hotel ("The Love Car Displacement") and tells Sheldon that "there's not a hair on my body I wouldn't let this woman trim" ("The Werewolf Transformation"), when Penny clearly has no desire to share a bed with Amy or cut her hair. Amy imagines a more extensive intimacy in their relationship than Penny actually offers, making herself a friendship bracelet and pretending Penny gave it to her ("The Isolation Permutation") and buying Penny a large, unflattering painting of the two of them together to commemorate what she perceives as the closeness of their friendship ("The Rothman Disintegration").[18] Amy quite clearly cherishes this friendship as one of the most important relationships in her life. In contrast, Penny and the others quickly pick up on the awkwardness caused by the dissonance between Amy's projection of their friendship and their relationship as it actually exists, though Amy remains undeterred.

Amy's interaction with a female peer group, mainly Penny and Bernadette, is also often awkward as she struggles to master social conventions of female friendship with which she has had little previous experience. Amy becomes part of this female friend group through such gendered rituals as a slumber party and shopping for bridesmaid dresses, as well as her privileged position as Bernadette's maid of honor—all of which she approaches with a homoerotic sexual charge. When Amy, Penny, and Bernadette have a slumber party, it is a first for Amy, who takes an intellectual approach by coming prepared with a list of conventional slumber party games, which she struggles to get the hang of, asking objective, scientific questions during "Truth or Dare," reciting Geoffrey Chaucer's "The Miller's Tale" when dared to tell a saucy story, and chatting about her gynecological health when they engage in "girl talk" ("The 21-Second Excitation"). The night takes a turn for the erotic when Amy reads that "slumber party guests often engage in harmless experimentation with lesbianism," leading her to make a pass at Penny ("The 21-Second Excitation"). Later in the series, Bernadette complains of Amy during the wedding planning, that "she keeps on telling us stories about bridesmaid traditions in other cultures and they're all about getting naked and washing each other" ("The Isolation Permutation"). Amy takes her maid of honor position very seriously, seeing her role as more important than that of the bride herself and taking an invasively proactive role in creating a video record of the pre-wedding preparations; she brings a camera as they try on dresses[19] and asks Bernadette personal questions, such as in which position she and Howard will have sex on their wedding night ("The Stag Convergence").

Compounding the complexity of these four female scientist characters' negotiations of intellectualism and sexuality is the fact that they are all inescapably compared to Penny, the most traditionally feminine character[20] in the series and the normative standard against which other women are measured and, more often than not, found wanting.[21] As the principal female character during the first couple of seasons, Penny is central to the group dynamic and a relatively well-integrated part of their social circle, though she still remains the only central character with no last name. She even begins to assimilate and take on some of the guys' nerd culture, such as using *Star Trek* metaphors more frequently as the series progresses, though she still remains a figure of the larger, non-geek culture. In fact, as Jayme Deerwester argues in the article "'Theory' Meets the Practice of New Female Castmates," when

Bernadette and Amy first appeared in the series, "the new girls ... needed Penny's tutelage, especially Amy" (Deerwester), on how to be more feminine and successfully navigate heterosexual relationships and social interactions in general. As such, Penny occupies a uniquely hybrid position, participating in and appreciative of both the more general culture and the specialized, scientific, geek discourse she picks up from the guys and later, Bernadette and Amy as well. As Bernadette and Amy struggle to balance their intellectualism and their sexuality, Penny is held up as a model of how to potentially occupy these two worlds simultaneously—though, like the female scientist characters, she does so only imperfectly.

In the context of a culture uncomfortable with brilliant women, representations of these women in popular culture are especially significant, and in the female scientist characters of *The Big Bang Theory*, the message is one of complex and contentious negotiation. Thus far, the series has featured four key female scientist characters: Leslie Winkle, Elizabeth Plimpton, Bernadette Rostenkowski, and Amy Farrah Fowler. Each of these women is accomplished in her scientific field and is unapologetically intelligent. However, when it comes to their enactment of traditional gender roles, social engagement, and sexual relationships, each is established as somehow aberrant. Leslie's performative gender roles when she and Leonard date are laughably over the top and her decision to engage in casual sex, and later to use sex to manipulate Howard, position her outside of commonly accepted relationship roles. Elizabeth is brilliant but shown as deviant in her promiscuity and desire for group sex. Bernadette's intellectual integrity wavers when she dumbs herself down to protect Howard's masculinity and when she engages in ill-advised laboratory experiments; she is also seen as not properly feminine in her dislike of children and lack of maternal instinct. Finally, Amy struggles to master social situations and gender roles, and embraces a nonconventional sexuality, achieving sexual pleasure with neurobiological brain stimulation and an electric toothbrush rather than a heterosexual romantic partner. In contrast, Penny is feminine, sexy, and desirable,[22] though she is often teased for her non-genius intellect, with Sheldon repeatedly referring to her interrupted scholastic career as a community college dropout.

In Amy and, to a lesser extent, Bernadette as well, we see these intellectual women striving to be more traditionally feminine, working to adopt mainstream, desirably feminine behavior and appearance. The results are often laughable and near-disastrous, though arguably it is, in some ways, this very failure that makes these characters so appealing to audiences of *The Big Bang Theory*: we like them *because* they're different, *because* they struggle with social gender cues. However, we also like them because they keep trying. Despite their likability and humor, here, as in other facets of popular culture, these intelligent women still continue to be considered less desirable than their more feminine and less intelligent counterparts. Viewing Penny as the normative woman and these four female scientist characters as outside the scope of that normativity, when it comes to female scientists in *The Big Bang Theory*, intellectualism, femininity, and sexuality still seem to be mutually exclusive propositions.

Notes

1. Biology is one of the few scientific fields in which women are fairly well represented, making up 44.1 percent of professionals in the field in 2000, according the American Association of University Women (AAUW), as opposed to 13.9 percent in physics in the same year (Hill, Corbett, and St. Rose 15).
2. Romantic comedies with a strong makeover theme, in which the nerdy, awkward scientist is revealed to have been beautiful all along, are an exception to this rule. As Suzanne Ferriss establishes this type of film in her article "Fashioning Femininity in the Makeover Flick," "makeover films are a dependable subgenre of chick flicks, where superficial, external changes are signs of an internal moral transformation: the female protagonist admits she needs love and companionship despite her apparent commitment to social and intellectual independence" (41).There are also several instances in which all it takes for a female scientist to be transformed from a plain Jane workhorse to a sexually attractive vixen is for her to remove her glasses and let down her hair, again pointing toward the intersection of physical appearance and performative gender roles: a woman at play or leisure is apparently sexier than a woman working, even if that work is making significant scientific discoveries. In *The Big Bang Theory*, Penny self-reflexively negotiates and subverts this smart and sexy paradigm when, after becoming self-conscious about whether she can compete with more intelligent women vying for Leonard's attention, she decides that "I don't need to be a scientist, I can just look like one" ("The Cooper/Kripke Inversion"), wowing Leonard with some newly acquired "nerdy" glasses and science vocabulary.
3. These women are addressed here in their order of appearance in the series. With the introduction of Bernadette and Amy, the characters become more central to the ongoing storylines, meaning that they also appear with far more frequency than the earlier female scientists, Leslie and Elizabeth. This organization allows a critical consideration of the increased inclusion of female scientists in general and the development of individual characters in particular, as well as providing a larger perspective on the development of gender politics and representations of female intellectualism in the series thus far.
4. Her reflection on this choice situates her earlier behavior as sexually aberrant, moving beyond casual sex to anonymous group sex. As she tells Leonard, "I guess there's just a time in every woman's life when she gets tired of wakin' up on a strange futon with a bunch of people she doesn't know" ("The Codpiece Topology"), a revelation that clearly disturbs Leonard.
5. This is true with the exception of Sheldon, who is frequently dismissive of Leslie's intelligence and accomplishments. However, since this relationship is reciprocal, with Leslie challenging Sheldon in turn, this does not necessarily undermine her intelligence or professional success in the larger scope of the series.
6. Later in the series Bernadette consistently laughs at Howard's jokes, but in this initial encounter, she questions him. As he explains that his definition of himself as suitable for microbiological study is a joke, she asks, "Are you sure?" She also shoots down his conversational

gambits of science fiction, role playing games, magic tricks, computers, and puppies; they end up initially bonding over their relationships with their overbearing mothers and the fact that their parents would object to their pairing, since her family is Catholic and his is Jewish ("The Creepy Candy Coating Corollary").

7. After Howard spends $2,500 to buy a used 3-D printer with Raj, Bernadette points out that she makes significantly more money than he does and, as Howard tells Raj, he has been "taken off the joint account until I learn the value of money" ("The Cooper/Kripke Inversion").

8. When Howard fails to clean and do the laundry while Bernadette is working late, she punishes him by hiding his Xbox ("The Tangible Affection Proof"). This also furthers the odd element of Howard and Bernadette's relationship where Bernadette serves as a type of mother surrogate to Howard, a role to which she is incredibly resistant, though the women share a handful of notable similarities, such as the tenor and rhythm of their raised voices.

9. At times Bernadette's irresponsible science threatens to overlap with her sexual relationship with Howard. At one point she tells him after they have sex that at her lucrative new job she has volunteered to be part of the premature ejaculation research team, since "it's not like either one of us has heart disease" ("The Roommate Transmogrification") and as they get ready to drink wine she stops abruptly because "I was working with penicillin-resistant gonorrhea in the lab today and I was just trying to remember if I washed my hands" ("The Boyfriend Complexity"), the former threatening his metaphorical manhood and the latter posing a danger to the organ itself.

10. She explains to Howard that this aversion comes, in large part, from having to take care of her younger siblings growing up and in another episode, when she helps the guys deal with a sleep-deprived Sheldon, she tells them that "I know how to deal with stubborn children. My mother used to run an illegal day care center in our basement" ("The Einstein Approximation"). It could be that having had experience as a surrogate mother, whether in caring for her siblings or helping her mother care for other people's children, Bernadette fully grasps the difficulty of childrearing and remains unconvinced by the sentimental discourse that regularly surrounds babies, children, and parenting. Interestingly, this isn't the first time that Sheldon takes on the role of a surrogate child: when Leonard and Penny fight ("The Guitarist Amplification") and later when they break up ("The Spaghetti Catalyst"), the relationship dynamic surrounding the three of them is very similar to that of separated parents catering to the needs of their shared child.

11. This is not seen as an especially serious or definitive conversation, so even though Howard has agreed to the familial paradigm in which he'll be a stay-at-home dad, it could be that he's clinging to the hope that Bernadette will change her mind or suddenly become overwhelmed by maternal instinct once their child is born rather than just a theoretical topic of discussion.

12. This is in keeping with the "mixed feelings" that Jessica Grose argues characterize the representation of childless by choice women in primetime television, where the predominant message continues to be that "having a kid is a pivotal, perhaps necessary landmark in a woman's life" and that women who choose not too are less feminine than their child-bearing counterparts. These representations reflect a larger cultural feeling described by Jessica Valenti in her book *Full Frontal Feminism: A Young Woman's Guide to Why Feminism Matters,* where she points out that, despite the advances of feminism and touting of women's power of choice in whether or not to have children, "women are supposed to want to have babies. It's our 'natural' inclination" (152). In her consideration of primetime TV representations, Grose looks specifically at the 2011–2012 television season representations of childless women in *How I Met Your Mother* ("Symphony of Illumination") and *Whitney* ("Up All Night"). Much like Bernadette, the titular character of *Whitney* (played by Whitney Cummings) is adamant about not wanting to have children until her boyfriend tells her that the issue is a "deal-

breaker" in their relationship; shortly thereafter, Whitney reconsiders, telling him that she can imagine having a family with him and reinforcing the idea that all women naturally want to have children and those who think they don't just haven't found the right partner yet. The childless by choice issue is addressed in a more nuanced way in *How I Met Your Mother* where Robin (played by Cobie Smulders), who has never wanted children, is shaken when she finds out that even if she wanted them, she is physically unable to have them.

13. Bialik herself has experience in this area, as she "got 'back in circulation' in 2009 thanks to an attempted makeover on TLC's *What Not to Wear* ... [with] the show's arbiters of style, Clinton Kelly and Stacy London" (qtd. in Deerwester).

14. This performativity is just as often negative as positive. Going with Penny and Bernadette to look at bridal magazines, Amy tells Sheldon, "sometimes you forget, I'm a lady. And with that comes an estrogen-fueled need to page through thick, glossy magazines that make me hate my body" ("The Isolation Permutation").

15. This becomes more inclusive of other female characters within the series when Penny, Amy, and Bernadette go to Disneyland and get "princess" makeovers. Despite her intellectualism and professional success, Bernadette is incredibly invested in being Cinderella, telling Penny and Amy that "this was my idea. I'm driving. I'm Cinderella. You bitches got a problem with that, we can stop the car right now" ("The Contractual Obligation Implementation"). This gender performativity intersects with the larger cultural issue of female intellectualism and participation in STEM fields. When it comes to young women pursuing math and science, as has been previously addressed, P.K. Electrical Inc. founder Karen D. Purcell explains that "the early lack of exposure can be detrimental to achieving gender balance in the STEM fields.... It begins when we are young and continues throughout our time in high school. Girls generally don't get to experience the level of exposure or encouragement in STEM fields that our male counterparts do. It is often subtle, but it's the first hurdle that confronts and confounds so many women" (qtd. in "Why STEM Fields Still Don't Draw More Women").The very topical issue of whether or not young girls are discouraged from STEM fields comes into play when Amy and Bernadette phone-conference in on a presentation encouraging teenage girls to pursue science, touting female intellectualism while physically embodying the girly princess beauty ideal; Amy tells the girls that "the world of science needs more women, but from a young age we girls are encouraged to care more about the way we look than about the power of our minds" as she looks in a mirror and applies lipstick. Finally, this performativity also engages with dynamics of heterosexual desire when both Howard and Leonard immediately disrobe upon seeing their respective partners all princess-ed up (ibid).

16. This discovery further complicates Sheldon and Amy's physical relationship, when Sheldon administers a spanking as punishment for her deception, which he intends to be a deterrent but which she finds sexually exhilarating.

17. This is significant in contrast to her refusal to flatter Sheldon, especially since the "boundless whimsy" upon which Amy is commenting is Penny making a shoebox talk, begging her to not return the out of her price range shoes inside.

18. This painting is also significant in terms of the sexual undercurrent Amy projects onto their relationship since, as Amy tells Penny, they were originally painted nude but she had clothes painted onto them after the painting was completed, making their shared nudity only a sponge wash away.

19. This is another moment in which Amy's perception of her and Penny's intimacy far oversteps Penny's comfort and personal boundaries, as Amy opens the dressing room door with the video camera trained on Penny in her underwear, invading Penny's privacy and engaging in dynamic voyeurism, as she turns the camera back on Penny even after Penny tells her to leave ("The Isolation Permutation").

20. Interestingly, Penny also has several traditionally masculine qualities, which set her apart from—and in superior position to—the male characters in the series, similar to the way

in which her successfully embodied femininity set her apart from the other female characters in the series. For example, when Howard is preparing to go on a fishing trip with Bernadette's father, it is Penny who shows him (and the other guys) how to bait a hook and gut a fish ("The Fish Guts Displacement").

21. Other traditionally female characters include Raj's sister and Leonard's one-time girlfriend Priya (Aarti Mann), who balances sexual attractiveness and a high-powered law career, though she remains insecure about Leonard's ongoing friendship with Penny; Sheldon's twin sister Missy (Courtney Henggler), upon whom all of the guys develop instant crushes, and who is outspoken and assertive, if not necessarily incredibly intelligent ("The Pork Chop Indeterminacy"); and Alicia (Valerie Azlynn), an attractive new neighbor who moves in upstairs from Leonard and Sheldon and has a more successful acting career than Penny, though the competition between Penny and Alicia is neutralized when Alicia manipulates the guys and takes advantage of their infatuation, once again establishing Penny as the ideal female ("The Dead Hooker Juxtaposition"). Attractive women from the science fiction genre also make appearances, including *Firefly* and *Terminator: The Sarah Connor Chronicles*' Summer Glau ("The Terminator Decoupling") and *Battlestar Galactica*'s Katee Sackhoff ("The Hot Troll Deviation"), though these women are either unattainable (Glau) or imaginary masturbatory fantasies (Sackhoff). Significantly, all of these are guest spots rather than regular cast members, leaving Penny's normative position as the ideal woman relatively undisturbed.

22. Sheldon also repeatedly pokes fun at Penny's sexual history and promiscuity, though since she fits the mainstream ideal of beauty, her active sex life is seen as more normal than that of the more intellectual, and thus presumably, less sexually attractive, women like Leslie and Elizabeth, and Sheldon is the only one who regularly comments upon it. For example, he uses mathematical principles to extrapolate Penny's estimated number of boyfriends and lovers ("The Robotic Manipulation") and when he identifies her as a "flag virgin" on his web show "Fun with Flags" he quickly jumps to explain that she's "not a real virgin" ("The Monster Isolation").

Works Cited

Anderegg, David. *Nerds: How Dorks, Dweebs, Techies, and Trekkies Can Save America (and Why They Might Be Our Last Hope)*, 2d ed. New York: Penguin, 2011. Print.
"'The Big Bang Theory': Amy's Gift to Penny is a Disturbing Portrait (VIDEO)." *Huffington Post*. The Huffington Post.com, Inc., 17 Feb. 2012. Web. 24 May 2013.
Deerwester, Jayme. "'Theory' Meets the Practice of New Female Castmates."*USA Today* 17 Nov. 2011: n.p. *Academic Search Complete*. Web. 15 Sept. 2012.
Ferriss, Suzanne. "Fashioning Femininity in the Makeover Film." *Chick Flicks: Contemporary Women at the Movies*. Ed. Suzanne Ferriss and Mallory Young. New York: Routledge, 2008: 41–57. Print.
Grose, Jessica. "Child-free on TV." Slate.com. 8 Dec. 2011. Web. 22 May 2013.
Heyman, Karen. "Talk Nerdy to Me." *Science* 320.5877 (2008): 740–741. Print.
Hill, Catherine, Christianne Corbett, and Andresse St. Rose. *Why So Few? Women in Science, Technology, Engineering, and Mathematics*. American Association of University Women (AAUW), 2010. Web. 15 Sept. 2012.
How I Met Your Mother. Created by Carter Bays and Craig Thomas. Perf. Josh Radnor, Cobie Smulders, Neil Patrick Harris, Alyson Hannigan, Jason Segal. CBS, 2005–present.
Murray, Noel. "The Changing Face of 'Nerds' (and Autism) in Popular Culture." AVClub.com. Onion Inc., 16 Jan. 2013. Web. 23 May 2013.
Inness, Sherrie A. "Who Remembers Sabrina? Intelligence, Gender, and the Media." *Geek Chic: Smart Women in Popular Culture*. Ed. Sherrie A. Inness. New York: Palgrave Macmillan, 2007: 1–9. Print.

Jones, Robert A. "'How Many Female Scientists Do You Know?'" *Endeavour* 29.2 (2005): 84–88. Print.
Sheffield, Rob. "Red-Hot American Geeks." *Rolling Stone* 1098 (2010): 26. *Academic Search Complete*. Web. 23 May 2013.
Steinke, Jocelyn. "Cultural Representations of Gender And Science: Portrayals of Female Scientists and Engineers in Popular Films." *Science Communication* 27.1 (2005): 27–63.Print.
Valenti, Jessica. *Full Frontal Feminism: A Young Woman's Guide to Why Feminism Matters*. Berkeley: Seal, 2007. Print.
Whitney. Created by Whitney Cummings. Perf. Whitney Cummings, Chris D'Elia. CBS, 2011–2013.
"Why STEM Fields Still Don't Draw More Women." *Chronicle of Higher Education* 59.10 (2012): B24–B27. *Academic Search Complete*. Web.

Failed Genders and Fragile Intimacies
Living in and After the Big Bang

BENJAMIN BATEMAN

It is easy enough to find feminist fault with CBS's immensely popular television series *The Big Bang Theory* for sometimes representing Penny as a witless, blond bimbo and the intellectually superior Amy Farrah Fowler as a sexually frustrated, socially awkward, and sartorially challenged outcast. Countless blogs and online commentaries have done so. But these critiques strike me as rather myopic given the show's overarching focus on haplessness played for humor. The central male characters, after all, hardly do better. Howard cannot attract women, and even when he succeeds—with the more financially and educationally successful Bernadette—he cannot overcome the oedipal task of breaking with his overbearing mother. Leonard, meanwhile, struggles to be "the man" in his on-again, off-again relationship with Penny, wanting to talk and define their dyad while she merely wants to watch football and drink beer. Raj's selective mutism prevents him, except when drunk, from even conversing with the opposite sex, and Sheldon—the show's singularly quirky star—fails almost entirely at deciphering interpersonal codes and romantic rules of engagement. And the men's failures are more than amorous. While it may be true that Penny's acting career and waitressing gig at The Cheesecake Factory lack the prestige of the men's scientific careers, her struggles to hit it big parallel their own inabilities to make major breakthroughs in their respective fields. Leonard spends years generating ultimately useless data, Raj worries he will be sent back to India for his underwhelming findings, Howard botches the toilet technology on the Mars Rover Spacecraft, and Sheldon, for all his talk of an impending Nobel Prize, is perpetually bogged down in string theory's endless dimensions and mathematical models.

So the following essay focuses not on the characters' relative successes but rather on their mutual failures—failures that, far from isolating or merely shaming them, stitch them together, sympathetically, into a community organized around non-accomplishment. Approaching their thirties—although the actors are older, visually accentuating the point this essay is about to make—the men of the show orbit more than they advance, return to the repetitive rhythms of their video games and comic books, genres which align them inexorably with adolescence, more than they propel forward in their professional pursuits. In her latest book, *The Queer Art of Failure*, Judith Halberstam writes of "practicing failure," which might perhaps "prompt us to discover our inner dweeb, to be underachievers, to fall short, to get distracted, to take a detour, to find a limit, to lose our way, to forget, to avoid mastery." "Failure," she offers, "loves company" (120–121). *The Big Bang Theory*, I argue, thematizes failure, particularly around matters of gender, sexuality, and intimacy. But the failure to love, or love properly, or be loved properly, or properly organize oneself to love and be loved, becomes a spur to sociality in the show, an opening for companionship that exceeds the proportions typically allotted a heterosexual male: the central figure of a wife and the auxiliary, lesser intimacies of male friends. Across episodes and entire seasons, the show allows its characters to fail—even revels in their failures—not simply for comic relief but for relief from capitalism's relentless pressures to succeed. Yes, the show trades in stereotypes about ditzy blondes and nellyish nerds, but the characters expand beyond these narrow parameters and begin to represent, the show's popularity might just attest, a common, fumbling effort to make and have a life in a swirling world whose codes, demands, and expectations—both genetic and social—bewilder as much as they inform.

After Darwin, psychoanalyst Adam Phillips writes, being human comes to feel "accidental" and "we have to work out what, other than specialness, might make our lives worth living" (xv). The scientists of *The Big Bang Theory* devote their lives to theoretical physics, experimental physics, and astrophysics, all enterprises that, even more so than Darwin's revolutionary insights, diminish the importance of humans in the universe or at least the impact of individual human lives. Ironically, then, attaining their goals and succeeding at their intellectual endeavors—rare occurrences on the show, as previously mentioned—reinforces these scientists' sense of their own inutility. And yet, Phillips elaborates, humans compensate for their lack of specialness, a specialness dangled in front of young infants to socialize and humanize them only later to be withdrawn by a world grown increasingly indifferent, by cultivating a sense of closeness (xv–xvi). Sheldon, for example, conceives of himself as practically pre-selected for a Nobel Prize and denigrates other modes of coming to feel special—through intimacies that, however compromised, salve the wound of the infant's original severance from the fulfilling mother—as so many evolutionary, hormonal, and genetic tricks. Where his adventures are cerebral, others' are corporeal, governed by instincts aligned with the very animals with whom Darwin rendered us uncomfortably proximate. String theory, in particular, promises to elevate Sheldon above the fray of precarious life because it is a theory of everything, a theory of the universe that subsumes and parameterizes particular species, bonds, institutions, needs, deeds, and feelings. Because it relies on the postulation of countless dimensions in the universe, string theory demands of Sheldon, or so he claims, a kind of unidimensional personality focused laser-like on science and thought rather than intimacy and camaraderie.

Sheldon's ongoing failure to string together string theory is accompanied by the nagging, if sometimes irritating, realization that he is strung to the social networks he so frequently disparages. In "The Vegas Renormalization," the man with an eidetic memory and an obsessive compulsive attention to detail locks himself out of his apartment, and with his crew vacationing in Vegas, he is forced to stay with Penny, his neighbor, whose companionship he at many moments professes to detest. While there, he inquires about the concept of "friends with benefits"—which he picks up from Howard's failed, casual relationship with the sexually aggressive scientist Leslie Winkle—and comes to realize, in his own peculiar and partial manner, that friendship is beneficial in ways that aren't purely utilitarian. At episode's end, with an outburst from the laugh track, he informs his roommate Leonard that Penny has instructed him in the concept, and although they have surely not engaged in sexual relations, he has indeed learned from Penny the salutary effect of her emotional presence in his life. A creature of habit—physical routines that simultaneously regularize his existence, and yet, because they must be repeated perfectly, persistently risk its deregularization—Sheldon cannot sleep in Penny's apartment, even after relegating her to the sofa and commandeering her bed. Conjuring his mother's ministrations in his sickly youth, Sheldon asks Penny to sing the "Soft Kitty" lullaby he requires as a soporific, explaining that homesickness from his apartment "is a kind of sickness." As Penny sings "Soft kitty, warm kitty / Little ball of fur / Happy kitty, sleepy kitty / Purr, purr, purr," Sheldon re-associates with those animal needs from which he seeks refuge at the same time as he is nurtured, succored, by another human, one whose "pussy," the obsession of his peers, holds no interest for him.

As Sheldon dozes off, he gently thanks Penny for letting him stay with her, and her pensive mien dissolves into the softest, warmest smile. She becomes the external sign of Sheldon's internal melting even as she herself radiates the possibility of interpersonal mingling, of selves becoming "mutually permeable," to borrow psychoanalyst Michael Eigen's phrase. For Eigen, the drives to succeed—to will oneself purposively and productively into the future—cause the self to congeal and to lose its ability, an urgent and enlivening ability, to live inside others and have others live inside it, to hazard its integrity and claims to proprietary ownership and exclusive responsibility (3). Sheldon aims at mastery, at sovereignty, and yet the show consistently underscores both his failures and the costs of approaching these states asymptotically—sadness, fear, mania, and exhaustion. Perhaps the most captivating aspect of the show is Penny's affect, which is frequently marked by disbelief, exasperation, and even anger at the guys' social cluelessness, but from time to time morphs into a receptive smile accompanied by a knowing glance, as if she already knows and yet is always anticipating the arrival of her companions' humanity, their capacities for transformative exchange and encounter. In "The Friendship Algorithm"—in which Sheldon, ridiculously, uses a mathematical approach to befriend his colleague Kripke for personal gain—Howard, upon seeing Penny's grimace at Kripke's more than unsolicited sexual advance, walks past and notes that he, by comparison, is "lookin' pretty good." Penny's cheeks flush, her smile broadens, and her eyes illuminate, releasing the tension not only from Kripke's unwelcome presence but from the larger worry that Howard and his friends could never occupy the same turf, be of the same mind, as a conventionally beautiful, starving artist with no scientific training. Which is to say that Penny's facial suffusions, repeated yet aleatory, serve as abiding evidence of the crew's openness to alterity, to sharing each other, magnanimously, just as they share meals, cars, beds, and living quarters. As the tension extinguishes from her face, we glimpse the possibility of a more relaxed existence, of a self made lighter by its combination with others, of life lived at a higher flame because of its susceptibility to outside fires, other lives. Penny, to push the point a bit further, is the crew's currency, the coin of the realm, the means by which it becomes apparent to itself as a force greater than the sum of its parts—a not outlandish assertion given the men's fascination with *Star Wars*, *Lord of the Rings*, and other animated extravagances. Another way of saying this is that Penny's magnetic presence marks the failure of discrete selves and betrays the lunacy at the heart of sovereignty. To return to Halberstam, failure loves company.

Where metatheories and totalizing ontologies purport to explain everything, *The Big Bang Theory* promotes what Arturo Escobar, following others in philosophy and theology, terms "relational ontologies," modes of being in the world fundamentally defined by—and not capable of being understood apart from—interdependency and emotional and imaginative interimbrication (39). Despite his best efforts at string theory, at deciphering the

Universe's Rosetta Stone, Sheldon finds himself inextricably threaded inside a social tapestry not of his own design and frequently beyond his comprehension. Relational ontologies, as Escobar explains, imply ethical responsibility, attentiveness, obligation, and reciprocity—he is thinking of them politically, in the context of nation-states and international relations—but they simultaneously lift the burdens of autonomous selfhood and liberate the self into communal ties that can depressurize the asphyxiating atmosphere of neoliberal individualism.

The episode "The White Asparagus Triangulation" is a touchstone for a number of the arguments this essay has been advancing but also a catalyst for thinking these arguments in relation to contemporary sex and gender politics. Triangulation immediately locates us within a relational frame, in this case Sheldon and Leonard's roommate relationship supplemented by Leonard's new girlfriend Stephanie, who earns Sheldon's esteem, unlike Leonard's previous romantic exploits, because she is a practicing physician. The episode predictably depicts Sheldon appealing to deterministic explanations of heterosexual romance but ultimately gives the lie to his determinism—fails determinism—at the same time as it exposes heterosexuality, or at least the couple form, as kind of failure in desperate need of nourishing company.

At the heart of the episode lies Sheldon's anxiety that Leonard will blow it with Stephanie, as he's done with previous girlfriends. To obviate this seemingly inevitable conclusion, Sheldon seizes upon evolutionary psychology and biology to reinforce Stephanie's budding desire and Leonard's tenuous appeal. In offensive fashion, he warns Penny to stay away from Leonard and to resist the urges of the hormones and pheromones coursing through her body, going so far as to check on the timing of her menstrual cycle. Although Penny insists that Sheldon need not worry about her incursions upon Leonard's new romance, he warns her that she is at the mercy of biological urges beyond her control. Immensely interesting here is the collision of essentialist and performative explanations of gender. Even as he ostensibly subscribes to essentialist explanations—those that naturalize gender identity as expressive of unshakeable, internal imprinting by genetics and pre-natal hormone exposure (brain organization theory)—Sheldon simultaneously nudges Penny's behavior, implying a social dimension exceeding biological determinants. This social dimension concatenates with concrete social networks, including Stephanie's virtual life on Facebook, where her "relationship status" is single, a source of anxiety for Sheldon, and where she is throwing sheep—again at great consternation to Sheldon—at some man named Mike. Even though Leonard and Stephanie have been dating for only two weeks, Sheldon warns, given her Facebook promiscuity, "we're losing her."

Before getting to the role of Facebook in contemporary dating, it is worth noting Sheldon's investment in Leonard's romantic life. Although he swears off sex for himself, he depends upon Leonard for support—materially in terms of car rides and practical advice but also for less tangible supplies such as emotional nurturance and companionship—and recognizes that Leonard's longevity as a friend depends upon the satisfaction of sexual needs beyond Sheldon's cognition. Thus Sheldon concerns himself with solidifying the sexual bond between Leonard and Stephanie, inserting himself into a date night so as to lubricate a conversation whose deficiencies he fails to recognize as the product of his own, unwanted presence. Believing Stephanie's adoration fleeting, he fabricates a masculinity test to prove Leonard an "alpha male," defending his proposal with the "scientific" rationale that if a woman sees her man best another man in competition, the oxytocin released in her brain will arouse her sexually and bind her to him. Grunting and groaning, Sheldon feigns an inability to open a can of white asparagus and delegates the task to Leonard, exclaiming unnecessarily volubly, so that Stephanie can hear, that he long ago accepted his status as "beta male" in his friendship with Leonard. Sheldon's willingness to be the "beta male" bespeaks his intellectual devotion to naturalizing accounts of gender while simultaneously undermining such accounts; after all, he does not really believe Leonard is stronger than he, and his failures to open the jar are as contrived as the gender polarities he seeks to stabilize. Far from viewing Leonard as essentially an alpha male, Sheldon wishes him to be so as to relieve himself from the pressures of heterosexual masculinity and to create space in which to be intimate (with Leonard and with Stephanie) without being sexual. Which is to say, Sheldon's asparagus experiment is less about proving a preexisting alpha male / beta male hypothesis than it is about testing it and establishing it so as to permit Sheldon to continue in his quite comfortable position as best friend to another man who happens, perplexingly to Sheldon, to crave sexual attention from women. Sheldon's scientific method, then, becomes an example of a performative science that enacts the knowledge it purports to trace; that creates the gender dichotomies it pretends to describe.

But performatives, as Michel Callon points out in his ruminations on economics as a performative science, generate counter-performatives, insurgent energies that interfere, to use the parlance of J.L. Austin, with the "felicity" of the performative endeavor. The conditions of Sheldon's experiment prove infelicitous as Leonard finds himself unable, even with his most herculean efforts, to pry the top from the tiny jar filled with mocking, semi-flaccid phalluses. It is worth nothing that asparagus most likely borrows etymologically from swelling (the Greek "spargan"), raising the question of what both men and women find tumescent and detumescent. Leonard, with coaxing from Sheldon, thinks a virile display will turn Stephanie on, when in fact, as we will soon see, her libidinal currents extend to softer and more sensitive versions of masculinity. Knocking the jar against the kitchen counter to loosen it, he instead shatters it and cuts himself, intimating both the inadequacy of his alpha masculinity and the lacerative impact of dominant masculinity—the unending toll it takes on the body as well as the psyche. Stephanie, the physician, hurries in to staunch the bleeding, but her ministrations only aggravate Leonard's sense of insufficiency, a state of affairs made visible by her larger size and height (by all appearances, she outmans him). When she insists his wound requires stitches and needles, Leonard vomits into the sink, despoiling Sheldon's defrosting steak, yet another signifier of raw masculinity gone down the drain. Later, at the hospital, we learn that Leonard cried while being sutured, which Sheldon expectedly characterizes as the last blow to his project of rendering Leonard an alpha male. In a humorous but also tender exchange, Sheldon turns to Leonard, while waiting for Stephanie to return with the discharge paperwork, and asks aloud why, given how lovable Leonard is to him, women find Leonard so difficult to love.

And so this performance of top dog masculinity, in which Sheldon was queerly willing to position himself as the bitch, is exposed as a simultaneous effort to protect his love for Leonard, to secure their intimate bond within a legitimating, heteronormative framework. Although black culture is frequently singled out in popular media for its homophobia—exemplified by the buzz over "no homo," the phrase in rap music that immediately follows admissions of male companionship—in truth homophobic disavowals abound in less explicit varieties. Stephanie is Sheldon's "no homo," the presence that allows his devotion to Leonard not to be absent, to be okay. Of course Sheldon, unlike the actor who plays him, is not gay, despite the show's humorous intimations of such a possibility; to the contrary, he is unapologetically asexual, profoundly perplexed by his peers' need for erotic gratification. Within heteronormative and homonormative logics, asexuality is made to appear as the absence of sexuality, when in fact for many it insists upon a sexuality fundamentally not oriented around an object, specifically a unitarily gendered object, a deconstruction that might in fact pave the way for thinking sexuality differently, more expansively, and through behaviors less tied to genital stimulation. Sheldon wants to be sung to, to have his ego stroked, to have his mind stimulated, and to share with all around him the vast wonders of the universe, but these desires do not count as a sexuality. Interestingly, it is Penny who most often, despite her recurring frustration and boredom with what she terms his "jibber jabber," takes his lessons to heart, surprising him at various moments with references to Star Trek and quantum mechanics, including the paradox of Schrodinger's cat. She, Penny, gives value, a little value, to Sheldon's alternative sexuality, a littleness she echoes when calling him, diminutively, "Sweetie."

Stephanie, a short-lived character on the show, also makes room for Sheldon, finding it cute when he tracks her and Leonard down at the movies and tags along on their date night. Thus far this essay has primarily instrumentalized her as the enabling condition of Sheldon and Leonard's homosociality, but in fact she surpasses such structural support, becoming an independent, if fleeting, voice in the show that exercises hospitality towards Sheldon's off-spots, neuroses (particularly his hypochondria), and unacknowledged need for companionship. If at the level of physical stature and tolerance for pain she outmans Leonard, she also becomes a new man in Sheldon's life, a surrogate father in a show replete with parental and familial substitutes necessitated by the failures of biological kinship. Sheldon's father died when he was a child, leaving him with an evangelical mother who regards his scientific accomplishments as the work of the devil. Penny's father is forever disappointed that she isn't a boy, a psychiatric diagnosis made by Leonard's mother, whose cold rationality and utilitarian worldview left Leonard so lacking for nourishment as a child that he contrived a robot to give him hugs. To the extent, then, that these characters struggle to become intimate with each other—and to engage one another in non-instrumentalizing, non-exploitative ways—it is in no small part because they were never instructed in how to do so and were left instead to draw nourishment from toxic sources. Living after the Big Bang means not simply establishing purpose and meaning in a rapidly expanding, decreasingly certain (and centered) universe conducive to apathy and anomie, but at the same time learning to assemble intimacy and sociality when the figures charged with modeling this behavior instead shattered and scattered, or never delivered in the first place, those feelings of specialness young infants so desperately need to grow in and into a fundamentally uncertain existence. Which is to say Stephanie's healing powers, for example, extend beyond the corporeal realm to provide emotional nourishment.

As it turns out, Stephanie is no more bothered by Leonard's crying and puking than she is by his inability to unscrew the lid of the white asparagus. Her responsiveness to his muted masculinity presages later episodes in which both Penny and Priya (Raj's sister) celebrate not his penetrative powers in bed but rather his passion and penchant for foreplay, for extending eroticism beyond intercourse and ejaculation. In earlier work, most notably *In a Queer Time and Place*, Jack Halberstam writes of the appeal to women of gentler, non-hyperbolic forms of masculinity that western culture is too quick to translate as femininity. Typically these alternative masculinities, such as those bodied forth by boy bands—who sing sweetly of soft caresses and fragile hearts—are considered appropriate for young girls but inappropriate for older women, who are supposed to trade in sensitive souls for rough and tumble cowboys (Justin Bieber for John Wayne, Corey Hart for Clint Eastwood). Arguing that this substitution is a social norm rather than a natural progression, Halberstam's work tethers ageism to heteronormativity and offers space in which to consider the lingering appeal to women of the Leonards of the world, short guys with nervous, nasally, stammering voices who sweat profusely in the presence of women in the absence of bodily exertion—men capable of appreciating, discussing, forgiving and sitting with feelings of insecurity, self-doubt, body-anxiety, inadequacy, and abandonment. A tall, solidly built woman like Stephanie might not just accept but actively seek out Leonard's heightened emotionality and corporeal vulnerability as a reflection of and complement to her own gender queerness. We need not speculate about the desirability of Leonard's masculinity, because it is already attested to by Sheldon, who loves what is supposed to be unlovable in a man—weakness, kindness, patience, and receptivity. Sheldon, we might argue, makes explicit what, according to Eve Sedgwick, is supposed to be repressed in men's bonds with one another, namely a desire for one another that exceeds the socially approved, mutual desire they share for a woman. Homosociality is set in sharp relief here even as it is given greater dimensions and finer texture. Stephanie is no mere alibi or proxy for these men's love of one another; she is a dynamic, self-aware, and pleasure-finding agent in its circulation, calibration and chronic overdetermination.

At the end of the asparagus episode, with Leonard back from the emergency room exhibiting his stitches—battle wounds that mock the chivalric, warrior masculinity he was meant to flaunt—to his friends, Penny barges in intrigued that Leonard has changed his Facebook relationship status to "in a relationship" after only two weeks with Stephanie. Declaring it a mistake, Leonard and the crew finally realize that Sheldon, worried Stephanie had been turned off by Leonard's chickenhearted reaction to the asparagus fiasco, hacked into the account and boldly made the first move on Leonard's behalf. Understandably furious, Leonard upbraids Sheldon even as he acknowledges that Sheldon lacks the emotional intelligence to appreciate fully the inanity of his move. As Leonard insists Sheldon not say another word, the otherwise mute Raj lets out a peep, which turns Howard's attention to the computer monitor and to the newsfeed update that "Stephanie Barnett is now in a relationship with Leonard Hofstadter." Against the group's expectations, Stephanie followed Leonard's (Sheldon's) suit and made official, and public, their nascent romance. Hazarding a smile reminiscent of Penny's, Leonard gently boasts, "Yeah, I guess I do have a girlfriend." Happening into a relationship as the result of Sheldon's virtual ploy, Leonard once again cuts the figure not of the cocky, dashing, take-charge hero but the soft-spoken, self-doubting, semi-passive adolescent on whom adult women are charged to take a pass. Even though he, courtesy of Sheldon, technically made the first move, he did so virtually, on Facebook, one of the many social networking platforms on which adults increasingly find themselves connecting—often with childhood friends—and relating in ways that feel adolescent. Halberstam describes particular queer lives as characterized by an "extended adolescence," by a continued and sometimes socially maligned participation in subcultures associated first and foremost with youth, but it is also the case that the virtualization of romance in an age in which people are dating and coupling at older ages means that "extended adolescence" might be turning into, even just as a set of affects, a broader social condition (175).

Ridiculous though they may sound, sheep-throwing, "liking," "poking," "following," "tagging," and "checking in" are quickly becoming the virtual means by which people exchange affection and recognition. Young people follow the leader, throw things, play tag, poke each other, ask their location constantly (are we there yet?), and sound off without hesitation about their likes and dislikes. Facebook, it could be argued, reignites the affectation of adolescence in the heart of adult interaction, love making, and community-building. Which means many adults now find themselves playing by the same codes they could never decipher as teenagers—because to be a teenager, in matters of love, is to be definitionally confused or at least deficient in or in excess of various reality principles. Dialing back the erotic clock, Facebook and other social networking sites throw a wrench in what Elizabeth Freeman calls "chrononormativity," the set of social norms dictating what behaviors, alliances, desires, and accomplishments befit particular moments in a person's life (4). Freeman, like Halberstam, thinks of queerness as a particular relationship to time marked by asynchrony, anachronism, and disconjuncture. Lives lived out of temporal joint frequently invite opprobrium as severe as that meted out to gays and lesbians who themselves have suffered historically from charges of immaturity and developmental delay. Where queer defined as desiring abnormally has struggled to achieve Eve Sedgwick's majoritizing ends, queer as Freeman and Halberstam define it, as not being at the right place at the right time, might just be expansive and supple enough to summon together a variety of marginalized populations, even those who remain privileged (straight bachelors, for instance) by their continued involvement in heteronormative practices.

The characters of *Big Bang Theory* appear queer, in my reading, less for their stated and sublimated longings, nonnormative though they may be (Amy's for Penny, Raj's for Howard, Stuart's for Raj, Sheldon's for Leonard), than for their mutual failures to grow and grow up at socially preferred intervals. The men's lingering and potent attachments to video games, action figures, science fiction, and superheroes betoken the persistence of adolescent imagination in their brilliant minds. Nearing thirty, and appearing quite a bit older, their need for sexual companionship conflicts with, but rarely supersedes, their needs for same-sex friendship and "juvenile" activity. And even when they get serious about heterosexual romance, they flail around, acting clueless and hopeless, a fumbling frenzy exaggerated by Sheldon and Amy's complex negotiations around holding hands and Howard and Bernadette's equally protracted conversations about not living with Howard's mother after their wedding. In fact, the crew's one instance of conjugal conventionality—Howard and Bernadette's union—is immediately followed by Howard taking off into space (and what boy doesn't aspire to be an astronaut?), where he continues, over video chat, to avoid telling his mother about his intentions to move out of her home. With heterosexual bliss literally suspended in mid-air, the newest episodes feature fraying ties between Leonard and Penny—the latter of which is rarely shown without a glass of wine intended no doubt to keep the pressures of womanhood, marrying and the like, at cognitive bay—and continued manual stimulation, at most, between Sheldon and Amy. And Raj continues to struggle to speak to women (though no longer mute), his silence standing in for the lacunae in love-making effected by the virtualization of public spheres and the invention of neoliberal, do-it-yourself dating technologies in which individuals frequently do not, indeed, speak to one another.

But what the show ritually holds out in consolation is the image of being-together and hanging out as mutual failures at love's long labor. Throughout this essay has used words like "friendship" and "community" as placeholders for nonlibidinal alliances, but even these words, one could argue, drip with the very kind of saccharine sentimentality the Sheldons of the world could never consciously appreciate or take seriously. And in fact the show's "friend" circle is riven with antagonisms, including Penny's disgust with Howard's dirty mind, Raj's laconicity, Sheldon's social anxiety disorder, and Leonard's nagging sense that he is bogged down in a social circle limiting his horizons. But they keep hanging out, keeping one another company, providing a kind of circular rhythm that keeps the beat of a different drummer, of a little boy who's not marching in time, who's not keeping pace, whose aspirations and imagination draw him away, even render him at odds with, the linear temporality of maturation he is meant to ascend and, if precocious, even accelerate. Even "The

White Asparagus Triangulation," which with nuance extols the queer virtues of a woman like Stephanie, ends not with Leonard and Stephanie in romantic embrace but with the regular gang sprawled across Sheldon and Leonard's apartment and Stephanie relegated to the virtual world of sheep-throwing. Which is to say that the show clings to, desperately and yet barely, nonvirtual modes of intimacy that are nonetheless virtual insofar as they never eclipse or become fully coeval with the normative modes to which all the characters, with perhaps the exception of Sheldon, pay some lip service. The characters need in fact to keep failing at what Sheldon calls "pair-bonding" in order to remain bound, however sadly or unfulfilling, to one another and to the depressurized space such mutual failure opens up—for spreading rather than succeeding, circling rather than aiming, playing rather than winning, dorking out rather than growing up.

Although Sheldon bumbles into his role as Cupid, his accidental success sounds yet another of the show's critical messages on which this essay will conclude. As I earlier said, the white asparagus experiment, intended to dramatize Leonard's masculinity, not only reveals gender as a performance from the outset—it is, after all, a hoax of sorts—but amplifies this revelation through Leonard's failure to dislodge the lid. No knightly feats are achieved, no oxytocin (the so-called "love hormone") is released, and yet Stephanie succumbs to Leonard's charms regardless. A hardcore social constructionist interpretation would insist upon this episode's denaturalizing approach to gender, its exposure of evolutionary psychology as so much hocus pocus and misogyny in new garb. Sheldon, by this account, might then be seen as a troglodyte using—ironically, given his assiduous devotion to objectivity—trendy, junk science as a substitute for the social skills he so sorely lacks. But if his dabbling in gender science proves flimsy and risible, his success in gender's social protocols, Facebook's rules of engagement, as it were, is equally brittle and happenstance. When Leonard realizes Sheldon's outrageous maneuver has paid off, Sheldon gets the episode's final, self-aggrandizing line: "Sheldon Cooper, for the win." But the game at which he has won is mostly a game of luck, of happy accident, unaffected by his personal genius or rigorous understanding, a fact attested to by his earlier befuddlement over what he worries are the amorous overtones of virtual sheep throwing. Like many of his peers, Sheldon is no better at decoding cultural codes of intimacy and gender interaction than he is at proving deterministic account of gender and sexual behavior.

One risk of pushing social constructionism too ardently is the unintended interpretation that if one simply knows the codes, one will succeed, or that if one simply understands that gender is a performance, one will be relieved of performance anxiety. Another way of saying this is that if one discounts too quickly the importance to human behavior of hormones and genetics and neurotransmitters and other pre-conscious inputs, one leaves the gendered subject with a sense of total responsibility, self-presence, and sexual sovereignty that becomes overwhelming, an impossible burden. Some of the most interesting scientific work in sex and gender of late examines the ongoing interaction between social and extra-social factors, between genetics and culture, hormones and gender heuristics (Young 182). This work argues that social factors not only matter but also that they cannot simply be tacked on to genetics in an additive manner; rather, they must be reckoned with in constant conversation with their biological codeterminants, flattened out with them so as not to be understood linearly or deterministically. If the relationship between biology and society is ongoing for each and every individual, then the struggle to make sense of or live inside the limits of one implies the concomitant struggle to make sense of and live inside the other—because, ultimately, they are intertwined, for better or for worse. *The Big Bang Theory* uniquely captures these interlocking struggles and attests to their depressive and demoralizing impacts upon modern individuals taught to believe they are masters of their respective destinies. Rather than offer biology or society, nature or nurture, as the explanation of modern personhood, the show plays up both in order to take pressure off the self, to demystify the ideologically enforced notion that through sheer will and determination the self can make anything happen. Nature and nurture are not offered as excuses but rather as uncontrollable and often unknowable forces that make life an ongoing experiment in failing and laughing and failing and laughing together without even being certain of at what it is we are failing and laughing.

Works Cited

Berlant, Lauren. *Cruel Optimism*. Durham: Duke University Press, 2011. Print.
Butler, Judith. *Gender Trouble: Feminism and the Subversion of Identity*. New York: Routledge, 1991. Print.
Eigen, Michael. *Damaged Bonds*. New York: Karnac, 2001. Print.
_____. *Toxic Nourishment*. New York: Karnac, 1999. Print.
Escobar, Arturo. "Latin America at a Crossroads." *Cultural Studies* 24.1 (2010): 1–65. Print.
Freeman, Elizabeth. *Time Binds: Queer Temporalities, Queer Histories*. Durham: Duke University Press, 2011. Print.
"The Friendship Algorithm." *The Big Bang Theory*. CBS. KCBS-TV, Los Angeles. 19 Jan. 2009. Television.
Halberstam, Judith. *In a Queer Time and Place: Transgender Bodies, Subcultural Lives*. New York: New York University Press, 2005. Print.
_____. *The Queer Art of Failure*. Durham: Duke University Press, 2011. Print.
Jordan-Young, Rebecca. *Brain Storms: The Flaws in the Science of Sex Differences*. Cambridge: Harvard University Press, 2011. Print.

Phillips, Adam. *Missing Out: In Praise of the Unlived Life*. London: Hamish Hamilton, 2012. Print.
"The Vegas Renormalization." *The Big Bang Theory*. CBS. KCBS-TV, Los Angeles. 27 Apr. 2009. Television.
"The White Asparagus Triangulation." *The Big Bang Theory*. CBS. KCBS-TV, Los Angeles. 24 Nov. 2008. Television.

Sexualizing Two Cultures
C. P. Snow, F. R. Leavis and The Big Bang Theory

Brian McAllister

Charles Percy Snow (1905–1980) delivered the 1959 Rede Lecture at Cambridge University. He chose for his topic what he perceived as the growing gulf of incomprehension between the arts, which he dubbed "traditional culture," and the sciences. C. P. Snow felt himself uniquely qualified to make such an observation. He had his PhD in physics (specializing in spectroscopy) from Cambridge and had held a number of civil service positions in the British government since 1940. He was also a published novelist. His first work, *Death Under Sail,* was a murder mystery published in 1932. Snow explained that he had "intimate friends among both scientists and writers" and that it was through this intimacy that he realized how little scientists and artists understood of each other (10). His lecture, subsequently published as a pamphlet titled *The Two Cultures and the Scientific Revolution,* coined the phrase the "two cultures," which still survives as "a vague popular shorthand for the rift ... that has grown up between scientists and literary intellectuals in the modern world" (Kimball n.p.).

Snow's idea was not new. Another Rede lecture, simply titled *Literature and Science* (1882), delivered by Matthew Arnold nearly eighty years earlier, had defended the classics as the proper focus of education against the incursion of the sciences into modern curricula as espoused by Thomas Henry Huxley's earlier essay, "Science and Culture" (1880). The often contentious relationship between the sciences and the arts had been material for discussion throughout the twentieth century. For example, according to Guy Ortolano, "in 1928 the Cambridge Union debated the proposition 'The sciences are destroying the arts.' In 1946 the BBC aired a series on the most pressing problem of the day: 'the wide gulf between the scientific and the humanistic approach to life'" (611). However, Snow's iteration of the topic captured the popular imagination, and continues to hold it, much more thoroughly than any of his predecessors. In 1963 F. R. Leavis noted, with much dismay, that the pamphlet "rapidly took on the standing of a classic" and that it was being quoted "not only in the Sunday papers," but was being assigned to students (29–30). Enthusiasm for Snow's idea has continued. The lecture has been reprinted by the Cambridge University Press as recently as 1993, and the 50th anniversary of the lecture in 2009 was noted by several journals, including *Nature Physics,* which praised Snow's term as a "succinct phrase, which still has currency" (Across the Great Divide 309). Of course, not all of the commentary generated by Snow's lecture was praise. Most famously F. R. Leavis's *Two Cultures? The Significance of C. P. Snow* (1962) was a scathing attack which may have inspired Snow's subsequent essay "The Two Cultures: A Second Look" (1963). The debate spawned by Snow and Leavis continues. The specific terms of that debate are reflected to a surprising degree of detail in the popular sitcom *The Big Bang Theory.* Further, perhaps revealing our own social prejudices, the program marks the divide between Snow's two cultures by the different sexualities of the program's characters.

In his lecture, Snow notes that his literary colleagues know little of science. For example, he points out their inability to explain the second law of thermodynamics. On the other hand, he also remarks that his scientific associates admit that they read very little literature. Thus, he sounds the alarm of an impending crisis: "I believe the intellectual life of the whole of western society is increasingly being split into two polar groups" (11). He elaborates,

> Literary intellectuals at the one pole—at the other scientists, and as the most representative, the physical scientists. Between the two a gulf of mutual incomprehension—sometimes (particularly among the young) hostility and dislike, but most of all lack of understanding. They have a curious distorted image of each other. Their attitudes are so different that, even on the level of emotion, they can't find common ground [11–12].

It is interesting to note here that Snow thinks the widest gap between the "two cultures" is the gulf between literary scholars and physicists. He observes of the physicists that their culture is nearly devoid of books, especially "books which to most literary persons are bread and butter, novels, history, poetry, plays" (19). However, he also makes the observation that "their culture ... doesn't contain much art, with the exception, an important exception, of music" (19). Snow admits that his dichotomy may be too simple. He notes, for example, a certain degree of snobbery between pure and applied science, claiming that "pure scientists have by and large been dim-witted about engineers and applied science. They couldn't get interested" (35). As further evidence, he also remarks that at one time the Royal Society had excluded the social sciences (note 64). Snow comments that the "complex dialectic between pure and applied science is one of the deepest problems in scientific history" (65). However, Snow decides that, for his purposes, the simple bifurcation of science vs. art is clear enough.

The most famous response to Snow's Rede Lecture was F. R. Leavis's Richmond Lecture of 1962, *Two Cultures? The Significance of C. P. Snow*. Leavis launched into an extremely vituperative rant. He attacks Snow's Rede Lecture specifically, saying that it "exhibits an utter lack of intellectual distinction and an embarrassing vulgarity of style" (30). He asserts that "if his lecture has any value for use in schools—or universities—it is as a document for the study of cliché" (36). He also insults Snow's work as a novelist claiming that "as a novelist he doesn't exist. He doesn't begin to exist. He can't be said to know what a novel is" (31). He claims, "Snow not only hasn't in him the beginnings of a novelist; he is utterly without a glimmer of what creative literature is, or why it matters" (38). Kimball reports that "literary London was stunned and outraged by Leavis's performance." Guy Ortolano adds, "Leavis overplayed his hand by deploying devastating *ad hominem* attacks against Snow and his novels, enabling critics to dismiss it as a mere personal attack" (610). The acerbic tone of Leavis's lecture obscures its merit. It is still, even in context of discussion about C. P. Snow, little quoted and often misunderstood. Leavis recognized Snow's bias toward the sciences; he saw that "to speak of 'the two cultures' is to convey regret, censure, and—since one is bold enough to name and appreciate a presumably unfortunate circumstance—superiority all at once" (Kimball). He also remarks that Snow had emphasized material wealth as a benchmark of progress. Kimball says that Leavis saw this as "the central philistinism, the deeply *anti*-cultural bias, of Snow's position." Further, much of Leavis's career had been influenced by the notion that the emergence of a mass media market had segmented what had been a shared common culture. Leavis saw Snow's use of the term "traditional culture" as a portent of this decline. He says that Snow's "'intellectual' is the intellectual of the *New Statesman* circle and the reviewing in the Sunday papers" (34). Ortolano explains that Leavis "identified Snow as the product of what he considered the true problem in modern culture: mass society and the decline of standards, symbolized by 'the culture of the Sunday papers'" (610). So Leavis feared the true crisis of the two cultures was that an aggrandizement of material success would ultimately lead to a cheap, mass-produced culture that would supplant a shared literary heritage. For Leavis, "it was not surprising that *The Two Cultures* so captured the public imagination; it did so precisely because it pandered to the debased notion of culture championed by established taste" (Kimball).

One final legacy of the Snow-Leavis controversy that has survived into twenty-first century discussion is the notion of a third culture. In his follow-up essay, "A Second Look," Snow anticipated the eventual rise of what he hoped would be a third culture. He predicts that when such a culture arises, "some of the difficulties of communication will at last be softened: for such a culture has, just to do its job, to be on speaking terms with the scientific one" (67). He finds the beginnings of such a culture in such interdisciplinary work as social history. The term "third culture" has entered the argot of some postmodern circles in a way that Snow, perhaps, did not anticipate and may find disheartening, for this particular use of the term does not represent a mutual respect between the sciences and the arts, but rather a kind of usurpation of the public square by scientists. Recounting Snow's vision in "A Second Look," John Brockman has appropriated the term to denote those scientists who have been able to articulate the meaning and value of their work to an intelligent general audience. Brockman states, "Literary intellectuals are not communicating with scientists. Scientists are communicating directly with the general public" (18). The result is that these scientists are the new cultural intellectuals and their popular writing has become the new public culture.

Especially during the first two seasons, all of the aspects of the Snow-Leavis controversy are played out among the original cast members of *The Big Bang Theory*: the gulf of miscomprehension and enmity between artists and scientists, the snobbery between pure and applied sciences and the worth of the social sciences, the supplanting of a literary heritage by mass media and popular culture. Even an observation as seemingly benign as Snow's remark that the one exception to most scientists' lack of appreciation of fine art is music is reflected in the sitcom. Among the scientists there is very little of what Snow or Leavis would have considered high literary culture. However, most of the principal science characters are appreciative of music. Sheldon Cooper plays the recorder, Leonard Hofstadter is a cellist, and Leslie Winkle is a violinist. When Amy Farrah Fowler joins the cast, we learn that she is a harpist. The only allusion to anything that would usually be considered high culture in the entire first season is a quip Sheldon makes in "The Jerusalem Duality." Lamenting a loss of prestige he feels at the hands of a younger colleague, Sheldon complains, "I've gone from being Wolfgang Amadeus Mozart to that other guy." And in an example of Sheldon's contempt for applied science, when Howard asks, "Antonio Salieri?" Sheldon laments, "Oh, God! Now I'm dumber than you!"

The Big Bang Theory program as a whole acts as both a celebration of and a commentary on Brockman's interpretation of the third culture. On the one hand, the show celebrates precisely those kinds of scientists and engineers that Brockman identified as the third culture—those who have written for the general public. Brian Greene, Stephen Hawking, Neil de Grasse Tyson, and

Steve Wozniak have all made appearances as themselves. The Nobel Laureate, George Smoot, also made a cameo appearance. It is interesting that Smoot, though he has not written for the general public, has become a public celebrity from an appearance on *Are You Smarter Than a Fifth Grader?*[1] On the other hand, these scientists are presented as celebrities along with such science fiction and pop culture icons as George Takei, Katee Sackhoff, and Stan Lee that present science as pop culture. This is a development to which Sheldon Cooper, despite his love of science fiction and comic book super heroes, is adamantly opposed. Sheldon has something negative to say to most of the scientist guest stars. Sheldon attacks what he sees as efforts to "dumb down" science for the non-specialist. For example, in "The Herb Garden Germination" Sheldon attends a lecture by Brian Greene. After asking Dr. Greene to confirm that he has dedicated much of his life to "educating the general populace about complex scientific ideas," Sheldon asks very pointedly, "Have you ever considered trying to do something useful?" This theme of Sheldon's distaste for the popularization of science is introduced early in the program. In the fourth episode of the first season, "The Luminous Fish Effect," when Sheldon is going to meet his new boss, Dr. Gablehauser, we learn that Dr. Gablehauser has written popular science books which Sheldon characterizes as "popular books that reduce the great concepts of science to a series of anecdotes, each one dumbed down to accommodate the duration of the average bowel movement." The two notable exceptions are Steve Wozniak, who is more an engineer than a scientist, and George Smoot, who does not fit neatly into Brockman's definition of the third culture.

Though *The Big Bang Theory* seems to celebrate, at least problematically, the third culture, it also explores Snow's two cultures and the mutual distaste often expressed between them. Sheldon certainly believes in two cultures and would keep them separate—and he would keep the sciences pure. Typifying Snow's remark that there is also enmity between pure and applied sciences and between physical scientists and social scientists, Sheldon consistently denigrates Howard's work as an engineer and Leonard's work as an applied physicist, and consistently characterizes the social sciences as "hokum." More importantly, Sheldon certainly feels superior to the arts and betrays a real enmity to all of the humanities. In "The Bad Fish Paradigm," for example, Penny wonders if Leonard would really be attracted to her since she is not college educated. She asks Sheldon in confidence if Leonard had ever dated a woman "who wasn't a brainiac." Sheldon recalls that Leonard had once dated a woman with a PhD in French literature. When Penny asks, "How is that not a brainiac?" Sheldon replies, "Well, for one thing, she was French. And for another, it was literature!" Another telling incident is in "The Benefactor Factor." Amy tries to motivate Sheldon to attend a reception to try to do some fund raising for the physics department. Sheldon is initially unconcerned, thinking that fund raising is beneath him; however, Amy is able to convince him to attend by telling him first to "prepare to be terrified." She then reports that if grant money isn't secured by the physics department it could go to geology, "or worse. It could go to the liberal arts." She continues, "Millions of dollars being showered on poets, literary theorists, and students of gender studies." Sheldon replies, in an obvious allusion to the radio broadcast of the Hindenburg disaster, "Oh! The humanities!"

Sheldon in particular exhibits the kind of philistinism Leavis pointed out in his Richmond lecture; he displays the crass superiority Leavis detected behind Snow's comments. For example, in "The Robotic Manipulation," Sheldon considers reproducing with Amy Farrah Fowler to produce "the first in a line of intellectually superior benign overlords to guide humanity to a brighter tomorrow." In another episode he is concerned about his twin sister's choice of mate as she carries genes similar to his own. Further, Sheldon measures the value of his world simply by the technological advancement of the sciences. A recurring trope in the show is that Sheldon dreams of one day transferring his mind into a robot.

During the first two seasons, all of the scientist characters of *The Big Bang Theory* live in the world that F. R. Leavis feared. The literary world of the four central male scientists is an amalgam of fantasy genre, mass produced movie and television science fiction, and super hero comic books. This is the mass culture Leavis predicted. And as Leavis feared, it removes the characters from a shared heritage with the rest of humanity. They treat these things as if they were great literature and sometimes discuss them in ways that literature is criticized. One of the recurring conversations between Leonard and Sheldon is their differing assessment of the artistic value of *Babylon 5*. However, as art, these things fail them utterly. Instead of leading them to insights into humanity, it inspires in them completely inconsequential thoughts such as whether or not one could ride on a giant ant or where Aqua Man defecates.

Snow's two cultures are represented in *The Big Bang Theory* by the scientists on the one hand and by Penny, an aspiring actress and playwright, on the other. So the sitcom depicts Snow's two cultures, but as it does so it identifies the characters' participation in either of the two cultures by their sexuality, more specifically their sexual dysfunctions or "otherness," and thus it sexualizes the divide. Penny, the artist, is presented as hypersexual. Science characters, on the other hand, are consistently characterized as asexual, either willingly so like Sheldon and Leslie, or asexual by unfortunate social awkwardness as in the case of Leonard, Howard, and Raj. Sheldon's asexuality is so entrenched as to be confusing to his peers. In his essay "I Went to Bed with My Own Kind Once: The Erasure of Desire in the Name of Identity," David Valentine has pointed out "erotic desires that fall outside the trinary of heterosexuality, homosexuality (either/or) and bisexuality, or which fail to make sense in terms of their basic logic of binary gender are rendered unintelligible" (16). Sheldon's complete asexuality is a challenge to the understanding of his peers. In "The Cooper-Nowitzki Theorem" this challenge is discussed directly by three characters:

> PENNY: I know it's none of my business, but I have to ask you guys—what is Sheldon's deal?
> LEONARD: Deal?
> PENNY: Women? Men? Sock puppets...?
> LEONARD: We've always operated under the assumption that Sheldon had no "deal."
> HOWARD: Over the years we've developed many theories on how he will reproduce. I myself am a strong advocate of mitosis.
> PENNY: Excuse me?
> HOWARD: I believe that one day Sheldon will eat an enormous amount of Thai food and split into two Sheldons.

Other examples of Sheldon's asexuality abound. In "The Dumpling Paradox," Leonard and Sheldon discuss the merits of Halo vs. sex. Sheldon declares, "As far as I know, sex has not been upgraded to include high-def graphics and enhanced weapons systems." Leonard responds, "All sex has is nudity, orgasms, and human contact," to which Sheldon responds, "my point." As the only other theoretical physicist, Sheldon's nemesis in the physics department is Leslie Winkle, who displays a similar asexuality to Sheldon's. Leslie does have sex, but apparently only rarely. In "The Hamburger Postulate," Leslie seduces Leonard during a string ensemble practice. It is interesting to note here that the seduction happens in the context of classical music, further associating the arts with sexuality. In fact, Leslie uses some admittedly crude double entendre about handling musical instruments to seduce Leonard. The next day, however, Leonard finds her unreceptive. When he asks why, she replies, "Well, I don't know about your sex drive, but I'm probably good until New Year's." In *Gender Trouble,* Judith Butler points out that those gender identities which "fail to conform to those norms of cultural intelligibility ... appear only as developmental failures or logical impossibilities" (24). Sheldon's and Leslie's desires, or lack of desires, are extremes, and they are presented as comic because their extremism seems unintelligible—a comic absurdity. The other three scientists in the central cast are consistently depicted as social/sexual failures.

Raj is worse off than Leonard. He cannot speak to girls unless he is drinking, and when he drinks, he behaves in sexually boorish ways. And, one of the running jokes of the show is that Raj and Howard form what Leonard's mother identifies as "an ersatz homosexual couple." In the first three seasons, Raj and Howard are always seen on the set together. When Raj is unable to speak because a woman is present, Howard is his interpreter. There are numerous examples of Howard and Raj having a verbal disagreement that seems like a lover's spat. Howard is an especially interesting character. He considers himself a lady's man, but usually just comes off as creepy. In fact, one of the running jokes through the first two seasons is Howard's strained and odd-ball strategies for meeting women: buying fake tattoo sleeves to impress women at a Goth bar, wearing an eye-patch to make himself look distinctive, trying to impress women with amateurish magic tricks.

Belying his own assertions of self-confidence, Howard, more than any other character, uses language strategies to assert his "hetero-normality." John Keisling, in a study of the language interactions of fraternity brothers, remarked that young men in same sex groups often referred to each other as women in a claim to dominance. He notes that a "language of heterosexuality … has a social construction that is primarily used by social actors to compete within same sex groups" (130). Howard often deploys this strategy. On one occasion, when Leonard whined about his troubles with Penny, Howard threatened to kick Leonard "in the ovaries." Though Howard is quick to attempt this method of dominance, it often backfires on him. In "The Luminous Fish Effect," Howard arrives at a reception with a tall blonde on his arm. He approaches the others with the greeting, "What up, science bitches? May I introduce my special lady, Summer?" Summer interjects, "I already told you touching's extra."

Like the incident with Summer, the few sexual encounters Howard has before the introduction of Bernadette are usually bought. He has an encounter in Las Vegas with a prostitute paid for by Leonard and Raj. In "The Dumpling Paradox," he has a fling with one of Penny's friends, whom he is told will sleep with any man as long as he keeps buying her things. Unfazed by this revelation and betraying his own sexual desperation, Howard treats the encounter as a triumph, and his language strategy reveals his desire to characterize the experience as triumphant. He greets his friends as "nerdmigos," willingly embracing what could be a pejorative. Cameron and Kulick point out that denigrated groups often willingly adopt labels attached to them "as a challenge to the ideological structures which make the subordinate status of the group appear natural, acceptable and inevitable" (25).

In the first three seasons, Leonard, Raj, and Howard all display some degree of sexual desperation, and each is depicted as a sexual failure. Perhaps the best summation of these character's sexual lives is in "The Killer Robot

Instability." Kripke wants to arrange a grudge match between fighting robots, but Leonard and Raj initially decline because Howard, the engineer of their robot, is absent. Howard is home moping because of an insult he received from Penny. When Kripke asks what is wrong with Howard, Raj volunteers, "He's depressed because he's pathetic and creepy and can't get girls." Surprised, Kripke answers in a querulous tone, "We're *all* pathetic and creepy and can't get girls. That's why we fight robots!"

As the scientist characters all display some degree or kind of asexuality or sexual failure, Penny, who as an actress and aspiring playwright represents the arts, is hypersexual. During the first two seasons in particular, she is seen with four different boyfriends. Played by Travis Schuldt, Allen Nabors, Brian Patrick Wade, and Brian Thomas Smith, these boyfriends are all unusually tall, muscular, and masculine looking men. Of course they contrast starkly with the relatively short, weakling scientists. And from the beginning of the program, her hypersexual behavior is fodder for humor. In "The Fuzzy Boots Corollary," she confesses to Leonard that her habit after a breakup is to find a partner for "rebound sex." She tells Leonard, "It's my pattern. I break up. I find some cute guy, and it's just thirty-six meaningless hours of … you know." Stunned by the number, Leonard asks, "I'm not sure that I do. Is that thirty-six hours spread out over, say, a long glorious summer?" In "The Hamburger Postulate," when Leonard is having his single encounter with Leslie Winkle, Sheldon notices the signal of the tie left on the doorknob and asks Penny what his actions should be as Leonard's roommate. Penny replies, "Gee, Sheldon, you're asking the wrong girl. I'm usually on the other side of the tie." We are also given to believe that Penny's sexual encounters are unusually loud and raucous. In "The Robotic Manipulation," Sheldon asserts his own asexuality to Penny by declaring that normal human reproduction is "messy, unsanitary, and, based on living next to you for three years, involves loud and unnecessary appeals to a deity." Penny exclaims, "Oh, my God," to which Sheldon adds, "Yes, exactly." In that same episode, Penny chaperones Sheldon and Amy on their first date. At dinner Sheldon and Amy entertain themselves by calculating the number of dates Penny must have had. Sheldon's calculations include the initial assumption that Penny probably began dating at age fifteen. Penny protests, but then admits she began dating at fourteen. Sheldon modifies his assumptions and estimates that Penny has dated one hundred and ninety three men. Amy asks if Penny had intercourse with all of these men, which inspires Sheldon to calculate the number of men Penny has slept with. He bases his calculations on the frequency with which he has seen men leaving her apartment in the morning, and the number of times he has seen her coming home wearing the same clothes she had worn the night before. He estimates thirty one partners. Pointedly, Amy Farrah Fowler interjects, "This is very interesting. Cultural perceptions are subjective. Penny, to your mind, are you a slut?" This scene emphasizes the sexual dichotomy between Penny, on the one hand, and Sheldon and Amy on the other. Penny's hyper-sexuality is revealed by Sheldon's calculations. Sheldon and Amy's asexuality is emphasized by their rationalistic discussion. For Sheldon, Penny's sex life is no more than fodder for an interesting arithmetic problem, and Amy's question is asked, not in a spirit of moral judgment, but simply as an interesting anthropological point.

It is important to note that the problem being explored here is not just that Penny is promiscuous—it is that the promiscuity is associated with Penny *as an artist*. *The Big Bang Theory* consistently associates sexual prowess and seduction with the arts. In "The Financial Instability," Leonard suggests to Penny that she may be able to solve her financial problems by moving in with him. Penny wrinkles her brow and speaks in a confiding tone. "Oh, Leonard, if we lived together I wouldn't be able to keep my hands off of you." Surprised, Leonard asks, "Really?" Penny's expression changes to an impish grin as she replies, "See, those acting lessons paid off!"

The sexualization of Snow's dichotomy in *The Big Bang Theory* is obvious and strong in the first several seasons, but with the introduction of Amy Farrah Fowler and Bernadette Rostenkowsky as characters, that dichotomy begins to shift, and that change is most prominent in the development of the character, Amy Farrah Fowler. When Amy Farrah Fowler is first introduced to the show, she is as asexual as Sheldon. In fact, she is introduced as a female counterpart of Sheldon. She is discovered when Raj and Howard decide to create an account on eHarmony using Sheldon's characteristics as their model. Her initial asexuality is strong. In fact, when she is first introduced to Sheldon, she announces, "all forms of physical contact up to and including coitus are off the table." Throughout most of the fourth season, her asexuality remains strong. Her visits with Sheldon are usually conducted through Skype. When she and Sheldon plan to reproduce, they assume that the embryo will be conceived *in vitro*. And Sheldon constantly reminds the other characters that Amy is not his girlfriend. However, most of the characters' sexualities change as the program develops.

As the plot lines evolve in later seasons, the asexual/hypersexual dichotomy between the characters is softened and then abandoned. As Penny and Leonard have their on and off again relationship, and as Leonard has a "normal" affair with Priya, Penny's sexuality is toned down. And once Howard marries Bernadette, the jokes based on his social/sexual ineptitude are no longer relevant. The writers instead begin to employ a set of clichéd jokes around Howard's ability or inability to negotiate the intertwined relationships with his wife and his mother. And with Howard married, the writers abandon the jokes concerning the homosexual undertones of his friendship with Raj. As these character situations develop, Amy Farrah Fowler begins to be portrayed, not as asexual, but rather as sexually confused. She finds an inexplicable attraction to Zack, Penny's muscular former boyfriend. At a girl's night with Penny and Bernadette, she thinks it appropriate to "experiment with harmless lesbianism." She tries kissing Sheldon. In one episode she sings to herself "I kissed a girl and I liked it." It is important to note that she is not being portrayed as truly bisexual. She seems to be lost as to her own sexuality and is still certainly socially, and, by implication, sexually inept. In one sense, she is still very much like Sheldon—she, like Sheldon, does not fit neatly into Valentine's trinary. Of course, what Amy Farrah Fowler and Sheldon also have in common, is their full immersion in their scientific fields. They, more than the other characters, rely on their background in science to negotiate their social world or to retreat from it.

As the program progresses, the strong dichotomy between science and art wanes. By the fourth season, the restrictive literary world of the scientists has expanded. In "The 21-Second Excitation," for example, Raj confesses that he has been moved by Elizabeth Gilbert's *Eat, Pray, Love,* and in "The Toast Derivation," Leonard and Priya find that they have in common, a love for Shakespeare's *The Taming of the Shrew*. Small literary allusions begin to show up in Sheldon's dialogue as well. Several times, for instance, he states ,"the moving finger has writ," paraphrasing Edward Fitzgerald's *Rubaiyat of Omar Khayyam*. Amy Farrah Fowler is also depicted as knowledgeable about literature as well as science. But that knowledge is a socially awkward hyper-intellectuality. For example, when asked to tell a naughty story at a girls' night in, to the complete confusion of Penny and Bernadette, she recites Chaucer's "The Miller's Tale" in the original Middle English—in its entirety. In making this shift, the writers have created a new dichotomy between hetero-normality on the one side, as represented by Leonard with his partners and with the marriage of Howard and Bernadette, and sexual otherness, as represented by Sheldon and Amy Farrah Fowler, on the other. In this new paradigm, an intellectual extreme is still marked by a sexual extreme. The hyper-intellectuality of Sheldon and Amy is directly associated with their sexual failure—Sheldon's continued asexuality and Amy's sexual confusion.

The high degree of correspondence between the terms of the Snow-Leavis debate and the various characterizations of the initial cast members in the first two seasons of *The Big Bang Theory* is ample testimony that Snow's perception of the respective worlds of the scientist and artist, and his perception of the enmity between them, is still very much part of the popular imagination. The sexualization of these notions is, perhaps, even more deeply revealing of our own social attitudes. Because all of the characters of the original cast are presented as comic extremes on either side of an implicit heteronormality, the writers' willingness to sexualize C. P. Snow's "Two Cultures" is also indicative of some of our culture's most deeply held prejudices. But those extremes are presented as implicated both in our popular notions of human sexuality and in our popular perception of the practice of science and art.

Note

1. *Are You Smarter Than a Fifth Grader* is a TV game show hosted by comedian Jeff Foxworthy in which contestants must answer questions gleaned from elementary school textbooks. George Smoot appeared as a contestant in episodes 321, aired September 11, 2009, and 322, aired September 18, 2009.

Works Cited

"Across the Great Divide." Editorial. *Nature Physics* 5. May 2009. 309. Web. 1 September 2012. Print.
"The Bad Fish Paradigm." *The Big Bang Theory: The Complete Second Season*. Writ. Steven Molaro and David Goetsch. Dir. Mark Cendrowski. Warner Brothers, 2009. DVD.
"The Benefactor Factor." *The Big Bang Theory: The Complete Fourth Season*. Writ. Chuck Lorre, Eric Kaplan, and Steve Holland. Dir. Mark Cendrowski. Warner Brothers, 2011. DVD.
"The Big Bran Hypothesis." *The Big Bang Theory: The Complete First Season*. Writ Chuck Lorre and Bill Prady. Dir. James Burrows. Warner Brothers, 2008. DVD.
Brockman, John. *The Third Culture: Beyond the Scientific Revolution*. New York: Touchstone, 1995. Print.
Butler, Judith. *Gender Trouble: Feminism and the Subversion of Identity*. New York: Routledge, 1999. Print.
Cameron, Deborah, and Don Kulick. *Language and Sexuality*. New York: Cambridge University Press, 2003. Print.
"The Codpiece Topology." *The Big Bang Theory: The Complete Second Season*. Writ. Bill Prady and Lee Aronsohn. Dir. Mark Cendrowski. Warner Brothers, 2009. DVD.
"The Cooper-Nowitzki Theorem." *The Big Bang Theory: The Complete Second Season*. Writ. Tom Doyle and Richard Rosenstock. Dir. Mark Cendrowski. Warner Brothers, 2009. DVD.
"The Dumpling Paradox." *The Big Bang Theory: The Complete First Season*. Writ. Lee Aronsohn and Jennifer Glickman. Dir. Mark Cendrowski. Warner Brothers, 2008. DVD.
"The Financial Permeability." *The Big Bang Theory: The Complete Second Season*. Writ. Richard Rosenstock and Eric Kaplan. Dir. Mark Cendrowski. Warner Brothers, 2009. DVD.
"The Fuzzy Boots Corollary." *The Big Bang Theory: The Complete First Season*. Writ. Bill Prady and Steven Molaro. Dir. Mark Cendrowski. Warner Brothers, 2008. DVD.
"The Hamburger Postulate." *The Big Bang Theory: The Complete First Season*. Writ. Dave Goetsch and Steven Molarno. Dir. Andrew Weyman. Warner Brothers, 2008. DVD.
"The Herb Garden Germination." *The Big Bang Theory: The Complete Fourth Season*. Writ. BIll Prady, Steven Molaro, and Steve Holland. Dir. Mark Cendrowski. Warner Brothers, 2011. DVD.
Kiesling, Scott F. "Playing the Straight Man: Displaying and Maintaining Male Heterosexu-

ality in Discourse." *The Language and Sexuality Reader*. Ed. Deborah Cameron and Don Kulick. New York: Routledge, 2006. 118–131. Print.

Kimball, Roger. "'The Two Cultures' Today: On the C. P. Snow-F.R. Leavis Controversy." *The New Criterion*. Web. February 1994. 4 April 2012.

Leavis, F. R. *Two Cultures? The Significance of C. P. Snow*. New York: Pantheon, 1963. Print.

"The Luminous Fish Effect." *The Big Bang Theory: The Complete First Season*. Writ. David Litt and Lee Aronsohn. Dir. Mark Cendrowski. Warner Brothers, 2008. DVD.

Ortolano, Guy. "Two Cultures, One University: The Institutional Origins of the 'Two Cultures' Controversy." *Albion: A Quarterly Journal Concerned with British Studies* 34.4 (Winter 2002): 606–624. Print.

"Pilot." *The Big Bang Theory: The Complete First Season*. Writ. Chuck Lorre and Bill Prady. Dir. James Burrows. Warner Brothers, 2008. DVD.

"The Robotic Manipulation." *The Big Bang Theory: The Complete Fourth Season*. Writ. Steven Molaro, Eric Kaplan, and Steve Holland. Dir. Mark Cendrowski. Warner Brothers, 2011. DVD.

Snow, C. P. *The Two Cultures: And a Second Look: An Expanded Version of The Two Cultures and the Scientific Revolution*. New York: The New American Library, 1964. Print.

"The Toast Derivation." *The Big Bang Theory: The Complete Fourth Season*. Writ. Chuck Lorre, Steven Molaro, and Jim Reynolds. Dir. Mark Cendrowski. Warner Brothers, 2011. DVD.

"The 21-Second Excitation." *The Big Bang Theory: The Complete Fourth Season*. Writ. Chuck Lorre, Steven Molaro, and Jim Reynolds. Dir. Mark Cendrowski. Warner Brothers, 2011. DVD.

Valentine, David. "I Went to Bed with My Own Kind Once: The Erasure of Desire in the Name of Identity." *Language and Communication* 23.2 (2003): 123–138. Print.

"The Vartavian Conundrum." *The Big Bang Theory: The Complete Second Season*. Writ. Richard Rosenstock and Bill Prady. Dir. Mark Cendrowski. Warner Brothers, 2009. DVD.

The American Female Dichotomy
Smart or *Sexy*

Abigail G. Scheg

> Culture stereotypes women to fit the myth by flattering the feminine into beauty-without-intelligence or intelligence-without-beauty; women are allowed a mind or a body but not both.
> —Naomi Wolf, *The Beauty Myth: How Images of Beauty Are Used Against Women*

The Big Bang Theory has rapidly grown in popularity in recent years due to its desirable, relatable, and likeable characters. Perhaps also, the show has gained popularity because of its blatant juxtaposition between "smart" and "not so smart" characters. In a time when television shows depict people eating scary foreign bugs for large sums of money and "real housewives" with too much plastic surgery, *The Big Bang Theory* has been a refreshing break in a way that is relatable to real life. The characters have jobs, relationships, and families, all of which are sources of both enjoyment and difficulty. In general, the characters lead a seemingly normal life.

A crucial aspect of this show has increasingly become the male-female relationships and, ultimately, the female characters. Season One began with the boys—Sheldon, Leonard, Howard, and Raj—with Penny as the lone female. Characters have come and gone, but there is now a core group of female characters in the show as well—Penny, Amy Farrah Fowler, and Bernadette. Though these ladies have many contrasting characteristics, they are now classified as friends and are often having fun, scheming, and relying on each other. However, one cannot help but notice the vast dissimilarities in characterization: Penny is inevitably shown as the "sexy" one, without as much investment in formal education as the others, or interest in becoming more intelligent in the subjects of the other characters. Amy, however, is characterized as the "smart" one, possessing a PhD in neurobiology and always caring about and furthering her research. Amy possesses little to no outward sex appeal, nor does she try. Bernadette, however, lies somewhere in the middle of this spectrum; blonde and buxom, one cannot help but name Bernadette as physically attractive, yet she also holds advanced degrees in microbiology and is undoubtedly smart.

Considering this more deeply, Penny demonstrates that she *is* smart in the episode "The Bat Jar Conjecture" in which she quizzes Leonard and Sheldon on pop culture. Although she does not know about physics, their desired field of expertise, she knows about other aspects of life. Likewise, she is consistently the person that the other characters go to for relationship advice, demonstrating that she is knowledgeable about that subject as well. Penny also beats Leonard in chess in her first few games; although she does not remember the correct terminology for the chess pieces, she wins quickly. Though there are areas where Penny demonstrates mastery, she is generally not considered a "smart" female, but rather a "sexy" female. Likewise, Amy's attempts to present herself as physically attractive are often the sources of jokes and ridicule in the show's plots. The female characters in the show play into stereotypes of females which makes it difficult to present a woman as more than one categorization. This means that the females are presented in a way that dichotomizes them, smart *or* sexy.

Thus derives the research question of this chapter: In American popular culture, can a female be both smart *and* sexy? By investigating sexuality in American popular culture, we garner a better understanding of the positioning of these *Big Bang Theory* characters. The foundation of this essay, therefore, relies on solid definitions of the terms "smart" and "sexy," as they relate to pop culture. Once the general status of female characterization in present day culture is defined, this essay will consider the combination of "smartness" and "sexiness" demonstrated by the three main female characters of *The Big Bang Theory*: Penny, Amy, and Bernadette. Although there have been additional female characters that played significant roles throughout the show thus far (Priya Koothrapali and Leslie Winkle, as examples), since these characters have not secured permanent roles on the show, they will not be considered in the discussions of this limited chapter. In order to apply the definitions to the characters, this essay will develop a continuum of smart-sexy in order to investigate whereupon the females would fit within the continuum in order to gauge if it is possible for a female to be *both* smart and sexy in American popular culture, using the main characters of *The Big Bang Theory* as gauges.

Defining "Smart"

One of the obvious standards to define if a character is "smart" on *The Big Bang Theory* is if they hold a PhD in their field of study. Throughout all of the seasons, characters are mocking Howard because he "only" has a master's in engineering, not a PhD, although he explains why the degree is unnecessary. Even Bernadette tells him, "If you don't want to get teased about that, get a doctorate. I have one; they're great" ("The Hawking Excitation"). A terminal degree, or education in general, seems like a foundational way to determine whether an individual is smart or not, according to *The Big Bang Theory*.

Monetary and personal successes also work towards the definition of one being "smart." For instance, in Season Two, Penny finds herself out of money when, combined with car trouble, her work hours are cut at The Cheesecake Factory. In this episode, she hides from the apartment manager in Sheldon and Leonard's apartment and shares her financial burdens with Sheldon. He responds, "You know, it occurs to me that you could solve all of your problems by obtaining more money" ("The Financial Permeability"). In fact, throughout all of the seasons, Penny is typically demonstrated in financial distress having infrequently had the acting opportunities she seeks. In order to help Penny, Sheldon retrieves one of his hidden stashes of money from the apartment. In true Sheldon fashion, he explains to her the percentage breakdown of his financial savings plan, including a savings account and various places around the apartment.

Stereotypically, "femaleness" is associated with less monetary value, as is evident in the numerous studies showing that male employees out earn their female counterparts. According to the Organisation for Economic Co-operation and Development (OECD), the gender wage gap has narrowed substantially, but the gap is still about 16–18 percent in recent years ("Gender Brief"). Within the show, a financial controversy arises within Bernadette and Howard's relationship when Bernadette is offered a new job in the fourth season. Although Bernadette is incredibly proud of her education and now, her professional accomplishment, Howard does not share her enthusiasm because she will be making more money than he does. The rest of the characters use this as an opportunity to mock Howard, calling him a "Trophy wife" ("The Roommate Transmogrification").

Generally, in American society, education and financial gain are good determinants of "smartness." However, beauty and physical appearance are something that has complicated these potentials. The inadvertent and unadvertised female figure and beauty seem to perpetually trap women in a cycle of stereotypes. In the American 1920s, burlesque performer, Gypsy Rose Lee, made a name for herself not only for her sexuality, but for her performances that exceptionally mocked American society and aristocracy. According to Jacki Willson's *The Happy Stripper*, "A potent combination of sexy stripping and intelligence had given this working-class girl the opportunity to live a life or riches and socialize with the intellectual elite" (32). As her career continued, Gypsy Rose Lee strove to represent the empowered female, demonstrating a sincere intellectual understanding of the challenges that femininity carried in American society and the daunting task of overcoming one's gender in order to make a place for oneself in contemporary society.

Willson's text continues with a socioeconomic view of the American depression as it relates to burlesque and female resourcefulness: "With the system weakened, women were both quietly and loudly challenging the legitimacy of "Business as a Man's World" (82). Women took the challenges of the American economy and capitalized on the opportunities, thus challenging their position and subjugation by males. Also, "middle-class feminists were using their female status as fragile and de-sexualized beings paradoxically, to acquire more power and experience in the public domain as fund-raisers, orators, politicians, negotiators and businesswomen" (82). The smart and sexy female was an anomaly; men, especially businessmen, did not necessarily understand that smart, sexy, and savvy women existed. This created unforeseen challenges for businessmen and opportunities for women to move forward. Women, who in this time period determined "85 percent of household expenditure," were assuming more personal freedoms and responsibilities towards financial gain and opportunity (80).

Putting the unique juxtaposition of burlesque aside, smart femaleness (or challenges thereabout) creeps its way into American popular culture throughout the years. Louisa May Alcott's *Little Women*, about the sisters of the March family is a consistent battle between Amy (the youngest) who wants to be constantly dolled up to attend theatre performances and begin courtships and her sisters (mainly Jo) who strive for increased education in any way it can be learned and challenges injustices in society. Another example would be the character Clarice Starling of *The Silence of the Lambs*, a young, scholarly trainee at the FBI Academy. As the story progresses, she demonstrates significant knowledge of the justice system, her potential career, and what is to be expected of an FBI agent. Yet another more recent example would be *Legally Blonde,* which chronicles Elle Woods' experience as a stereotypical blonde sorority girl transitioning to becoming a successful defense attorney. Although the story occurs because she is initially following an ex-boyfriend to Harvard Law School, Elle's character discovers her true potential in education and law.

Perhaps most notably are the female teams that are presented in popular culture: *Thelma and Louise, Fried Green Tomatoes, Steel Magnolias, A League of their Own, First Wives Club, Divine Secrets of the Ya-Ya Sisterhood, Waiting to Exhale,* and, of course, *Sex and the City.* In these teams, females are presented as strong, smart, full of potential, and bouncing their strengths off of the other members of their female teams only creates additional strength and opportunity for the characters as individuals and as a team. The female characters of *The Big Bang Theory* also demonstrate strength, intelligence, resourcefulness, and beauty, which make them an ideal focal point for the examination of intelligence and sex appeal.

In order to provide summative points for the definition of smart, please consider the following points as comprising the definition of "smart": In progress of or has completed higher education; holds steady, successful career; holds lucrative career or is otherwise skilled with money; confidence in ones' abilities, skills, and knowledge; and demonstrates potential for growth in one or more of these categories.

Defining "Sexy"

Naomi Wolf discusses the professional beauty qualification (PBQ), which perpetuates much of the visual American culture: flight attendants, waitresses, secretaries, and many more professional positions. PBQ has a lengthy historical background including being tied to the lawsuit, *St. Cross* v. *Playboy Club of New York,* in which a waitress, Margarita St. Cross, was fired from the Playboy Club "because she had lost her Bunny image." The required beauty standards of this position are as follows:

1. A flawless beauty (face, figure, and grooming)
2. An exceptionally beautiful girl
3. Marginal (is aging or has developed a correctable appearance problem)
4. Has lost Bunny Image (either through aging or an uncorrectable appearance problem) [Wolf 32].

The PBQ perpetuates all facets of popular culture, including recent news highlights rumoring that Ann Curry was fired for refusing to dye her gray hair. Somehow, an imaginary standard of beauty perpetuates American culture despite the number of after-school specials that are hosted around the country and number of celebrities who proudly share their experience with an eating disorder to dissuade other young individuals to remain true to themselves.

There has been long-standing discussion across academic disciplines as to what constitutes beauty. In particular, scholars strive to define cultural considerations of beauty and navigate the changes made to such cultural views. In Milton Rokeach's 1943 article "Studies in Beauty: I. The Relationship Between Beauty and Women, Dominance, and Security," Rokeach defines three aspects of beauty: anatomical aspects, cultural determinants, and psychological determinants (186). Anatomical aspects, Rokeach argues, "are certain absolute standards as to what is beautiful. Probably, a hunchbacked cripple is considered ugly in any culture. Malformed and distorted bodies are universally perceived as ugly" (187). While lacking in appropriate discussion and political correctness by today's standards, the same concepts still apply: able-bodiedness is still favored in American popular culture as the "norm," whereas deviations from abled-bodiedness are still generally considered unattractive.

Rokeach's second point, cultural determinants, are the most superficial considerations. Such details include "ever-changing styles in clothing, hair, figure, and facial make-up" (187). Clothing, hair, figure, and make-up are details of beauty that have shifted over time, which are chronicled in detail in Mazur's article "U.S. Trends in Feminine Beauty and Overadaptation." Mazur discusses American culture's perception of beauty as a shifting phenomenon, one that changes with the popularization of individual females, movie stars, models, and popular trends of the time.

Rokeach's third point, psychological determinants, refers to two concepts, "(a) how they perceive themselves ... and (b) how they imagine and desire others to perceive them" (187). Therefore, as he argues with this point, beauty is not entirely about the physical, but can also include the psychological aspects of a female perceiving themselves as beautiful, as well as their actions and reactions to popular culture's notions of beauty that are reflected upon them.

In "The Construction of Beauty: A Cross-Cultural Analysis of Women's Magazine Advertising," Katherine Frith, Ping Shaw, and Hong Cheung identify specific characteristics of beauty as represented in American media. In order to best represent characteristics of beauty, these authors separated depictions of women into eight categories: Classic, Feminine, Sensual, Exotic, Cute, Girl-Next-Door, Sex Kitten, and Trendy (4). In particular, the authors found, Classic and Sensual/Sex Kitten were the two most popular representations of women in American popular media (8). "Classic" beauty they define as "a classic elegant look, model is slightly older than average. Fair skin, feminine, glamorous and sophisticated. Usually wears soft, demure, feminine apparel and is not heavily accessorized" (12). "Sensual/Sex Kitten," defined as "Sexually attractive, usually wears sexy attire or revealing, tight clothes. Model can also be dressed in normal clothes but posed in an unnatural way, such as an uncomfortable, "cheesecake" pose (chest thrust forward, back arched) (12). These characteristics are seen in more than just print media; they pose in grocery store check-out lines, educational advertisements, young adult fiction, and of course, television shows such as *The Big Bang Theory*.

The iconic American images of femaleness include the likenesses of Marilyn Monroe, Jackie Kennedy Onassis, Elizabeth Taylor, Audrey Hepburn, and so forth. What are the overlapping physical characteristics of these individuals? These physical characteristics include able-bodied females, clear complexions, symmetrical facial structure, make up, clean and straight teeth, beautiful clothing, shiny and well maintained hair, complimentary hair styles, thin or desirably curvy body structure, voluptuous breasts and buttocks, thin-waisted, beautiful accessories, and an ability to photograph well. Although the iconic photographs associated with these individuals are, in some cases, decades old now, they still maintain the American standard of classic beauty and sexuality upheld today. Perhaps the specifics of the look of American sexy have adapted to incorporate the likes of Britney Spears and Cindy Crawford, but the general categories of sexy remain the same.

Nancy Etcoff's *Survival of the Prettiest* adds another facet to the definition of beauty: youth. Etcoff explains the historical context of this notion:

> For most of human history, people mated in their teenage years and conceived a first baby by age twenty: being a teenager was all about courting and choosing. In many parts of the world it still is. When anthropologist Suzanne Frayser surveyed four hundred and fifty-four traditional cultures, she found that the highest frequency of brides was in the twelve to fifteen years old age category, and the largest age category for grooms was eighteen. Girls at this age are preternaturally beautiful [57].

From there, Etcoff chronicles the discovery of models at young ages: Christy Turlington at thirteen and Kate Moss at fourteen. Associating youth with beauty and sexuality is another aspect of the American stereotype with a long history, as is evident by the social-anthropological survey discussed above. With aging come changes to complexion, hair texture, hair color, reaction to and need for makeup, and many more characteristics that are diametrically opposed to the above mentioned definition of sexy.

In order to provide summative points for the definition of sexy, please consider the following points as comprising the definition of "sexy": Thin to moderately healthy height/weight ratio; thinness preferred; young; able-bodied; clear complexion, makeup enhanced skin; pleasant physical presentation in terms of makeup, clothes, hair style, and body; voluptuous, proportionate buttocks and breasts.

Applying "Smart" and "Sexy" to The Big Bang Theory Females

In order to apply these terms to the female characters of *The Big Bang Theory*, this essay will discuss a continuum of smart-sexy to evaluate where the characters would place based on American popular culture standards.

The Continuum of Smart-Sexy

Smart: In order for a character to be placed at the far left of the continuum, she would have to be incredibly smart, based on the aforementioned definitions, but entirely lacking the elements of sexuality.

Sexy: In order for a character to be placed at the far right of the continuum, she would have to be incredibly sexy, but entirely lacking the characteristics in the definitions of being "smart."

Smart and Sexy Balance: In order for a character to place in the very middle of the continuum, Smart and Sexy Balance, the character would have to demonstrate an equal amount of physical sexuality *as well as* the characteristics in the definition of being "smart."

Smart   **Smart and Sexy Balance**   **Sexy**

Placing The Big Bang Theory Characters on the Continuum

Penny—In terms of the definitions of smart, Penny does not meet many of the qualifications listed above. As is described in the course of the show, Penny dropped out of community college before she could finish. Therefore, she possesses no degrees of higher education, nor does she frequently make mention of a desire to continue her education. She did re-enroll in community college courses, but it is unknown if she just registered for classes on a part-time basis or is working towards a degree.

Penny does not hold a steady, successful career. Rather, she works part-time at the Cheesecake Factory while attempting to become a famous actress. However, her acting opportunities are few and far between and typically the source of mockery and humor in the show's early plots. Penny typically demonstrates some confidence in her acting abilities, although she has not been received well at auditions.

Penny does present knowledge in various subjects outside academia, such as popular culture, playing chess, cow tipping, weaponry, fighting, and much more. However, by the definitions of "smart" established earlier in this chapter, these characteristics do not add considerable weight to this consideration of Penny as being "smart."

As was previously discussed in the chapter, Penny often does not make enough money to pay her required monthly expenses. She does, however, like to shop for new clothing and expensive shoes, thus demonstrating that she is not particularly skilled with money.

Penny does demonstrate potential for growth in all of these categories. She wants desperately to become a successful actress and, at some times, demonstrates the drive to make that a possibility for herself. Should that possibility become a reality, Penny's opportunities for career and financial growth would grow exponentially. Penny also has the potential for educational growth, should she choose that path.

In terms of the definitions of sexy, Penny does meet all of the criteria in the definition. Physically, Penny is thin waisted with a proportional (albeit underweight) figure. Penny is young; she is in her twenties in the duration of the show. She is able-bodied and demonstrates no outward physical disabilities deriving her from a stereotypical American standard body image.

Penny's complexion is always clear and the majority of the show time she does have makeup enhancing her facial appearance. Although there are times when she does not have makeup, it is typically for comedic purposes and limited to a scene or two within an episode.

Generally, Penny has a pleasant physical presentation. She typically wears revealing or tight clothing which accentuates her figure. Likewise her hair and makeup are almost always done well.

Again, Penny's physical body image is well-presented. She has a stereotypically desirable body with voluptuous (and typically displayed) breasts and buttocks. In terms of Rokeach's psychological determinants, Penny is quite aware of her physical appearance and uses it throughout the show to help achieve things for herself or others. In the episode "The Tenure Turbulence," Penny tries to support Leonard's endeavors to achieve tenure at his university. Leonard is unable to understand how she can help, so Penny bends over in front of him pretending to tie her shoe; Leonard is then able to see that Penny plans to use her sex appeal to assist his tenure process. To a subsequent university event, Penny wears a very low cut dress with significant cleavage in order to entice the older male members of the tenure committee. Penny's behavior in "The Tenure Turbulence" demonstrates that she has a psychological awareness of her sexuality and uses it to her advantage.

Considering these factors, Penny will be placed almost entirely on the "Sexy" end of the spectrum. She possesses only one (perhaps almost two) parts of the definition of "Smart," which move her slightly towards the left on the continuum. See below:

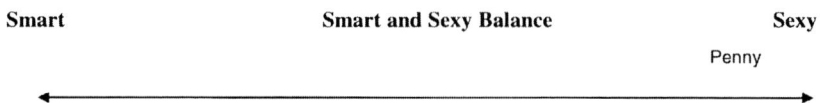

Amy Farrah Fowler—Regarding the definitions of "smart," Amy does successfully meet all of these criteria. Amy holds a PhD in neurobiology and is consistently working in her lab, on new projects and new research.

Although her monetary situation is not typically mentioned in the show, she seems to share the same financial tendencies as Sheldon and is therefore sufficiently (or more than sufficiently) compensated for her advanced degree and exceptional research. Amy's apartment is used as a set in a few episodes and the appearance of her apartment likewise suggests financial successes. She also lives alone in her apartment, indicating that she does not need a roommate to supplement rent payments.

Amy does appear to be quite confident in her knowledge and research. She does have some notable successes with her research and publication throughout the show, which are immediately downplayed by Sheldon's overconfidence. However, Amy is aware of her capabilities and propensity to excel in her field. When Sheldon does not respond appropriately to a successful publication that Amy earned, she does not permit him to belittle her academic achievements and he must make up this relationship misstep with her ("The Shiny Trinket Maneuver").

Likewise, Amy demonstrates the potential for growth in any of these categories. Should she choose a new field or additional education, she has already proved successful in that endeavor. Amy has an abnormally high IQ and therefore possesses the ability to learn about and potentially achieve skill in many areas.

Considering the definition of "sexy," Amy does meet some of the criteria (which could solely be because she is a television character and not a "real person"). She is thin to moderately healthy in terms of her height and weight ratio.

Amy's age is not given in the show, but given her extensive education, we can deduce that she is older than Penny. However, she generally "fits in" with the other group of characters. Therefore, she could potentially be late twenties to early thirties.

Amy is an able-bodied female, like Penny, displaying no outward physical disabilities. She does have a clear complexion, but does not typically wear any makeup.

In comparison to Penny, Amy does not have a noticeably pleasant physical presentation. She does not wear any makeup (typically) to enhance her natural features. Also, she wears glasses. Mostly, the clothing that she wears is very conservative and not flattering to her female figure. She wears a lot of layered clothing, giving the visual impression that she is larger or heavier than she actually is. She has tried on some occasions to give in to popular conventions of dress, such as high heels; however, she was not very successful in this endeavor and typically maintains her conservative look. Her hair is always shiny and healthy looking, but she does not style it in an interesting or noticeable manner. Typically, she wears her hair straight down or with a headband, which does not compliment her face or physical appearance in any way.

Amy does seem to have a pleasant body shape, but again, she is typically covered almost neck to toe in layers of clothing, including tights or long socks. Therefore, this is not a considered factor in Amy's appearance.

In terms of Rokeach's psychological determinants, Amy does believe that she has sex appeal and often attempts (unsuccessfully) to utilize this sex appeal with Sheldon. However, she does look to Penny as a mentor on sexuality and physical appearance and generally makes perceived inappropriate comments about Penny's beauty being idealistic. This demonstrates that Amy is aware of her physical presentation, but does not consider sexualizing her identity as a critical factor in her identity creation. Penny, Amy believes, is far more successful and experienced at such an endeavor.

Considering these factors, Amy will be placed towards the left side of the continuum, towards smart, but not entirely on the left side. There are physical features leading to a definition of Amy as "sexy," that allow her name to be placed slightly towards the middle of the continuum.

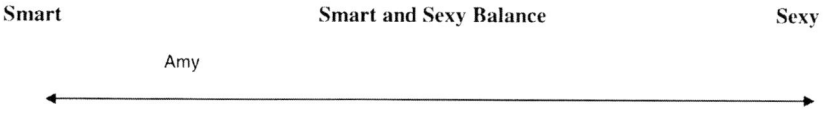

Bernadette—Following the established characteristics of a "smart" character, Bernadette meets all of the required criteria. She holds advanced degrees, including a PhD in microbiology and, like Amy, is always working on new developments in the field.

Upon earning her doctorate degree, Bernadette is offered a job with a pharmaceutical company conducting research into medications suitable for treatment of premature ejaculation. She seems to constantly be amused and entertained with her work, sometimes much to the disbelief and disgust of the other characters.

As previously discussed in the essay, Bernadette's position with the pharmaceutical company is a highly lucrative career. She seems to be confident with money handling, giving Howard a Rolex watch upon receipt of her new job. These are the only times in the show when Bernadette's financial situation is discussed.

Bernadette, though seemingly quiet, shy, and polite, does appear confident in herself, especially in her career path. She consistently makes forward progress with her research plans and developments. She likewise seems confident in herself, as well as in her relationship with Howard. Bernadette is admittedly absent-minded or somewhat careless when it comes to her career; in "The Justice League Recombination," Bernadette is unable to attend a party with the others because she is quarantined after consuming Jell-O shots from Petri dishes used to test yellow fever samples. This instance, and other examples, demonstrates her absent-mindedness or poor decision making skills in some situations. However, per the definitions previously explored in this chapter, absent-mindedness is not a negative addition to the consideration of a woman's intelligence and will therefore, not be factored into the continuum.

Bernadette does also demonstrate enormous potential for growth in any of the aforementioned categories. She possesses the education, abilities, and drive to continue to move forward in her career and her life to the best of her abilities, continually accomplishing tasks and goals.

Physically, Bernadette is of a healthy height to weight ratio. Her height is a source of contention at some points, but she is physically proportionate and typically wears clothing to accentuate her feminine curves. Bernadette's age is also not discussed in the show, but, like Amy, given her educational experience, we can place her within the late twenties to early thirties range. Bernadette is also an able-bodied female character in the show. She does have a clear complexion, which is typically enhanced by a light amount of makeup. She typically goes for a natural look with her makeup.

Bernadette always has a pleasant physical presentation in terms of her light makeup, clothing, hair styles, and body. Her clothing is typically more reserved than Penny's wardrobe, but not quite as covered up as Amy's. She often wears dresses that compliment her hourglass figure without being too tight or revealing. Bernadette's hair is always well maintained, although the style does change for the episode and occasion. The physical body is not presented as such an obsession as the other characters: Penny flaunts her sexual physique and Amy desperately tries to flaunt hers. Bernadette is reserved in her outward sexuality and physical presentation.

Bernadette does have a voluptuous, female body shape that is often accentuated with her choices of clothing. Her buttocks and breasts are adequately (but not overtly) displayed in her clothing throughout the show.

Considering all of these factors, Bernadette will be placed in the middle of the continuum, having met the criteria for the "Smart and Sexy Balance" category.

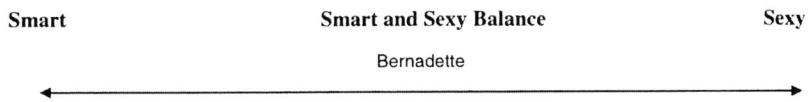

Now that all of the characters have been described, compared to the American popular culture definitions of "Smart" and "Sexy," let us place them together on the continuum to understand their characteristics in conjunction with one another.

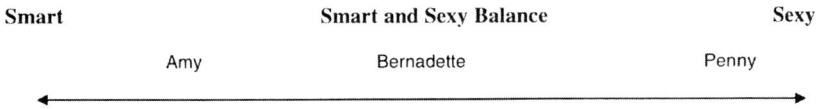

So, Can a Female Be Both Smart and Sexy in American Popular Culture?

Determining definitions for "smart" and "sexy" in terms of American popular culture is a difficult task. As with all features of pop culture, definitions and ideals change in the drop of a hat, with a slip of Jessica Simpson's tongue or Janet Jackson's nipple. In order for television characters to be developed, there is a large reliance on stereotypes in any capacity and *The Big Bang Theory* is no different. Once definitions were established, a core group of characteristics was identified to help distinguish smart and sexy.

In following these characteristics taken from popular culture, this essay has determined that a female character in American popular culture *can* be both smart and sexy, which, in the case of *The Big Bang Theory* is emulated by Dr. Bernadette Rostenkowski-Wolowitz. Additional female characters emulating a balance of smart and sexy may be achieved in this show, such as Priya Koothrapali, but for the purposes of this chapter, only the three main, permanent characters, Penny, Amy, and Bernadette, were considered. Bernadette's education, experience, potential and physical appearances balance each other out in such a way that she demonstrates both smartness and sexiness. For a show that places significant emphasis on Penny's sex appeal (in the first show she is shown as the new, gorgeous, scantily clad neighbor), it does not immediately instill confidence that education (or anything other than sex appeal) is a valued characteristic. However, all of the female characters do have a unique place in the show and all of the females together create a strong balance of varying types of individuals.

Conclusion

American popular culture has, in recent years, glorified appearance, physical presentation, and talent rather than education, depth, and meaningful experience. Developing the context of this conversation was a challenging experience; so many key fixtures of American culture could go into the development of any examination of female depictions. However, since the scope of the project was *The Big Bang Theory*, considering more recent aspects of popular culture (in particular other television shows and film) seemed like a wise feature.

Each of the female characters of *The Big Bang Theory* has a unique place on the continuum of smart-sexy. Once the definitions were analyzed, Penny placed towards the "sexy" end of the continuum, not demonstrating many of the prescribed characteristics of "smartness" in American popular culture. Conversely, Amy Farah Fowler placed more towards the "smart" end of the continuum, possessing some of the characteristics of "sexy." Bernadette's character lies in the middle of the continuum, demonstrating indications of being both smart and sexy in an equal manner.

Perhaps the most telling feature of this piece is the propensity of individuals to study *The Big Bang Theory* in such a scholarly manner throughout this text. Although it may seem like a time when unintelligence is consistently rewarded, recognizing the success of a show like *The Big Bang Theory* is a tremendous step forward on a number of levels. Specifically, glorifying female characters with education, work ethics, and potential places a positive pop culture potential on what it means to be female.

One way that this brief study could be enhanced would be through a systematic review of American popular culture in a limited period of recent time. Perhaps only the past year in television and film could be considered. Or, for a larger scope of a project, five years, ten years, a century, and so forth. The definitions of "smart" and "sexy" as used in this chapter are admittedly quite limited, but a more extensive view would prove telling. Likewise, the scope of this project was limited to the television show *The Big Bang Theory*, which, as a larger study would demonstrate, may or may not be a crucial piece of the pop culture puzzle.

Works Cited

"The Bat Jar Conjecture." *The Big Bang Theory*. CBS. CBS. 21 April 2008. Television.

"The Financial Permeability." *The Big Bang Theory*. CBS. CBS. 2 February 2009. Television.

Frith, Katherine, Ping Shaw, and Hong Cheng. "The Construction of Beauty: A Cross-Cultural Analysis of Women's Magazine Advertising. *International Communication Association* (March 2005): 1–16. Print.

"Gender Brief." *Organisation for Economic Co-operation and Development*. OECD.org. 2012. Web. 2 October 2012.

"The Hawking Excitation." *The Big Bang Theory*. CBS. CBS. 5 April 2012. Television.

"The Justice League Recombination." *The Big Bang Theory*. CBS. CBS. 16 December 2010. Television.

Mazur, Allan. "U.S. Trends in Feminine Beauty and Overadaptation." *The Journal of Sex Research* 22.3 (1986): 281–303. Print.

Rokeach, Milton. "Studies in Beauty: I. The Relationship Between Beauty in Women, Dominance, and Security." *The Journal of Social Psychology* 17 (1943): 181–189. Print.

"The Roommate Transmogrification." *The Big Bang Theory*. CBS. CBS. 19 May 2011. Television.

"The Shiny Trinket Maneuver." *The Big Bang Theory*. CBS. CBS. 12 January 2012.

"The Tenure Turbulence." *The Big Bang Theory*. CBS. CBS. 4 April 2013.

Willson, Jacki. *The Happy Stripper: Pleasures and Politics of the New Burlesque*. London: I.B. Tauris, 2008. Print.

Wolf, Naomi. *The Beauty Myth: How Images of Beauty are Used Against Women*. New York: Harper, 2002. Print.

The Androgyny of Rajesh Koothrappali

Ann-Gee Lee

> Raj: Listen, there's something I want to talk to you about. I wasn't ready until now, but I think it's time.
> Raj's Father: It's finally happening. You're coming out of the closet, aren't you?
> Raj's Mother: We love you, and we accept your alternate lifestyle. Just keep it to yourself.
> Raj: No, I'm not gay. If anything, I'm metrosexual.
> Raj's Father: What's that?
> Raj: It means I like women as well as their skincare products.
> —"The Transporter Malfunction"

In "How America Unsexes the Asian Male," David Mura recounts what fellow actor Marc Hayashi once said to him: "Every culture needs its eunuchs. And we're it. Asian-American men are the eunuchs of America." This is a common sentiment among some in this particular population of males who may feel inferior to western males. In *The Big Bang Theory*, it seems a similar manifestation of Asian male inferiority has occurred with Raj. A running trope on the show is the question of Rajesh Koothrappali's sexuality. In many ways, Raj is not so masculine since his selective mutism allows him to become silenced or colonized by the others. He also has preferences for things females might like. While at times he is perceived as weaker than some of the females, his androgyny is actually acceptable in Indian culture, and to some extent, western culture.

One reason why Raj may seem like a stereotype at first glance could be due to the nature of characters on the show. According to an interview he did with Gabrielle Compolongo, actor Kunal Nayyar, who plays Raj, does not see the potential in the role he is portraying:

> I think that, predominantly, these characters don't have room for much personal growth. These guys are very set in their ways, very comfortable in their world. Except

for Leonard, who's constantly trying to reach out into the real world or grasp basic understand of social relationships in the real world. The rest of the guys, they don't change much, so I don't see Raj growing much as a person.

This interview was done in 2011, about the middle of Season 4. It is interesting to note that the actor had doubts about his own character, who has, in actuality, grown significantly.

About a year later, Adam B. Vary lamented in an *Entertainment Weekly* article that there is not much to Raj's character, as he is not allowed to grow: "Every other major character on this show has had a chance to grow beyond their initial archetype.... But Raj is pretty much the same guy in season 5 he was in season 1, except more desperate." Although the tone is somewhat negative, Vary implicitly mentions that there could be potential with his character. I would like to argue that when culture comes into play, it is difficult to make a flat character stay flat. The writers can play with Raj's androgyny, through his mannerisms and his preferences, to perplex the show's characters along with the audience. In doing so, they can achieve character growth.

On the other hand, Nayyar and Vary are correct in some ways. More specifically, I would like to point out that this so-called stereotyping of the emasculated Indian male may be seen as a form of dark comedy, even as a way to normalize the non-traditional roles the other male characters represent. Despite ridicule, Raj does not give up his beauty regimen or "feminine" hobbies to impress girls despite pressure or teasing from his friends. This differs from Leonard Hofstadter, the most desperate and insecure of all the young men of their cohort and the quickest to abandon things he likes or loves to impress girls. Leonard even tries to sell and give away everything "geeky" he owns because he thinks Penny will like him then. On the other hand, fans can easily see how none of the main characters in the show fit the "masculine" mold, but they are nonetheless successful professionally and, to a certain extent, in relationships. The whole premise of the series is the fact that the nerd can also get the girl although for a while, Raj seems to be acting as a foil to the premise. Despite continuous emasculation from the others, he is actually much more comfortable with, and confident in, his sexuality, interests, and preferences than his male compatriots are—even if he does express doubt and concern on occasion. Exploring ideas of masculinity and applying various theories can allow the audience to have a larger discussion of Raj's place in the show.

Often when discussing differences between east and west, ideas of gender tend to emerge. The title character from *M Butterfly*, Song Liling, states: "The West thinks of itself as masculine—big guns, big industry, big money—so the East is feminine—weak, delicate, poor" (qtd. in Eng 1). Along the same line, in "Identity Crisis and Gender Politics: Reappropriating Asian American Masculinity," Jinqi Ling stresses the fact that

> the traditional Western concept of masculinity—which values men as embodiments of civilization, rationality, and aggressiveness and devalues women as embodiments of primitiveness, emotion, and passivity ... was extended to account for the West's sense of economic and political superiority over Asia by projecting the latter as a diametrically opposed feminine Other [qtd. in Cheung 314].

Ling reveals a clear line between east and west, with west as strong and east as weak. Without directly saying so, Ling has touched on concerns expressed in Orientalism, Edward Said's theory that captures the western and eastern dichotomy, which is also one of the canonical works of post-colonial literature. In a nutshell, Orientalism is an ethnocentric way of western thinking that makes assumptions about the East, which usually connotes negativity. Said refers to Raymond Schwab, who provided an encyclopedia entry for Orientalism in his book, *La Renaissance Orientale*, published in 1765 to 1850. While Said does not directly tell us what Schwab said, he states, "Schwab's notion is that 'Oriental' identifies with an amateur or professional enthusiasm for everything Asiatic, which was wonderfully synonymous with the exotic, the mysterious, the profound, [and] the seminal" (51). Said even divulges that the concept of the Orient was perpetuated by writers such as Chaucer, Mandeville, Shakespeare, Dryden, Pope, and Byron who "designated Asia or the East, geographically, morally, and culturally" (31).

Breaking down Said's complex theory, John McLeod lists various stereotypes regarding the Orient. He refers to the "effeminate Oriental male," who was "frequently deemed insufficiently 'manly' and displayed a luxuriousness and foppishness that made him appear a grotesque parody of the ... female" (45). Moreover, "the East as a whole is 'feminised,' deemed passive, submissive, exotic, luxurious, sexually mysterious and tempting; while the West becomes 'masculine'—that is, active, dominant, heroic, rational, self-controlled and ascetic" (45). McLeod also points out that Oriental people were seen as "degenerate" and stereotypes such as "cowardliness, laziness, untrustworthiness, fickleness, laxity, violence, and lust" were imposed upon them (46). These ideas perpetuated the idea that those in the Orient were immoral and uncivilized. Thus, such stereotypes justified Western reasons for colonialization.

Especially discussing *The Big Bang Theory*, Dhanuka Bandara points out that Raj captures the ideas from Spivak's "Can the Subaltern Speak" due to the fact he cannot speak in front of women and because he is depicted as "effeminate and exotic." Moreover, "he is used as a foil against which the other white male characters are contrasted and through this contrast their superior masculine attributes are fore grounded." Bandara also states, "Raj functions as a medium through which the orientalist views about India are conveyed. Raj then functions as a 'native informer' who validates orientalist conceptions." Bandara highlights the fact that Raj is often subjugated by his friends, the other Caucasian males. As one of the few Indian characters on television, it does not help that his character provides the lens for which stereotypes of Indians are seen. Bandara also cites the example of Fez, the foreign exchange student (FES) on *That 70s Show*, who is also shown to be effeminate. Viewers are also unsure of where he is from despite his Latin American accent. Thus, he "becomes a colonial stereotype in the light of the United States' colonialist intervention in Latin America" (Bandara). To others who encounter him, Fez, being an international student, is the embodiment of the world and everything foreign in it. Although his friends may know his real name and where he is from, the audience is not allowed to know despite various hints. Like Fez, Raj has been depicted as exotic and mysterious, though unlike Fez, Raj's masculinity is often questioned.

Western culture often sees silence as weakness. Therefore, Raj's most obvious weakness is his selective mutism. He cannot converse with women and sometimes even effeminate men ("The Middle Earth Paradigm": Season 1, Episode 6). What is interesting about Raj's character is that he brought the problem of selective mutism to public attention although it is one of the show's comedic tropes. Though he often has more luck with girls than his friends, he has a debilitating quirk—he cannot converse with females unless he is intoxicated (from Season 1 to the end of Season 6). Raj cites his selective mutism as a real medical condition though it often gets the best of him.

Raj's trouble speaking with girls began at a young age. He exclaims in "The Grasshopper Experiment" (Season 1, Episode 8), "Ever since I was a little boy, my father wanted me to be a gynecologist, like him. How can I be a gynecologist, I can barely look a woman in the eye!" This fear of his, although his parents rarely mention it, has prevented him from following in his father's footsteps. Following the stereotype that Asian parents are strict and put extreme pressure on their children, Raj feels like he has failed his parents, especially his father. As the son, he has the responsibility of finding a woman to marry and give them grandchildren to continue the family line.

When Raj's parents arrange for his marriage to a childhood friend, Lalita Gupta, whom he has not seen in years, Raj is anxious about his impending date while Leonard tries to console him:

> LEONARD: Look at the bright side. [Lalita] might turn out to be a nice, beautiful girl.
> RAJ: Great, then we'll get married, I won't be able to talk to her, and we'll spend the rest of our lives in total silence. ["The Grasshopper Experiment"]

While the situation seems drastic for him, for us the idea of a married couple not speaking to one another is unfathomable and hence provides us with a sense of comedy. Raj feels that although he will not be able to speak around his wife, at least he would have a life partner, which is expected of him. Despite how hard he tries to fulfill his duties as a son or a male, his selective mutism tends to get the best of him. In the previous episode ("The Dumpling Paradox," Season 1, Episode 7), Penny spends the night, and Leonard and Sheldon are going off to bed. Raj is standing by himself in the kitchen in the dark, eating a sandwich. Since Penny was in the room, and she is a beautiful female, he was unable to speak to let them know of his presence. They had no idea he was still there. This situation provides sympathy for his character while also providing a comedic moment to the show. It still, however, depicts his subjugation. Much later, Sheldon once again points out Raj's weakness in "The Pants Alternative" (Season 3, Episode 18):

> RAJ: These methods of meditation come from the ancient gurus of India and have helped me overcome my own fears.
> SHELDON: And yet, you can't speak to women.
> RAJ: True, but thanks to it, I am able to stay in the same room with them without urinating.

Again, like the idea of a mute couple, this situation is humorous to the audience because he is so serious about the issue, though having a nervous bladder is also amusing. In this rare instance, Raj draws comfort from his own culture, although Sheldon's retort leads to his admittance of his weakness.

Therefore, before he meets his potential bride, he finds another way to construct his masculinity. The date with Lalita is the first time viewers are introduced to the cure for his selective mutism—alcohol. Drinking alcohol removes his inhibitions—he says exactly what is on his mind and offends his dates or important women, which often leads to disaster. He becomes overly confident and often ends up insulting the women and driving them away instead of seducing them. This depiction of Raj as a "loser," when it comes to pursuing women, may contribute more to the notion that he might be homosexual.

To gain a deeper understanding of Raj's sexuality, however, one needs to become more acquainted with Hindu culture. Raj is often portrayed as the submissive Asian, much like the *hijra* is in South Asian culture. According to Serena Nanda, "The *hijra*, an institutionalized third gender role in India, is 'neither male or female,' containing elements of both. The *hijra* are commonly believed by the larger society to be intersexed, impotent men, who undergo emasculation" (qtd. in Parker and Aggleton 237). Nanda describes her first encounter with *hijras* in the 1970s, a time when the concept was strange. She says that *"hijras'* ... lives [appear] shrouded in great secrecy and around whom there appeared to be a conspiracy of silence" (xvii). Raj is actually a complex character, although the omniscient audience does not really get to know much about Raj—he is not necessarily a protagonist but merely a member of the group.

In another article she wrote for the Safra Project, Nanda elucidates the ideas of gender in Indian culture, particularly in Hinduism. While the male and female dichotomy "[represent] the most important sex and gender roles in society" (1) they are not considered the only ones. Nanda elaborates, "The interchange of male and female qualities, transformation of sex and gender and alternative sex and gender roles, both among deities and humans, are meaningful and positive themes in Hindu mythologies, ritual and art" (1). Nanda goes on to explain that this is actually quite common in Hindu deities—the fact that some are also "sexually ambiguous or have dual gender manifestations" (1). She lists peace-loving Vishnu and the youthful Krishna as ones who are depicted androgynously.

In many cultures, children's names are chosen in relation to their gender. Parents like to choose strong names for sons and delicate names for daughters. Raj's personality does not quite fit his name. By looking at Raj's full first name, Rajesh, from gleaning Indian culture through the media (i.e., Disney's *Aladdin*), viewers might know that a *raja* means a king. Several baby name websites and books have confirmed that any male named Rajesh is much more elevated than just the ruler of India—he is the king of kings. The administrators of the Birth Village website provide further details:

> Rajesh is ... above human life, law, government or creation because He is the essence of creation Himself. This is a name attributed to Lord Shiva, who is the great lord of all. There is nothing higher or greater than Rajesh. He is the supreme One that lives in all beings and pervades every atom. All is motivated by Rajesh and all is in Him. His power is everywhere and all-pervading. He also represents the highest, spiritual knowledge that is attained only through inner stillness. Through meditation one can know the state of Rajesh.

Raj has been given the most masculine and powerful name Indian parents could give their sons. Also, being the first-born son, his parents have high intentions for him and disapprove of his whims. To them, his effeminate qualities thwart the cultural significance of his chosen name.

Going back to the idea of the *hijras*, I would like to point out that they are already emasculated men and seen as neither men nor women; therefore, they are looked down upon and seen as abnormal. If they are being depicted in Bollywood films, *hijras* are often used for comic relief. One of the most popular ways of poking fun at Raj's sexuality is through interactions with Raj and his family. "The Grasshopper Experiment" (Season 1, Episode 8) is one of the few episodes that highlights Raj's family relationships.

He has just begun Skyping with his parents, who have managed to set him up on a semi-blind date with a childhood friend. After introducing Leonard, he moves on to Sheldon and tells them that Leonard and Sheldon live together. His mother says, "Oh, that's nice, like Haroon and Tanvir." She is referring to two homosexual family friends. While Raj is protesting that Leonard and Sheldon are not actually like "Haroon and Tanvir," she goes on to tell about how even Haroon and Tanvir had just adopted a baby. Raj is standing up for his more masculine friends although he is the one most confused as being gay. This conversation is actually important because it almost seems his mother does not have a problem with homosexuality. She seems to care more about the possibility of having grandchildren, though it does not help that his parents infantilize him, further emasculating him in front of his friends.

While Raj is chatting with his parents via Skype, his friends overhear their banter:

RAJ'S MOTHER: You are wearing the boxers we sent you, Rajesh?
RAJ: Yes!
RAJ'S MOTHER: Because you know what happens to the samosas when you wear the tighty-whities.
RAJ: Can we please stop talking about my testicles?

The conversation can be interpreted in various ways. First, most young people do not like to speak of their own sexuality in front of their parents, particularly in front of their friends; that is probably because they are often disgusted with the thought of their parents' sexuality. Secondly, "having balls" is slang for being brave, daring, and masculine. Not having any, on the other hand, results in emasculation. By teasing him, his parents are embarrassing their son and making him lose face in front of his other male friends.

After being emasculated and continuing to have trouble with women, he submits to his parents' wishes. Much later, in "The Transporter Malfunction" (Season 5, Episode 20), since his best friend, Howard Wolowitz, is getting married, Raj feels the pressure of dating and marriage and finally begs his parents to arrange a marriage for him. His parents are relieved because they were expecting him to "come out" since Lalita, the woman from his first near arranged marriage (from "The Grasshopper Experiment": Season 1, Episode 8), noted the rumor that he was "more comfortable in a sari." This is when he emphasizes that he likes girls ... and their facial products.

This second set-up date is just as disastrous as the first: Laksmi, the new girl, discloses that she is a lesbian and is only getting married to please her parents. Raj, who dislikes the idea of being lonely for the rest of his life, agrees to the marriage. Lakshmi, on the other hand, also thinks he is homosexual and merely thinks she is entering a "lavender marriage," in which the bride and groom are both homosexual. After Raj has decided to go through marrying lesbian Lakshmi, his concerned friends talk him out of it—with a puppy.

> BERNADETTE: I think we've found someone for you to cuddle with.
> RAJ: Oh my goodness, aren't you the cutest little Yorkie ever? You got him for me?
> HOWARD: Her. We thought you two would hit it off.
> RAJ: I think we already have. Thank you guys so much. Let's see if you fit in my man purse ["The Transporter Malfunction"].

When the delighted Raj goes to look for the man purse, Bernadette's response is "Metrosexual my ass." The humor in this scene is twofold: a puppy is thought to be a substitute for a heterosexual relationship and the fact that Raj uses a man purse. However, a post-colonial lens demonstrates that even the Caucasian female has seen him as homosexual, hence inferior to herself.

Another blatant way he is emasculated is through the character of his sister, Priya. In "The Raj Prototype," Anita Felicelli points out that Raj's sister, Priya, who is attractive and well-educated, aggressively pursues Leonard. Felicelli claims, "The stereotype of the sexually aggressive minority female is emphasized when one character notes that Priya has 'the smoldering sexuality of a crouched Bengal tiger' and that she comes from the culture that wrote the book on sex." This is a different take on Orientalism since Oriental women are inferior to Oriental men. Furthermore, the juxtaposition of an aggressive younger sister with the effeminate older brother and their banter is entertaining to the audience.

Besides being upstaged by his sister, he has been colonized by his friends. Since he cannot speak in the presence of girls, he whispers what he wants to say into Howard's ear, and then Howard becomes his mouthpiece. Howard's responses often show the wit that Raj actually has but is unable to express. Another instance of his subjugation occurs in "The Zarnecki Incursion" (Season 4, Episode 19) when Leonard lies to Raj's sister, Priya. Priya has just happened to call Raj because Leonard missed her call, which prompts Raj to respond thusly:

> Hello, Priya. What's up? How would I know if Leonard's at work or not? Don't be suspicious. Look, if you want your relationship with Leonard to continue, you're going to have to believe whatever wild-eyed cockamamie excuse the white devil has the nerve to offer you. Okay? Yeah, bye-bye.

This allows Raj to implicitly inform Priya that Leonard is probably lying, but could also represent dissatisfaction of colonization and/or subjugation.

Although Leonard is his friend, perhaps his second best friend, he has called him "white devil," showing a difference between their races. He is also being protective of his sister's honor, which could be considered a more masculine trait. Further standing up for his sister in "The Recombination Hypothesis" (Season 5, Episode 13), he says to Leonard,

> RAJ: Did you forget what Penny did to you? It took two years and defiling my sister to turn that frown upside down.
> LEONARD: I didn't defile your sister; we had a relationship.
> RAJ: I heard you called her "Brown Sugar." In my book, that's defilement.

Besides the fact they were engaging in premarital sex, which is frowned upon in cultures with arranged marriages, he found the term, "brown sugar," to be demeaning because it was related to skin color, hence racist and post-colonial.

Besides being colonized by Leonard, Sheldon also upstages him. In "The Grasshopper Experiment" (Season 1, Episode 8) during Raj's date with Lalita Gupta, Sheldon, who is amazed that she looks like one of Sheldon's favorite childhood story characters, ends up charming her. When they leave together, nobody can fathom what has occurred since Sheldon has always been considered asexual. What is ironic about this episode is that although Raj has been seen to get the girl in more than one instance, Sheldon actually ends up stealing his date. Once again, Raj, who is trying to begin a relationship with someone of his own culture, is overpowered by the "white man." Sheldon wins again when he, although asexual, is able to get a steady girlfriend, the eccentric Amy Farrah Fowler, before Raj.

In "The Terminator Decoupling" (Season 2, Episode 17) when they are on a train to see Nobel Prize–winning physicist George Smoot at a conference, actress Summer Glau, being of *Firefly* and *Terminator: The Sarah Connor Chronicles* fame, is on the same train. Raj manages to procure alcohol and begins smooth-talking her; Glau is quite charmed by him until Howard points out later that the beer is non-alcoholic, which renders Raj speechless, once again. Although Howard is unpopular with Glau, as is Leonard, Raj has once again been overpowered by the "white man."

There are also the humorous instances in which Sheldon tries to school him in his own culture and make him feel inferior, thus emasculating him through intelligence. While Raj's parents are planning his first arranged marriage, Sheldon responds, "[W]hile arranged marriages are no longer the norm, Indian parents continue to have a greater than average involvement in their children's lives." Raj's retort is "Why are you telling me about my own culture?" ("The Grasshopper Experiment": Season 1, Episode 8). The audience probably wonders the same thing.

In another instance in "The Pirate Solution" (Season 3, Episode 4) when Raj is in danger of being deported since his research has come to a dead end, he listens to his friends making Thanksgiving plans and says that he will miss "Beefaroni" most of all. This prompts Leonard to say, "I've always been a little confused about this. Why don't Hindus eat beef?" Raj solemnly says, "We believe cows are gods." Sheldon interjects, "Not technically. In Hinduism, cattle are thought to be like God." Once again, Raj's response to Sheldon is "Do not tell me about my own culture, Sheldon! In the mood I'm in, I'll take you out, I swear to cow!" ("The Pirate Solution") While the audience's first inclination would be thinking that Sheldon is merely being a know-it-all and find the situation amusing, Sheldon's character could actually be educating them as they watch. However, since Sheldon is the one informing the audience, and due to the fact he is the white male who dictates everything his peer group does, he is, in fact, colonizing Raj. It is in scenes like this that the audience can see his dissatisfaction of being perceived as less than masculine. Moreover, it does not help when his character is not allowed to be the mouthpiece of his own culture, as he does not enjoy having that pointed out by a person who is a stickler for facts and accuracy and seems to know more than he does.

Besides making him feel inferior, Raj's friends already have their suspicions about his sexuality, and then other characters have a tendency to agree with their assumptions. In "The Maternal Capacitance" (Season 2, Episode 15), Leonard's mother appears for the first time. After his mother tells embarrassing stories about Leonard's childhood, Leonard deflects the conversation by pointing out the fact that Howard lives at home while Raj cannot speak in the presence of females. This leads to Howard and Raj's bickering, often seen in couples, which prompts her diagnosis of their "ersatz homosexual relationship."

In "The Guitarist Amplification," Raj's parents refer to Howard as their daughter-in-law, although Raj insists that he can find his own woman. Raj could be considered somewhat homosexual because he is always with his male friends, which leads us to the term "bromance." While homosocial relationships are nothing new, the term "bromance," appeared in 2004 (Merriam Webster), a portmanteau of "brother" and "romance." While the word may connote homoeroticism, it actually constitutes a non-sexual relationship. Often, young men who have trouble socializing with females tend to stay together, leading others to believe they might engage in homoerotic activities. The actor who plays Raj also sees this. In an interview with *New York Post*, Kunal Nayyar says,

> There's definitely a bromance there. That's what is so lovely about this season: you're seeing that they can't live without each other... I think Raj and Howard are endearing. I also love that Raj is becoming more needy and effeminate, like the wife in their relationship [Wieselman].

Nayyar's response indicates amusement of the idea of his character becoming effeminate, perhaps because he also comes from a culture in which androgyny is acceptable. While it may provide comedic contribution to the show, queer-platonic relationships are actually quite normal and have been misdiagnosed as homosexual relationships. Therefore, it is important to mention his interest in, and ability to form and maintain, nonstandard relationships in regards to his atypical masculinity and heterosexuality.

Raj might also be considered homosexual due to his various preferences. He has expressed his love of *Sex in the City* ("The Precious Fragmentation": Season 3, Episode 17), *Annie* ("The Speckerman Recurrence": Season 5, Episode 11), and Sandra Bullock's movies (various episodes). He has revealed that if he were to get a tattoo, he was thinking about either a hummingbird or dolphin on his ankle ("The Ornithophobia Diffusion": Season 5, Episode 9). He enjoys putting together potpourri ("The Flaming Spittoon Acquisition": Season 5, Episode 10), which is not a manly hobby in the West, but is common in the East in the form of religious incense. He enjoys baking and has taken a dance aerobics class. While society has been opening up their minds to the idea of beta males, or males who stay at home while their wives work, many can agree that several of his extracurricular activities are not exactly masculine, and thus, he is ridiculed.

Also related to the possibility Raj is homosexual, out of all the young men in his cohort, he is the most sensitive. Any little thing can set off his tears. For example, in "The Apology Insufficiency" (Season 4, Episode 7), Sheldon wrongs Howard and presents him with his spot on the couch as an apology gift; Raj begins crying and tells Howard to forgive Sheldon. In "The Wiggly Finger Catalyst" (Season 5, Episode 4), Raj is feeling more depressed as Howard and Bernadette's wedding is around the corner—he binge eats and cries at the cake-tasting. Penny, feeling sorry for Raj, decides to set him up with her friend, who is the perfect date for Raj—she is deaf. Unfortunately, she is only dating him for his money. His parents threaten to cut him off and when he confesses to his girlfriend, she leaves him. Raj is seen crying and drinking at Penny's house. From a young age, western males are told to be strong, to "suck it up," and not openly express their feelings, particularly those related to sadness. However, Raj is very open with his feelings, even when he uses Howard as a mouthpiece. However, in the western culture, males who openly express their emotions are often perceived as weak or womanly.

How Raj argues with others who question his sexuality is through the concept of metrosexuality. Though Raj has yet to don a dress—as Indian *hijra* tend to do—he does take extra care in his appearance, grooming, and hygiene and calls himself a "metrosexual." To support Raj, I would like to go over the history of the term. In 1994, Mark Simpson wrote an article for *The Independent* entitled "Here Come the Mirror Men: Why the Future is Metrosexual." This was the first mention of the word "metrosexual," for which Simpson had enclosed in quotation marks. Simpson begins his article by describing the trend through Britain's first exhibition for men called "It's a Man's World," organized by *GQ Magazine*. One young man in his early twenties says that the trend has "...been kept underground for too long" (qtd. in Simpson). Simpson states that "male vanity's finally coming out of the closet.... And it's busy filling the new-found space in there with expensive clothes and accessories ... male narcissism is here and we'd better get used to it" (Simpson). What is interesting about this quote by the observer is the idea of "male vanity finally coming out of the closet." The colloquialism for someone confessing his or her homosexuality is "coming out of the closet." Therefore, by using that term, the writer has somewhat feminized the term, metrosexuality.

Bear in mind also that metrosexuality began in a time when grunge prevailed, grunge being the style of unkempt hair, torn jeans, baggy clothing, and so on. Perhaps metrosexuality was an opposition to the sloppy style and perhaps a different permutation of the yuppie. Simpson further stresses in another article, "Mark Simpson's Metrosexual Reflections,"

> Metrosexuality is about men becoming everything. To themselves. In much the same way that women have been for some time. It's about men finally realizing that if women can appropriate hitherto "male" behavior and practices for their own enjoyment and advancement, then why can't men do the same thing? And if women won't be women for men any more, why on Earth should men be men for women?

Along with Simpson's thoughts, many males actually acknowledge that they are just as vain as females. With the availability of men's hygiene and beauty products, though still not nearly as many as the women have, males have the means to improve their grooming. Raj has mentioned that he considers himself metrosexual when people are dubious of his sexual preferences. This insistence of being called "metrosexual" indicates that he does not want to be associated with homosexual, hence overcompensation.

Simpson states in another article, "Metrosexuality and whatever comes after it, when all is said and done, isn't really about men becoming 'gay' or 'girly'" (*Out Magazine*). Raj adamantly tells his parents that he does like girls, yet the 'but' that ensues reveals that he also likes their beauty products. This kind of shows that despite the availability of men's products, he might prefer women's versions, which does make him more effeminate. Although he is trying to validate his manhood, he contradicts himself with that addition.

In fact, Simpson reveals, interestingly in an interview with himself, "metrosexuals themselves didn't want to confront who they really were. They were ashamed, not of their love for themselves, of course, but of what the world would think of it. They feared, probably correctly, that their partners and friends wouldn't understand, didn't want to understand" (Salon). Just like homosexuals feel tentative about revealing their true sexual preferences to loved ones, some metrosexuals are afraid to disclose their product and lifestyle preferences. Raj insists that he is metrosexual, while his family and friends do not cease with the teasing that he might be homosexual.

Due to the fact everyone assumes Raj is gay and he cannot convince them otherwise, he has to overcompensate with his masculinity. In "The Middle Earth Paradigm" (Season 1, Episode 6), he ultimately dresses up as Thor at Penny's Halloween party. After his friends have interesting altercations with other characters, he has been missing: viewers see him in bed with an attractive girl. Though he has been unable to speak to his one-night-stand, she is happy because "he is a good listener" and she falls asleep. He smiles and puts his arms around his head in victory. Also, he always follows Howard around, trying to score. They even go to unsafe locations, such as thematic bars (gothic and country) to look for places to have casual sex.

Raj's overcompensation also leads him to sometimes objectify women. He blames American media in "The Wiggly Finger Catalyst" (Season 5, Episode 4) for creating images of "streets paved with beautiful blond women with big bazongas." Viewers might think that he objectifies women because before coming to the United States, he saw them as something to just conquer. However, when paying close attention, the audience can see that he actually respects women. In "The Thespian Catalyst" (Season 4, Episode 14), Bernadette wants to find out why he has been avoiding her and Howard. Little does she know, Raj has had a crush on her and thus begins his Bollywood fantasy, not necessarily in a Kama Sutra–like or sexual way, but in a Bollywood way. They are surrounded by people dancing. She is not scantily clad—moreover, she is a protagonist along with him in his fantasy.

Another interesting point is his wish to be like Indira Gandhi, Prime Minister of India from 1966 to 1977 and from 1980 to 1984. During his almost first arranged marriage, Raj whines, "I had such plans. I had dreams. I was going to be the Indira Gandhi of particle astrophysics ... but with a penis, of course" ("The Grasshopper Experiment": Season 1, Episode 8). Despite his short accolade of the female leader, he is quick to add that he is a man, who requires a phallus to maintain his masculinity. At first listen, the audience may find a male wishing to be female to be somewhat homosexual, though in actuality, it may also demonstrate the respect he has towards female authority figures; Indira Gandhi was the first female Prime Minster in India.

Similarly, in "The Wheaton Recurrence" (Season 3, Episode 19) when the bunch loses a bet to actor Wil Wheaton and they are forced to dress up in female superhero costumes, he finds that wearing Catwoman's suit is actually very empowering. In reference to the movie *Catwoman*, the title character played by Halle Berry, she is a strong female protagonist instead of villain, as she is portrayed when juxtaposed with Batman. The examples of Indira Gandhi and Catwoman show that he may be more comfortable in a female role and overcompensates by mentioning something sexual.

Despite his redeeming qualities, viewers can see, more often than not, Raj is emasculated by society, his family, and his friends. For the majority of the seasons, his selective mutism has prevented him from social productivity and maintaining a healthy heterosexual relationship; it also keeps his circle of friends small. Moreover, he is not seen or appreciated for being himself because everyone around him has been questioning his sexuality and finds his preferences and idiosyncrasies to be eccentric. However, his androgyny is what makes him interesting. In fact, what is ironic about Raj is that he carries so many effeminate qualities that would make him an ideal friend, boyfriend, or husband. Due to his selective mutism, he is unable to communicate with them, except of course, when he is intoxicated. Even when he does finally get an equally socially-awkward girlfriend in Season 6, there are still assumptions about his sexuality, although the new girlfriend finds his quirks to be endearing. It seems the majority of the series can be seen as commentary on the social construction of masculinity. In fact, Raj seems to be slipping between being emasculated and possibly being homosexual—he requires an unfixed masculine identity for the purpose of humor.

At the end of Season 6 in "The Bon Voyage Reaction," as an aftermath of his breakup with Lucy, viewers witness substantial growth in Raj: he is able to speak in front of females without alcohol. In some way, Raj has reclaimed his masculinity by being able to speak for himself. However, when the female characters find that they are going to be unable to shut him up, he is back to being feminine for being a "chatty Cathy." With such events as this, fans might be amused and intrigued by the mystery of whether Raj is gay or not, but they may never know. His character is flexible, either pushed or pulled along a stereotypical continuum, sometimes to make the other male characters manlier and to empower the female characters. Nevertheless, his androgyny provides even more complexity to his character.

Works Cited

Bandara, Dhanuka. "Who Does the Culture Work Now?" The Nation.lk. Rivira Media Corporation, Ltd., 18 Mar. 2012. Web. 1 Apr. 2014.

Compolongo, Gabrielle. "Exclusive: Kunal Nayyar Speaks on 'Surreal' Big Bang Theory Renewal." *TV Fanatic*. She Knows Entertainment, 17 Feb. 2011. Web. 1 Apr. 2014.

Eng, David L. *Racial Castration: Managing Masculinity in Asian America*. Durham: Duke University Press, 2001. Print.
Felicelli, Anita. "The Raj Prototype." *India Currents*. India Currents, 8 Apr. 2012. Web. 1 Apr. 2014.
Ling, Jinqi. "Identity Crisis and Gender Politics: Reappropriating Asian American Masculinity." *An Interethnic Companion to Asian American Literature*. Ed. King-Kok Cheung. Cambridge: Cambridge University Press, 1997. Print.
McLeod, John. *Beginning Postcolonialism*. Manchester: Manchester University Press, 2000. Print.
Mura, David. "How America Unsexes the Asian Male." *New York Times*, 22 Aug. 1996. Model Minority, 2012. Web. 1 Apr. 2014.
Nanda, Serena. "Hijras: An Alternative Sex and Gender Roles in India." *The Safra Project*, 2001–2011. Web. 1 Apr. 2014.
_____. "The Hijras of India: Cultural and Individual Dimensions of an Institutionalized Third Gender Role." *Culture, Society, and Sexuality: A Reader*, 2d ed. Eds. Richard Parker and Peter Aggleton. New York: Routledge, 2007: 237–249. Print.
_____. *The Hijras of India: Neither Man nor Woman*, 2d ed. Belmont: Wadsworth, 1999. Print.
"Rajesh." *Birth Village*. Lucky Orange, LLC, 2012. Web. 1 Apr. 2014.
Said, Edward W. *Orientalism*, 25th anniv. ed. New York: Random House, 1994. Print.
Simpson, Mark. "Here Come the Mirror Men: Why the Future Is Metrosexual." *Mark Simpson*, n.d. Web. 1 Apr. 2014.
_____. "Mark Simpson's Metrosexual Reflections." *Out Magazine*. Here Media Inc., 8 June 2011. Web. 1 Apr. 2014.
_____. "MetroDaddy Speaks!" *Salon*. Salon Media Group, Inc., 5 Jan. 2004. Web. 1 Apr. 2014.
Vary, Adam B. "'The Big Bang Theory': How Do You Solve a Problem like Raj Koothrappali?" PopWatch. *Entertainment Weekly*, 30 Mar. 2012. Web. 1 Apr. 2014.
Wieselman, Jarett. "'Big Bang Theory' Star Answers Fan Questions!" *New York Post*. NYP Holdings, Inc., 22 Mar. 2010. Web. 1 Apr. 2014.

About the Contributors

Lauren R. **Archer** is a doctoral candidate in the Department of Communication at the University of Washington. Her research focuses on the rhetoric of science and medicine, especially as it emerges in public forums. She is particularly interested in understanding the ways in which public discourse, from policy debates to popular culture, influences public understanding of science as a process and a product.

Benjamin **Bateman** is an associate professor of English and women's, gender, and sexuality studies at California State University, Los Angeles, where he also directs the Center for the Study of Genders and Sexualities. His areas of research include modern and contemporary literature, queer theory, and popular culture.

Alissa **Burger** is an assistant professor of English and humanities at SUNY Delhi, where she teaches writing, literature, and women's studies courses, including Introduction to Women's Studies and Women in Literature, both of which explore representations of women in popular culture. She has written about representations of intelligent women elsewhere as well.

Raewyn **Campbell** is a PhD candidate in the Faculty of Law, Humanities and the Arts at the University of Wollongong in Australia. Her research examines shifting discourses surrounding nerd/geek identity and the ripple effects these shifts have throughout society, particularly in regards to gender and power.

Nadine **Farghaly** is a PhD student at the University of Salzburg. Her research interests mainly focus on gender representations within popular culture. She is the editor of a collection on *Resident Evil* (McFarland, 2014) and is working on a collection about *Sherlock Holmes*, with many more projects in progress.

Ann-Gee **Lee** is an associate professor of English at University of Arkansas–Fort Smith. Her research interests include composition studies, covert rhetoric (secret codes, scripts, languages, silence, body rhetoric), civic discourse, women's studies, disability studies, language pedagogy/theory, multiliteracies, film, television, art, and design.

Eden **Leone** is a PhD candidate in rhetoric and writing at Bowling Green State University in Bowling Green, Ohio. Her research interests focus on popular culture, argumentation, and detective fiction.

Brian **McAllister** is an associate professor of English at Albany State University in Albany, Georgia. He specializes in modernist literature and is especially interested in the intersection of science and the humanities during the twentieth century.

Andrea **McClanahan** is a professor in the Department of Communication Studies and the coordinator of the Women's Studies program at East Stroudsburg University of Pennsylvania. Her research focuses on the intersections of popular culture, persuasion and interpersonal relationships.

Abigail G. **Scheg** is an assistant professor of English at Elizabeth City State University in North Carolina where she mostly teaches composition. She researches, publishes, and attends conferences in the areas of online pedagogy, first-year composition, social media, and popular culture.

Janice **Shaw** is a lecturer in critical and creative writing, film and media studies and children's literature at the University of New England, Australia. Her publications include articles on the Australian writers Frank Moorhouse and Beverley Farmer in the peer reviewed journals *Antipodes, Clues* and *Body, Space, Technology*. She has also written essays for several collected volumes.

Julia **Spiegel** graduated from Indiana University Bloomington. While there, she was the recipient of several Jewish studies program scholarships, and spent a year studying at the University of Buenos Aires in Argentina. She is a corps member in AVODAH: The Jewish Service Corps and works as a legal advocate at a domestic violence agency serving immigrant women in Chicago.

Index

adolescence: boundaries with adulthood 72, 74, 79, 82, 84, 85n1, 85n7; games quest 72, 74, 80, 81, 83; lifestyle 75, 76, 84; quest for ideal woman 72, 76; sexuality and masculinity 77, 79, 80, 81, 82, 83; stereotype of nerd 77, 82, 83, 84
Allen, Woody 52, 58, 62, 70; *see also Oedipus Wrecks*
American Jewish Humor 58, 69
androgyny 174, 175, 179, 184
Antler, Joyce 54, 62, 68, 70
"The Apology Insufficiency" (episode) 184
Apsell, P. 28
Arnold, Matthew 146
autonomy 98

Ball, Peter M. 32
Barth, Belle 52, 55–56, 58, 65–66
bathroom humor 52–53, 56–58, 60–69
Baudry, Leo 80
beauty culture 163
Bennett, Tara 32
Bhabha, Homi 53–54, 70
Blatterer, Harry 72, 75
Bloom, Stuart 123
BlueSky 81; *see also* Kendall, Lori
Boiarsky, G. 26, 30
Bollywood 179
"The Bon Voyage Reaction" (episode) 187
Brockman, John 149
"bromance" 183
Bruce, Lenny 56, 70
Butler, Judith 57–58, 70, 82, 152

Cameron, Deborah 153
Catwoman 187
Chambers, David Wade 29–30
Chaudry, Laksmi 181
chivalry 72, 73, 80, 83, 85
Cohen, Sarah Blacher 55–56, 65–66, 69
colonization 174, 176, 177, 181–182, 183
computer 75, 78, 81, 84; *see also* games; quest; science
Condit, Celeste M. 31, 33
Connell, R.W. 12, 13, 14, 21, 85n3
Cooper, Missy 130n
Cooper, Sheldon 112, 113, 114, 120, 121, 122, 123, 124, 127n, 129n, 149, 151–52, relationship with Amy Farrah Fowler 154–55, 178, 180, 182, 183
cosplay 76–77
courtly love 83, 85

discipline 92–93, 105
disembodiment 52, 61, 66–68
Dudo, Anthony 26, 29
"The Dumpling Paradox" (episode) 178

Eglash, Ron 81
Eigen, Michael 135
emasculation 174, 175, 176, 177, 178, 179, 180–181, 182, 183, 184, 187
ethnic, as cue of otherness 52–53, 65–67

Falconer, Rachel 85n2
Feasey, Rebecca 72
female scientists 112–131
Female Spectacle 54, 57, 70
feminine 80, 82
femininity 89, 90, 92, 103, 104, 109; hegemonic 103–105; queering of 97, 106, 109
feminism 54, 57
Feuer, Jane 73
Fighting to Become American (Riv-Ellen Prell book) 60, 69–70
"The Flaming Spittoon Acquisition" (episode) 184
Foucault 92–93, 105
Fowler, Amy Farrah 112, 113, 114, 116, 118, 120–125, 126, 129n, 149, 151, 156; relationship with Sheldon Cooper 154–55, 182
Freeman, Elizabeth 141

Gablehauser, Ira 150
games 72, 74–76, 79–81, 83; *see also* computer
Gandhi, Indira 186, 187
gender 52–53, 57–58, 60, 66–67, 69, 72, 75, 76, 80, 82, 84
Gender Trouble 57–58, 70, 152
Gerbner, George 28, 30
girth 55–58, 65–66, 69
Glau, Summer 130n
Glenn, Susan 54–55, 57, 70
"The Grasshopper Experiment" (episode) 177, 180, 182, 186

191

Greene, Brian 149–50
Grunewald, Elizabeth 32
guilt 54, 57, 64
"The Guitarist Amplification" (episode) 183
Gupta, Lalita 177, 178, 180, 182

Halberstam, Judith 133, 141
Hartley, John 73
Hawking, Stephen 149
Hayward, Keith 73–74, 85*n*7
hegemony 97, 103
heterosexual imaginary 89, 90, 91, 95, 97, 105
heterosexuality 88–90, 91, 109
Hijra 178–180, 184
Hinduism 178–179, 183
Hofstadter, Leonard 112, 113, 114, 115, 116, 120, 127*n*, 149–53, 156, 175, 177, 178, 180, 181–182, 183
Holmes, Linda 32
homosexuality 178, 180–181, 183–184, 185, 186, 187
How to Talk Dirty and Influence People (Lenny Bruce book) 56, 70
Huxley, Thomas Henry 146

imagination 91
intelligence 161

Jenkins, Henry 9, 10–11
Jewish father 66
Jewish mother representation: as excessive 54–55, 57, 59–61, 66–68; nagging 54, 62, 67; overprotective 52, 62–63; sexual 54–56, 61, 65, 67–68; undesirable 54, 57–59
Jewish son: as lens on mothers 52–53, 57, 60, 62, 65; mother/son paradigm 52, 60, 68; Oedipal complex 57–59, 61–62
Jordan-Young, Rebecca 142

Keisling, John 153
Kendall, Lori 11, 12, 14, 75, 80–81
Kidult 72, 85*n*2
Kimball, Roger 148
Kimmel, Michael 85*n*3
knight 72, 76, 79–80, 83, 85*n*4
Koothrappali, Priya 130*n*, 155–56, 181–182
Koothrappali, Rajesh (Raj) 112, 116, 120, 128*n*, 151, 155–56, 174–187; relationship with Howard Wolowitz 152–53
Kripke, Barry 154
Kulick, Don 153

LaFollette, Marcel C. 26–30, 37
Leavis, Frank Raymond 147–48, 151, 156
Lee, Stan 150
Literature and Science 146
Long, M. 26, 30

masculinity 11, 12, 13–14, 16, 18, 22, 72, 73, 89, 90, 92, 96, 100, 101, 107, 109, 175–176, 178, 179, 180, 182, 184, 186, 187; hegemonic 5, 11–12, 13–15, 17, 21, 22, 97–103; queering of 97, 98, 99, 101–102, 103, 109
"The Maternal Capacitance" (episode) 183
mathematics 72, 75, 77, 81, 84
Mazursky, Paul 52, 58, 62, 70
metrosexuality 174, 180, 181, 184–186
"The Middle Earth Paradigm" (episode) 177, 186
millennium 72–74, 76, 79, 84
Mulvey, Linda 34

Nabors, Allen 154
narrative analysis 93
National Science Board 28
Nayyar, Kunal 174–175, 183–184
Neale, Stephen 84
Nelkin, Dorothy 28
nerd 5–22, 85*n*5, 85*n*6, 85*n*8; adolescent quest 72, 82, 83; bullied 77, 80; female 5, 12, 16, 19, 21–22, 73, 82; as knights on a quest 72, 76, 83; masculinity 72, 73, 76, 80, 81, 84; stereotypes 72, 73, 74, 75, 80, 81, 84; *see also* adolescence; masculinity
Next Stop, Greenwich Village (Mazursky film) 62, 70
Nisbet, Matthew C. 29
normality 73, 75, 82, 84
Nowotny, Helga 28

objectification 81, 82, 83; consumerism 75; of women as idealized patroness 72, 73, 76, 83, 85; *see also* patroness
Oedipal complex 57–59, 61–62
Oedipus Wrecks (Allen short film) 62, 70
Orientalism 176–177, 181
"The Ornithophobia Diffusion" (episode) 184
Ortolano, Guy 146, 148

"The Pants Alternative" (episode) 178
patroness 72, 76, 79
Penny 112, 114, 117, 120, 121–122, 124–125, 127, 127*n*, 150, 151, 153, 156; and boyfriends 154–55, 175, 178, 182, 184, 186
performance 91
Phillips, Adam 133
"The Pirate Solution" (episode) 183
Plimpton, Elizabeth 112, 113, 114, 116, 117, 126*n*, 130*n*
politics of plausibility 5–7, 8, 11, 12, 13, 14, 16–17, 19, 22
Polo, Susana 32
popular culture 160
Portnoy's Complaint (Roth book) 62, 70
power 92–93
Prady, Bill 7
"The Precious Fragmentation" (episode) 184
Prell, Riv-Ellen 60, 69–70
princess culture 129*n*
punishment 92–93, 105

Quail, Christine 81–82, 84
quest 72; adolescent 77–79; for adult play 73–

76; computer games 72, 74, 79, 80, 81, 83; for the cool kid 81–83; for masculinity 73, 74, 76, 77, 80, 82; in a millennial context 72, 79; for power 79–81; for sexual fulfilment 78, 80; *see also* adolescence; computer; games, religious, as cue of otherness 52–53, 65–67, 69

"The Recombination Hypothesis" (episode) 182
Rivers, Joan 55, 69
role 74; of chivalry 80; model 80, 82; normative 77, 79; play and cosplay 76, 80
Rostenkowski-Wolowitz, Bernadette 112, 113, 114, 116–119, 120, 121, 122, 125, 126, 127n, 128n, 129n, 155, 181, 184, 186
Roth, Philip 52, 58, 62, 70; *see also Portnoy's Complaint*

Sackhoff, Katee 130n, 150
Said, Edward 176–177
Schiappa, Edward 45–46
Schuldt, Travis 154
Schwab, Raymond 176
science 72, 74, 75, 76, 77; *see also* computer; technology
science fiction 73, 74, 75, 77, 80, 84
selective mutism 107–108, 174, 177–178, 187
sexual 54–56, 61, 65, 67–68
sexual identity 77, 79, 82
sexual scripts 90, 91–92, 97
sexuality 72, 80, 83
sexy 163
Sinfield, Alan 5, 6, 13, 16–17
Smith, Brian Thomas 154
Smoot, George 150, 157n1
Snow, Charles Percy 146–48, 149, 150, 151, 156, 157
"The Speckerman Recurrence" (episode) 184
Spivak, Gayatri Chakravorty 176
Star Trek 74, 76, 77, 80
Steinke, Jocelyn 26, 30
stereotype 52–54, 56–57, 59–60, 67–70, 159; adolescence of millennial adults 78; male scientists 74; of masculinity 72, 85; nerds 72,

73, 74, 75, 77, 80, 82, 83, 84; in quest 83, 85; *see also* nerds; normality

Takei, George 150
technology 79, 81; *see also* computer
"The Terminator Decoupling" (episode) 182
textual criticism 93
That 70s Show 177
Thayer, G. 26, 30
"The Thespian Catalyst" (episode) 186
The Third Culture: Beyond the Scientific Revolution 148–49, 150
Thor 186
"The Transporter Malfunction" (episode) 174, 180, 181
Tucker, Sophie 52, 55–56, 58, 65, 69
Turkle, Sherry 72, 85n4
The Two Cultures and the Scientific Revolution 146–48, 150, 157
Two Cultures? The Significance of C.P. Snow 148
Tyson, Neil de Grasse 149

Valentine, David 152

Wade, Brian Patrick 154
"The Wheaton Recurrence" (episode) 186–187
Wheaton, Wil 186–187
"The Wiggly Finger Catalyst" (episode) 184, 186
Winkle, Leslie 112, 113, 114–116, 117, 126, 127n, 130n, 149, 152, 154
Wollock, Jennifer G. 83
Wolowitz, Howard 112, 116, 117, 118, 119, 120, 121, 128n, 149–51, 154–55, 180–181, 182, 183, 184, 186; relationship with Rajesh Koothrappali 152–53
Wozniak, Steve 150

Yiddish 55–56, 58, 61–62, 65–67
You Never Call! You Never Write! A History of the Jewish Mother (Antler book) 54, 69–70

Zack 156
"The Zarnecki Incursion" (episode) 181